D1503118

LIBRARY OF LATIN AMERICAN
HISTORY AND CULTURE
GENERAL EDITOR:
DR. A. CURTIS WILGUS

ETHNOLOGY
OF THE WESTERN MIXE

BY

RALPH L. BEALS

WITH A NEW INTRODUCTION.

COOPER SQUARE PUBLISHERS, INC.
NEW YORK
1973

Originally Published 1945
New Introduction Copyright 1973
Published by Cooper Square Publishers, Inc.
59 Fourth Avenue, New York, New York 10003
International Standard Book Number 0-8154-0481-6
Library of Congress Catalog Card Number 73-75846

Printed in the United States of America

INTRODUCTION FOR THE COOPER SQUARE EDITION, 1973

BEFORE THE first publication of THE ETHNOLOGY OF THE WEST-
ERN MIXE in 1945, most ethnographic knowledge of the group consisted
of limited comments by Frederick Starr included in his *Indians of Southern Mexico* (1899) and *Notes upon the Ethnography of Southern Mexico*
(1900). Starr, indeed, was the only anthropologist to visit the group before my study in 1933. Even the scanty ethnohistorical sources for the
Mixe were inaccessible to most anthropologists. Francisco de Burgoa had
not then been reprinted and only two copies of the original printing of
his history and geographical description existed in the United States, one
in the Newbury Library in Chicago and the other in the Bancroft Library
in Berkeley. Not only was I the second anthropologist to visit the area
but, except for a few days' visit by the geographer, Oscar Schmieder, apparently I was the only North American who had visited the western
Mixe since Starr.

My study was made possible by Elsie Clews Parsons who not only fi-
nanced it but first enlisted my interest. Parsons' concern for the Mixe
arose from contacts she had made with Mixe visitors in the course of her
study of the Zapotec community of Mitla in the course of which she
elicited an invitation from the political boss of Ayutla to conduct a similar study in that town. In a sense I was her surrogate in responding to
that invitation, a circumstance that greatly aided my acceptance in Ayutla.
As a result I was drawn immediately into the preliminary activities for
the fiesta of the village's patron saints, San Pedro and San Pablo, and
within twelve hours of my arrival had been a guest in some twenty houses.

Parsons was one of the first anthropologists to recognize that the Indian
cultures of Mexico were not merely evolved aboriginal cultures but were
the complex product of interaction between native and Spanish cultures
through processes of acculturation occurring mainly in the early colonial
period some three centuries before. Her belief that these cultures de-
served study in their own right as vigorous on-going social groupings is
evidenced by her study of Mitla (Parsons, 1936) but her larger ultimate
interest was in throwing light on the general processes of acculturation
responsible for their modern form. A necessary step toward this goal she
manifestly believed to be the identification as far as possible of the various elements entering into the formation of the modern cultures.

Some students recently have criticized Parsons' preoccupation with
identifying elements of aboriginal and Spanish provenience and have ac-

cused her of mistaking lists of such traits for analysis of the processes of acculturation. Her reply, if she bothered to make one, I imagine would have been to point out that to analyze past acculturation processes it is necessary first to establish their existence by showing that the modern cultures include elements derived from two different sources. In any case, her concern with the study of the Mixe sprang from reports that their culture retained an unusually high proportion of manifest Indian origin.

In any case, my interests and views in 1932 were very similar to Parsons'. This is evident in my COMPARATIVE ETHNOLOGY OF NORTHERN MEXICO, essentially an ethnohistorical study to establish the nature of pre-Hispanic cultures in the area before significant Spanish influences. My first field work in Mexico among the Yaqui and Mayo of southern Sonora was framed as a study of acculturation but initially I still saw these as cultures, so manifestly different from that of the surrounding mestizos, as influenced by and in some cases incorporating Spanish elements, but still basically representing evolved Indian cultures. Thus my first approach was much the same as that of most ethnographers dealing with the moribund or memory cultures of the Indians of the United States and I first conceived the task as one of rediscovering or reconstructing the past aboriginal culture. In the field situation it soon became evident that the existing and closely similar cultures of the Yaqui and Mayo had to be studied in their own right as active on-going cultures. Ultimately, I published two separate monographs on these groups, one an attempt at reconstructing their aboriginal cultures, the second an account of their contemporary cultures. In neither, I realize now, did I really come to grips with the problems of acculturation. In this change of views Parsons contributed, both during some weeks she spent with me in the field, and later in visits to other Indian and mestizo communities in Mexico. With her much better knowledge of Spanish culture she also made me much more aware of the degree to which colonial Spanish culture had influenced the formation of the modern Indian cultures of Mexico.

With this background of interests it may be that I spent an undue amount of time and eaort in an all too brief field trip in seeking information about possible aboriginal ritual survivals, subjects about which considerable secrecy existed. On the other hand, these rituals and the associated belief system were an integral part of the modern Mixe culture. This apparently is still true. As recently as 1972 a priest resident among the Mixe visited in Los Angeles to discuss with me methods of learning more about them. He is convinced that they still are important to many Mixe and that without adequate knowledge of them he could not carry on his functions properly.

The ETHNOLOGY OF THE WESTERN MIXE still is the major source of information about the group although some additional short articles about them have appeared. The principal contribution of these articles has been to disclose some fairly extensive persistences of aboriginal calendrical forms, especially among the more eastern villages which I did not visit. Two points in my monograph I feel have not had adequate recognition. One is the discussion of the civil-religious "ladder" hierarchy of officials which has been largely ignored in later publications dealing with this phenomenon in other parts of Meso-America. The second is the discussion of Mixe barrios in which I suggest that they and similar phenomena, including the moieties of the Pueblo region of the United States, possibly developed as civil-religious organizations and that any kinship functions they have in some places have been secondary accretions. In Mexico, I suggest, discussions of the calpulli, which may be an antecedent aboriginal organization, have gone astray by trying to fit them into antiquated evolutionist viewpoints concerning clans and moieties.

An important omission in the study I recognize now is the failure to point out the ability of the Mixe to compartmentalize some aspects of their culture. This is most evident in their religious and ritual life. Catholic ritual and belief, although still carried on in most villages without benefit of clergy, is a simple but remarkably well preserved form of colonial religious practices with few alterations or contaminations from the parallel non-Catholic observances. In at least one village a stone idol moved onto the altar and in several others sacrifices have moved to the outside church walls. Burning copal (a gum from one of the tropical pines) now is used as incense in the churches, despite early missionary attempts to extirpate its use, but this has occurred in many other parts of Mexico and Guatemala. Chicken eggs and candles were incorporated into the sacrificial non-Catholic rituals. But in the main the two traditions have affected each other very little. Rather they serve different needs or, in some cases, form alternative or supplementary means to desired ends. A turkey may be sacrificed with accompanying rituals for the benefit of a sick relative or a candle may be burned to a saint in the church along with appropriate prayers. Or both may be used as a double insurance. But what is of greatest interest is the fact that many Mixe were able to keep the two traditions separate for several centuries (and I presume some still do).

Certainly changes have occurred among the western Mixe since 1933. Schools have been improved and a boarding school was established in Ayutla some years ago. Isolation has decreased. Daily buses and numerous trucks now reach Ayutla and the road is being pushed farther into the mountains. The Mixe now export chile peppers and avocados as well as coffee. Maize is imported and the threat of famine reduced while a wider variety of external goods are now available to them. There have been shifts in the power structure. The most influential political boss now is in Zacatepec rather than in Ayutla, a shift dating since the political murder of Coronel Daniel Martinez of Ayutla outside the Governor's office in Oaxaca. The number of traders and cultural "brokers" and the percentage of Spanish-speakers has increased. In the main, however, I believe Mixe culture has altered relatively little since 1933.

Certainly there is still need for further research, whether it be studies in greater depth, or as a setting for testing specific propositions, or to examine the effects of changes in the last forty years. And of course the eastern Mixe communities, many of them located in somewhat different environments, are basically unstudied. Despite the improved access to Ayutla, students of other communities will still face isolation, absence of transport, restricted food supplies, nonexistent medical facilities, and, depending upon location, such hazards as onchocerciasis, typhus, vampire bats, cold fogs, and heavy rainfall. Rewards, aside from the possibilities of study, are the magnificent scenery and the attractions of dense cloud or rain forests and extensive stands of virgin pines.

RALPH L. BEALS

CONTENTS

ETHNOLOGY OF THE WESTERN MIXE

BY

RALPH L. BEALS

INTRODUCTION

THE MIXE first came to my attention near the end of a rather long stay among the Mayo and Yaqui of Sonora in northern Mexico. In the spring of 1932 Dr. Elsie Clews Parsons, noted Southwestern authority, visited me in the field for some weeks, familiarizing herself with these two peoples. During the two previous years Dr. Parsons had been making an intensive study of the valley Zapotec town of Mitla, Oaxaca.[1] Since Mitla is not far from Mixe territory, she met several Mixe, particularly Colonel Daniel Martínez, principal man in the tribe. As a result she became interested in the possibility that the Mixe might have retained more of their aboriginal culture than have other tribes of southern Mexico. We discussed the Mixe at some length, and Dr. Parsons' interest, enthusiasm, and assistance determined my trip to the Mixe. When, in 1933, I left Mitla the latter part of January for a stay of over three months among the Mixe it was with the pleasurable excitement of visiting not only a virtually unknown people but an almost unknown land.[2]

Because of the notorious shyness of the Mixe as well as their distrust of strangers, it seemed wise to begin work in Ayutla, home of Colonel Martínez. This is the nearest Mixe town to the valley of Oaxaca. With the limited amount of time at my disposal it also seemed advisable to concentrate my efforts as much as possible in one place. This, as it later developed, was unfortunate. Had it been otherwise, this account might be fuller. Yet despite many inadequacies in the field data, the picture of Ayutla and the western Mixe may be a useful one despite its incompleteness.

With the Mixe, as with most aboriginal groups in Mexico, a series of problems are met which do not confront the ethnographer in most parts of the world. Nowhere in Mexico is there an aboriginal culture which is intact, uncontaminated by European influences. Not even the memory of purely pre-Hispanic conditions survives. For from three to four centuries processes of disintegration, absorption, and reconstruction have made the Indian cultures new and distinct. Every tribe has received in varying degree an increment of Spanish-Mexican civilization. Apparently everywhere in Mexico the acceptance of these "foreign" influences has been periodic. At the first shock of the Spanish conquest and for a varying time thereafter a great many cultural elements were taken over by the Indian. These were absorbed, reworked, and amalgamated with native culture to form a functioning cultural entity, new, unique, and individual, but no longer Indian. On the other hand, neither is it European. Today these mixed Indian-Spanish cultures retain European or, more specifically, Spanish elements which have long disappeared in the culture from which they were originally borrowed. Such elements are now regarded as Indian by the natives themselves and by the Mexicans about them. Later periods of unrest

---

[1] Mitla: Town of the Souls (Chicago, 1936) was the result of this work.
[2] It should be understood that the facts here presented are as of 1933. Since that time changes have occurred in the contemporary picture. For example, there is now a boarding school at Ayutla.

[1]

seem to have been characterized by new changes in the Indian civilizations. The wars of independence, the reform period culminating in the French intervention, and, finally and most importantly, the revolutionary epoch beginning in 1910, each appear to have modified the cultures of the Indian groups, although in differing degrees. The Mixe, owing to their retired situation, seem to have been affected primarily by only the first and last periods. Even these contacts have been tenuous. During the early period, few Spaniards other than the Dominican friars who performed a bloodless conquest seem to have entered the Mixe area. It lacked mines, wealth, and hacienda sites. No rebellions called for troops. Even in the last revolutionary period, soldiers reached only one Mixe village on a rather daring raid. Consequently, the Mixe have been affected primarily by the general intellectual ferment of the times rather than by direct contacts or by any physical dislocation of their mode of life.

Contemporary Mixe culture thus presents several historical layers. These consist of borrowings from Spanish culture of the sixteenth and seventeenth centuries, often distorted or changed, the remnants of the original Indian culture, and later changes and borrowings. Sometimes aspects of the two civilizations may coexist side by side with little overlapping. Thus a mass and a turkey sacrifice may be paid for by the same man. The later introduction of Spanish-Mexican culture among the Mixe is relatively simple, owing to its recency. However, the mechanisms, the cultural processes, by which these elements are adopted are interesting. Particularly striking is the selection accompanying the recent changes, for even now the Mixe are by no means taking over European culture in its entirety.

The rapid changes being undergone by native or local cultures in Mexico at the present are proceeding at varying rates of speed in different communities. This is true even in a limited area like that of the Mixe. Neighboring villages show great differences. Roughly, Mixe villages may be divided into two classes, progressive and conservative. Of the former class Ayutla, Juquila, Zacatapec, and Totontepec may be considered the only full-fledged representatives. Tlahuitoltepec, Metaltepec, and Cacalotepec are intermediate. The rest are purely conservative. From what I heard I doubt if there are any progressive villages among the central and eastern Mixe with the possible exception of the Nexapa group.

The progressive villages are characterized by a number of *ladino* (i.e., Spanish-speaking Europeanized) people who are politically in the ascendancy, not only in their own villages, but throughout the region.[3] They are generally ignorant of the non-Christian rituals and beliefs practiced by their fellow tribesmen and, when they come in contact with these beliefs, persecute those who practice them within their own villages. Thus *curanderos* who use anything other than herbal remedies are forced to leave the village of Ayutla by the Colonel's orders. The inhabitants of the conservative villages, on the other hand, believe in and practice non-Christian rituals almost without exception. In the progressive towns there is also a certain amount of secret observance of the non-Christian rites, usually by people who live most of the time on ranches. The townspeople or those who live much of the time in the town proper are usually *ladino.*

This situation naturally leads to a certain amount of secrecy concerning the non-European elements of the culture. The necessity of using *ladino* interpreters, to-

---

[3] *Ladino* is used here in its original sense, not as it has been used in Guatemala to mean mixed bloods or *mestizos.*

gether with the normal suspicion of strangers, made it impossible to ascertain fully the character of the conservative culture, particularly in its religious phases. It is also probable that the surviving elements in various sections of Mixe territory differ considerably. Chisme, for example, is considered the great center for witchcraft, while Alotepec is said to be greatly influenced by the magical character of the mountain of the same name, and it is possible, to judge by various hints I was given, that there still exists a considerable body of folklore in this village. Isquintepec makes its sacrifices openly: one of the schoolteachers reports having seen them many times, but when he asked about them he was told plainly they were none of his business. Mazatlán has strange curing rites on the hilltops in which bonfires figure. Undoubtedly there are other differences, but it was physically impossible to visit or collect data from more than a fraction of the towns and even those of the western or Zempoaltepec Mixe could not all be visited.

Knowledge of these differences, of course, was acquired only after some weeks in Mixe territory. Shortly after my arrival in Ayutla, the Colonel left for Mexico City for a stay of over a month. This also hampered my work, for even in Ayutla it was much more difficult to secure coöperation in his absence. Even here it was harder to find good informants and interpreters than among any people I have ever visited. This was not because it was difficult to overcome their suspicions: the drawback lay in the fact that among the progressive Spanish-speaking peoples there is no interest in their native culture. Only those things which are from outside, those things which are "modern," interest them. For their own ways they have little respect. They have lost all pride in their own culture and have become apologists for a new way of life which they do not understand.

Upon first arriving at Ayutla and for some time afterward my feeling was one of distinct disappointment. My primary interest in visiting the Mixe was to seek aboriginal survivals. Except for the general crudity of living conditions, there was at first little to suggest that the Mixe preserved any more Indian culture than the valley Zapotec of Mitla, if as much. It was only after several weeks that I began to get hints that behind the external and conventional Christianity of the Mixe lies a stratum of religious observances, beliefs, and customs which retain much of their primitive character. This, it developed, is the type culture of the conservative town. Had it been possible at the beginning to establish my headquarters in a conservative town, that aspect of this study would be more complete. Living conditions, the difficulty of securing a suitable and willing interpreter, and lack of time all prevented. Consequently this report deals primarily with the progressive village of Ayutla plus some comparative material from other western towns.

The difference between the progressive and the conservative town is the most interesting aspect of Mixe culture, with the exception of the somewhat unrelated problem of environmental adaptation. In these differences the processual mechanisms are most apparent. As is almost inevitable with any Mexican ethnographic study, the problem of acculturation consequently could not be ignored, despite the primary interest in primitive survivals.

In the following pages I have attempted first of all to give a sympathetic and as full an account of the Mixe and their way of life as my time there permitted. The importance of Mixe environment suggested that it be given rather full treatment. Since the geographical setting is markedly different from that of the neighboring peoples and is little known even in Mexico, I have spent some time in describing the approach to the area in order to afford a contrast. When possible, I have suggested the origins of various culture traits. Comparisons with other peoples are sometimes given, but no systematic comparative work was done. Native terms, unless they are essential to understanding, are omitted from the text but are listed in an appendix.

At the close of chapter i, I have mentioned the Mixe who helped me most. Here I wish to thank them collectively for their friendship and aid. The Mixe are given a hard name by their neighbors and in literature, so it is a particular satisfaction to say that they are loyal and affectionate friends, even though sometimes difficult to win. Here also I wish to express my appreciation of the aid, encouragement, and advice given me by Dr. Elsie Clews Parsons.

I should not close this introduction without a word of acknowledgment of other services rendered. Don Rafael and Doña Angelica Quero y Toro of Mitla, keepers of the inn of La Sorpresa, arranged my trip, sent word to the Colonel of my coming, and performed many important personal services. But above all I wish to express my appreciation for the many courtesies extended me—often including food and lodging—by the group of self-sacrificing and poorly paid schoolteachers, who did everything in their power to assist me and to make my stay comfortable. For them I shall always have the highest regard and admiration.

CHAPTER I

THE LAND AND THE PEOPLE

A THOUSAND MILES south of Galveston the cornucopia of Mexico swings sharply
eastward and pinches together to form the Isthmus of Tehuantepec.[1] Here is the
geographical dividing line between North America and Central America. The
easterly trend of the Pacific Coast is accentuated until the shore line bends north-
ward for a short distance, forming the Gulf of Tehuantepec. At the Isthmus, the
Pacific lies to the south, the Gulf of Mexico to the north. The territory of the Mixe
extends westward from the Isthmus on both sides of the backbone of the continent.
It is a long and relatively narrow strip of rugged mountains extending from the
Isthmus to within some forty air-line miles of the city of Oaxaca, capital of the state
of the same name. From the low, steaming Isthmus, its highest point less than eight
hundred feet above the sea, the land rises abruptly to the west, culminating sixty
miles away in the enormous fog-bound, rain-drenched mountain knot of Zempoaltepec, "The Twenty Mountains," nearly fourteen thousand feet high (pl. 2, a). On the
flanks and ridges of this mountain mass the western Mixe live. With this western
third of Mixe territory this report is primarily concerned.

The most frequently used approach to the western Mixe is from the Zapotec
village of Mitla at the end of the eastern arm of the valley of Oaxaca. The route
crosses the pass at the end of the valley to the village of San Lorenzo.[2] From San
Lorenzo the trail skirts the edge of a canyon tributary to the Río Tehuantepec.
San Juan del Río, Santa Ana del Río, and other Zapotec settlements are situated at
the bottom of the gorge. After skirting the upper arms of the canyon, the trail passes
through Santa María Albarrados, a small, compact Zapotec village. The boundary
of Mixe territory lies at the summit of the first rise out of Santa María. With good
horses, which are hard to get, Ayutla may be reached in one day from Mitla. With
poor horses it is usually necessary to stay overnight at Santa María.

An alternative approach to the western Mixe is from the town of Tlacolula a few
miles west of Mitla. The trail from Tlacolula crosses a pass through the mountains
north of the town and goes to Yalalag, the largest Zapotec town in the Cajones
River drainage system. From there a number of Mixe towns can be reached. The
trip from Tlacolula to Ayutla requires two full days' travel.

For such towns as Totontepec, the best route is to continue from Yalalag through
mountain Zapotec country to Villa Alta. This is an old Spanish-Tlaxcalan garrison
town, the second oldest Spanish settlement in the state, "a Virgilian paradise, where
the fruits vie with the flowers, and the fruits of the tropics with those of the
temperate zone," according to old Father Burgoa, who knew and evidently loved
the place.[3]

Either route is difficult and justifies Father Burgoa's description:

... Villa Alta de San Ildefonso, whose pueblos lie in a great expanse of mountains so rugged that
the Alps and Pyrenees, which are so celebrated when one sees them coming from the Kingdom

[1] Part of this paragraph, of course, is written for readers unfamiliar with Mexican geography.
[2] This is a Mixtec-speaking settlement established by the Spanish in the sixteenth century to
utilize a grove of palms near by, since the Zapotec of the region did not weave from palm. The
villagers are still regarded with distrust by the Zapotecs and most Zapotec travelers avoid it
as much as possible.
[3] Burgoa, 1:131.

of France to Spain, [are] but a third as high. . . . There are rough roads and dangers from the cornices of the cliffs which one necessarily passes by, and great depths of canyons and gorges with extensive muddy places at intervals. Between rough rocks and marshes one passes ascents and descents to turbulent rivers with bridges of vines which appear, in the movements they make, to tremble from the torrential and thunderous course of those violent waters confined between massive rocks.[4]

Although the mountain Zapotec and Mixe countries are fundamentally similar in their geology and physiography, there is a great difference in appearance of the two regions. The western Mixe area is generally a little higher and somewhat more rugged. The major differences, however, are due to variations in rainfall with resulting changes in the vegetation. The Zapotec country is less heavily forested, mostly with dry-land oak and pine associations. There are extensive grass-covered areas which are brown in the dry season. On the other hand, the Mixe country, with some few exceptions near the Zapotec borders, is always green and almost everywhere forested except for farm clearings.

Precipitation varies with area and altitude. Although there are no official figures, it is estimated that the dryest part of the Mixe country receives an average of sixty inches of rain a year. In many places the total is probably double that amount. Consequently, a large part of the Mixe country is covered, or was formerly covered, with oak rain forest or cloud forest. In some spots this type of forest reaches elevations of as much as ten or eleven thousand feet (pl. 3, *a*). In many parts of the area pine forests are found, both above and below the cloud forests. In the dry season it is quite clear that the distribution of the two types is affected primarily by the elevation and route followed by fog and clouds drifting in from the north or the Gulf of Mexico. March and April are the only months regarded normally as dry, although in some years the heavy rainy season may not start until June. When this happens, the crops are seriously damaged. Even in March and April heavy fogs, drizzles, and two- and three-day rains are common. A completely clear day from sunrise to sunset is a rarity even in the dry season. However, the heaviest rains usually begin in May and continue through September or October. At this time of year, rain may fall continuously for periods of as much as fifteen days.

In Mixe country, streams are larger and more numerous; only rarely is one out of the sound of rushing water. Bridges are common over the larger streams but only a few of them are large enough for animals. These bridges are of logs, the suspension bridge of vines recorded by Burgoa no longer being made.[5]

The heavily forested country begins at the higher levels on the east side of the slopes of the Cajones River gorge and basin and extends to the Isthmus of Tehuantepec on the Gulf side of the continental watershed. The oak cloud forest in particular rarely crosses the divide. A very striking example of the abrupt demarcation line may be seen on much of the trail from Juquila Mixes to Tepuxtepec, which follows the sharp crest of the divide for a number of miles. Though the correspondence between the change of environment and the boundary between the Mixe and Zapotec is not exact, there are few places in which cultural, tribal, and ecological boundaries are so nearly identical.[6]

In pre-Conquest times the Mixe were one of several peculiar enclaves of peoples

---

[4] Burgoa, 1:89.   [5] Burgoa, 1:299.
[6] A fuller account of the geography and climate is given in Appendix I, p. 129.

of simple culture in the midst of the higher civilizations of Mexico. To the south, west, and in part of the north lived Zapotecs with a relatively high culture. Some of the eastern Mixe were in contact with peoples speaking Mayan languages, although whether the latter shared the high civilization of most of the Maya has not yet been determined. It is probable that the Mixe had some contact with the Aztecs; at least they have a native word for Mexico City, newin, "by the water," indicating a knowledge of the lacustrine situation of the Aztec capital of Tenochtitlan. Yet every reference in the scanty early literature indicates that then, as now, their cultural level was much below that of all their neighbors, except the Chinantecs living to the north of them and their close relatives to the east, the Zoque.[7]

Anciently the Mixe were a warlike people. Passing along the trails through the dense woods, one wonders how the Spanish ever managed to subdue them. Actually, the conquest was one of souls, begun by an intrepid Dominican missionary and carried on by others who had the patience and determination to learn the Mixe tongue. Except for a few raids, it is doubtful if Spanish military forces ever entered the country. Christianity consequently became what it still is in the nonprogressive villages, an adjunct to the surviving native religion. The church is merely another shrine at which sacrifices are made and where, until very recent years, idols were often kept openly on the altar with the images of the saints.

If Spanish troops made few entries into the area, since independence military incursions have been even more rare. Felix Díaz is said to have traversed the region during the French intervention; the Carranzistas entered Juquila Mixes over two decades ago—and were fortunate to get out alive. Federal troops entered Isquintepec for a short time in the latter 1920's to pacify a village quarrel—at the request of the political boss, who could not settle the difficulty without losing prestige. With these exceptions, bandits, Zapatistas, and others have kept strictly out of Mixe territory. And small wonder! There is little or no loot or political advantage to be had for the pains of toiling across precipitous ridges and through dense woods inhabited by a population easily angered by any outside intrusion and possessing guns which it uses with disconcerting accuracy.

As for travelers, the situation is little better. Dr. Moisés Sáenz, then Subsecretary of Education, was told in 1928 that he was the first visitor since Felix Díaz—a slight inaccuracy, for, as we know, Frederick Starr entered at Juquila near the end of the nineteenth century. Starr also refers to a naturalist, E. W. Nelson. Furthermore, there have always been some priests. Within the last twenty-five years there have been a few schoolteachers in the border towns, while since 1928 schools have been established in all the towns. School inspectors and, in some of the border villages, tax collectors are occasional visitors. Nevertheless, in many of the towns, particularly in isolated ones such as Mixistlan, I may well have been the only visitor, except for the priests and schoolteachers, for over half a century (and this village is only six hours from the populous Zapotec center of Yalalag).

The poverty of Mixe civilization may be ascribed in part to the habitat. Almost of necessity the Mixe live close to the bitter level of bare subsistence. Their country is beautiful and picturesque, but it is also extremely inhospitable. The magnificent

---

[7] Linguistically the Mixe belong to the Zoquean family. Recent writers suggest that Zoquean is a remote member of the Mayance family or that Zoquean and Maya are part of a Macro-Penutian group. Mason proposes Mizocuavean as a new term to include Mixe, Zoque, and Huave. Mason (pp. 72–73), summarizes various opinions on the subject.

forests are still a tremendous obstacle to the extension of their crude hillside agriculture. If today it is only by grueling toil that a man may carve a field out of the forest, the difficulties in the days of stone axes must have been tremendous. The cold and humid climate saps men's energies in the constant effort to keep warm with insufficient clothing and inadequate housing. An abundant fauna preys upon the fields and at times upon the men. Dangerous parasites and insects attack the Mixe and communicate unusual, debilitating, and often fatal tropical diseases. When fields are cleared, they usually lie on precipitous slopes down which boulders hurtle at any time. Fields or houses are often liable, particularly in the rainy season, to be swept away in great landslips. Much of Mixe life must be spent in combatting and foreseeing these endless contingencies and in wresting an inadequate subsistence from the soil and from the forests. The Mixe have few diversions in a life of unremitting discomfort and toil, except their fiestas and the constantly employed alleviation of sodden drunkenness. In the rosy glow or sullen stupor induced by mescal, aguardiente, tepache, or pulque they forget for the time the cold, the poor food, the unending labors, the whole sordid routine of a barely successful struggle for mere existence.

Yet environment does not account for all the simplicity of Mixe culture. Although Mixe life in many respects is a weak reflection of the civilization of the more advanced peoples near by, particularly the Zapotecs so far as we know them, there is much which suggests the archaic, much which cannot be ascribed to late-Zapotec influence. Particularly in material aspects it is difficult to believe that there was much Zapotec influence in aboriginal times. Rather does Mixe civilization appear to be a culture of the lowland humid tropics, ill adapted to the rainy, cold, and foggy mountains and suggesting influence from north and east rather than from the Zapotec in their relatively dry climate. The most typical Mixe houses with great high roofs and ample ventilation suggest the need for airiness found deep in tropical jungles, not on windswept foggy mountain heights. The habitually scanty clothing—in a region where snow sometimes falls many still wear light cotton garments without even a blanket for covering at night—and the methods of cultivation and rotation of fields are all better adapted to the warm lowlands. What few characteristics the Mixe possess in common with the Zapotecs, aside from the rather easily identifiable post-Spanish contributions, may quite possibly spring from a common cultural substratum which had its origins in some other direction or far back in time.

Not only does Mixe culture suggest archaic features. It is also a makeshift in many respects; it lacks standards of quality. Everywhere there is variation, and though some of it is caused by importations due to the post-Conquest civilizing influence of the Zapotecs (rather than of the Spaniards directly), much of it must be earlier. Not only does village differ from village in an endless variety of details in dress, speech, houses, and customs, but within each village these things are widely variable. Some of this variation may be ascribed to the wide climatic range. Each village has lands in two and sometimes three well-recognized climatic zones: cold, temperate, and hot or tropical. (These regions as classified by the Mixe are considerably colder than lands so termed in most of Mexico.) Yet far more important seems the lack of any feeling for style, for doing things in the right way. Only a small part of the population possesses a standard which carries it beyond necessities. The rest get along with what works, and no nonsense about it. A torn shirt is patched with whatever colored fragment of cloth is conveniently at hand at the moment and a new hat is bought when the old one has so disintegrated that no amount of crude repair will hold it together. This is true even of people who, by Mixe standards, are relatively well off. Throughout my stay among the Mixe I was constantly reminded of Kroeber's characterization of the Seri:

The crudity [of Seri culture] is due to the lack of standard, order, and interest in finish which pervades all Seri cultural manifestations and which rests ultimately on their essential isolation and self-sufficiency in an unusually forbidding environment. What a Seri is interested in is not a neat job but one that will substantially meet his immediate need.[8]

The Mixe environment of course is inhospitable in a quite different sense from that of the Seri. Neither is the isolation as great. Such isolation as exists, however, is essentially a function of the environment, granting the timidity of the Mixe about going into other territory. The poverty-stricken culture and forbidding landscape operate to exclude outsiders. Consequently the culture is more self-sufficient than is common in most of Mexico.

The Mixe occupy the highest, most rugged, and isolated region of the mountainous state of Oaxaca. Burgoa's description of the Zapotec country about Villa Alta to the north and west is entirely inadequate to describe the Mixe habitat. It is a region of heavy forests, torrential rains, clammy fogs, and fine drizzles which reduce the dry season to a mere two months of the year. Peaks are often snow-capped in winter. There is scarcely a level spot to be found and most of the country is precipitously mountainous. Houses and villages cling precariously to little artificial terraces on the hill slopes or perch dizzily on the summits of ridges. Possessing one of the few apparently unmineralized regions of Oaxaca, the Mixe have been left very much alone in their mountains. The main trails all shun the region to pass through the scarcely less high but more open, less abrupt, and drier Zapotec mountains.

Geologically and morphologically the mountains of the Mixe belong in a general way with the area occupied by the mountain Zapotecs. Although little geological study has been done in the state, this mountain region is considered a unit block which has gradually lifted over a long period of time and which may still be in process of uplift (pl. 1, *a*). In a region of high rainfall, the surface is so highly dissected that there is practically no evidence of the original land surface. From the character of the mountain slopes one may deduce that the uplift and subsequent acceleration of the erosional processes has been somewhat periodic. The very highest valleys have wider, smoother contours, suggesting that they are remnants of a period of fairly static conditions in which the stream valleys became wide and fairly level. Below this are found deep gorges where erosion processes are obviously taking place at a rapid pace (pl. 2, *a*). It is evident that these canyons are working back toward the headwaters of the streams. At a still lower level east of Zempoaltepec one again finds wide, fairly level valleys.

The region discussed in this book is that occupied by the western, or Zempoaltepec Mixe. It is to some extent a geographical unit, although I do not know that it is an ethnologically justified division. All of the towns visited, except possibly Juquila Mixes, may be considered to lie on lands which are wholly or partly situated on the

[8] Kroeber, p. 24.

outlying ridges of Zempoaltepec.[9] No map at present is more than an approximation of this area; all existing base maps are highly inaccurate. Though in map 1 I have made rough corrections of what seemed unmistakable blunders in the base maps and have added the approximate locations of many towns which are not to be found on any map, the map remains a rough sketch and should not be considered accurate.

Map 1. The Villages of the Western Mixe. Broken line shows author's route. Dots are Zapotec or Mexican towns.

The location of the Mixe towns is undoubtedly a relic of aboriginal habits. Burgoa speaks of the Mixe living in rancherias on the slopes and inaccessible gorges,[10] and the Nexapa Mixe are described as living on high hills.[11] This is equally true today. There is good evidence that some towns, such as Yacoche, Mixistlan and Tepuxtepec, are on the sites of ancient settlements or but slightly removed from

---

[9] The towns of the following list are those on the slopes of Zempoaltepec or on ridges connected with the mountain. Those starred are towns actually visited. With three exceptions the rest have all been seen from a distance. When available, approximate altitudes (in meters) are given as taken by one of the school inspectors with a not very accurate barometer.

*Ayutla, 2110	Metepec, 2050	*Zacatepec, 1500
*Tamazulapan, 2120	Tepitongo	*Atitlan, 1600
*Tlahuitoltepec, 2300	Ametepec, 2000	*Cacalotepec, 1800
*Yacoche, 2500	Chichicastepec, 1900	*Juquila, 1540
*Mixistlan, 2270	*Totontepec, 1900	*Tepuxtepec, 2350
Tiltepec	*Moctun, 1750	Tepantlali
Huitepec, 2100	*Ocotepec, 1400	Ayacaxtepec
Jareta, 2000	*Jayacastepec, 1630	Otepec or Ocotepec
	*Metaltepec, 1600	

A complete list of Mixe towns is given in Appendix I, pp. 130–131.

[10] Burgoa, 2:305.

[11] Santa María y Canseco, p. 36.

them. Mixistlan (pl. 9, *a*) is just below what would appear to be the ancient location on the absolute summit of a mountain where house terraces and pottery are abundant. The western Mixe villages are situated either on isolated and inaccessible peaks (Mixistlan), or on or near the summit of very steep ridges or spurs (Yacoche, Huitepec, Metepec, Jareta, Moctun, Jayacastepec [pl. 7, *b*], Metaltepec, Zacatepec, Cacalotepec, Tepuxtepec), or on high benches less steep and more accessible but still isolated, or on terraces on the upper hill slopes (Ayutla [pl. 7, *a*], Tamazulapan [pl. 8, *b*], Tlahuitoltepec, Chichicastepec, Totontepec [pl. 8, *a*], Ametepec, Atitlan).[12] Juquila and Ocotepec are unique. The former is situated in a fairly open small river valley but is protected by high ridges and canyons. The latter is in the bottom of a river canyon on a steep slope, but this is a modern location. The old Ocotepec may be seen high above on a projecting spur of Zempoaltepec. It may be noted in passing that nearly every one of these towns has lands better suited for settlement. A few miles west of Ayutla, for example, are the attractive and fairly level pinelands of Mata Gallina, which are more centrally situated and possess adequate water. The climate is drier and from ten to fifteen degrees warmer.

This habitual choice of location calls for some explanation. It has been suggested that warfare was originally the cause for the selection of these inaccessible sites. Although this would seem the most obvious explanation, I suspect there is a deeper reason springing from habits extending back to an earlier location of the Mixe. Mixe towns with few exceptions lie at altitudes of from forty-five hundred to eighty-five hundred feet, that is to say, within the cloud belt. The tropical rain forest within this cloud belt reaches its greatest luxuriance. Indeed, during the dry season the tropical rain forest follows very closely the lines followed by the fogs, so that the relative locations of pine forest and rain forest seem largely determined by moisture conditions and in particular by the areas most frequently visited by dry-season fogs. These are in the main the summits of the ridges and a belt along the slope of Zempoaltepec. It is suggestive and I think significant that nearly all the western Mixe villages are in or near the present borders of the tropical rain forest, although in many localities deforestation for agricultural purposes has made it difficult to determine the actual nature of the original forest near the villages. If, as is suggested by several features of the culture, the Mixe were originally dwellers in tropic forests in a warmer climate, the location of the villages may possibly be due to a very ancient habit. (For a more detailed description of vegetation, rainfall, and climate, see Appendix I, pp. 129–130.)

Beautiful though the forests and the mountain scenery may be, the Mixe country has its less attractive features in the humidity and the rough and dangerous trails. The Spaniards liked it very little. Neither did they care much for the people. Speaking of the founding of Villa Alta, Burgoa remarks:

The bold might and valor of the Mixes made the timid Zapotecs esteem the presence of the Spaniards . . . [as a protection] against the invasions of those brutal bandits. These [the Mixe], as they grow up about the highest mountain and the roughest peaks which are known in this kingdom of New Spain, are people who fight with wild beasts and pass among [the mountains] without horror of the leopards, lions [pumas], jaguars, bears, and snakes which are nurtured

---

[12] Starr (1900), p. 53: "They live in a magnificent mountain region and their towns are on the heights. With a few exceptions it may be said that they are in one of three lofty positions—(*a*) on the very crest of ridges, (*b*) just below the crest, on the slope, where they will be sheltered from the wind or (*c*) on the crests of high spurs jutting out from the main ridges. Probably many of their town sites are ancient."

by the abundance of waters which descend from that high mountain. Although the summit [of Zempoaltepec] is visited by the sun, the clouds may weep rains on the slopes below and one may hear the thunder on its sides, the summit being exempt from its terrors. [Observing] the thickness of the trees of various species that crown [the peak while] . . . visiting those houses, I felt a great painter was demanded by the beauty of so many attractive meadows between the crystal waters hastily bathing the leafy trunks and the jagged rocks in the dark shadows made by the canyons. Between the frightfulness and fearfulness of [the forest] awnings sing sonorous choruses of birds . . . which like sirens of the earth provoke one to diversion and invite one to the danger of its paths. . . . From Totontepec to Juquila there are twenty-two leagues of travel [about fifty-eight miles] of such dangerous trails through mountains, profound canyons, and turbulent rivers, that today, despite great care, the ministers fall from the rocks and are caught on others, as happened a few years ago when were precipitated Father Master Friar Juan de Noval, and Friar Lorenzo de Olivera, and others. . . . Although the lack of ministers at first piously recommended to our Lord to guard them from these risks and misfortunes, yet the distance between places, and the ruggedness of the trails occupied their days, while nights sleeping in wastes among rocks and wild beasts, without shelter from the rains nor clothing for the snows, necessitated prolonged exposure to the rigors of these embarrassments. They arrived at the villages fasting, dismayed, broken and milled as by haircloth by falls and always without spirit in their bodies.[13]

Even with some improvement of trails in recent years, this picture is not overdrawn. I have traveled the route mentioned by Burgoa from Totontepec to Juquila on foot, and it is far from the worst trip in Mixe territory (pl. 1, *b*). In many of the towns living conditions are difficult. Outside of Ayutla, Totontepec, and Juquila, unless the schoolteachers were in the town and provided me with other food, my diet was restricted to tortillas, a little dried salt beef, an occasional egg or sometimes beans, and coffee. If the schoolteachers fed me, the improvement consisted largely of the assurance of more eggs and beans with occasional vegetables; but I knew I was consuming supplies which it would be impossible for them to replace. Consequently, long stays in the conservative towns were impossible without finding means to bring food from a distance.

Among other people in Oaxaca the Mixe have a bad reputation. In their rare visits outside their own territory the Mixe are readily distinguished by their dress, physical type, and behavior. They rarely emerge from their mountains except in groups, the members of which keep together and remain quite aloof from strangers. The Zapotec traders who visit their territory insist that they are disagreeable and rather dangerous. In my own experience I found them shy, suspicious, uncommunicative, and often inhospitable. On the other hand, they are never uncivil or belligerent toward strangers, and often they betray a pathetic eagerness for the good opinion of visitors. Their inhospitality is frequently born of either poverty or suspicion. Actually, nowhere in Mexico, after the first few weeks of adjustment, have I traveled alone with such a feeling of confidence and safety.

Like most of the peoples of Oaxaca, the Mixe are short, with an average stature of 1,575.6 millimeters (5 ft. 2 in.). Rarely there are individuals who are greatly over the average (pl. 10, *b*). The mayor of Ayutla in 1933 was well over six feet. Despite their short stature and the evident malnutrition of many individuals, the Mixe are a sturdy, stocky people. They are generally more heavily built than the Zapotecs, with broad shoulders, deep chest, and short arms. Their features are usually broad and flat for Indians and the lips are somewhat thick. The head shape is round and tends to be flattened in the occiput with a receding forehead and high

---

[13] Burgoa, 2:271, 300.

crown, resulting in a "sugar-loaf" shape. A similar feature is found among some Zapotecs, but, subjectively, I am of the impression that the Zapotec forehead is higher and that the Zapotec and Mixe "sugar-loaf" types can be readily distinguished by a person resident for a few weeks in the region. The chin development is light and there is a slight prognathism. Despite this somewhat unattractive summing up, the Mixe are of rather pleasing appearance. The women are usually slight, even in old age, and girls often have faintly pink cheeks.

The significant figures available are as follows: the arm index (proportion between arm length and stature) is the lowest in Oaxaca, 44.6. The finger index (distance between tips of fingers with arms outstretched) is 103.3, indicating very broad shoulders when taken in conjunction with the short arms. The shoulder width index is 22.6, the cephalic index 81.8.[14]

Starr, who has made the only physical observations for the area, reports a considerable percentage of reddish tinted hair in the town of Iscuintepec. Actually, it is of frequent occurrence in other towns. As it is common in other parts of Mexico also and is referred to in quite early documents, it is probably pre-Cortesian. Certainly the high incidence in Mixe territory cannot be due to outside influence since there are almost no other indications of mixture, and mestizo types are almost completely lacking.

Some albinism occurs. At Tepuxtepec I was told there are five albinos, all related. I saw one of these, a boy, with almost white hair, pinkish weak eyes, and very white freckled skin. Elsewhere I observed albinism only among the Yalalag Zapotec.

Goiter is a fairly common ailment, as Starr notes, although the incidence varies greatly from town to town. I know of only three cases in Ayutla, although there are many individuals with indications of enlarged thyroid. Malaria is common but it is contracted only in *tierra caliente*. Onochcercosis (a peculiar and little-known Central American Filaria causing blindness and death and believed borne by flies and gnats) is a great plague in some of the warmer towns. Tiltepec is reported to have a 95-per cent infection. I saw no indubitable case of trachoma—a very surprising absence. Typhoid is relatively rare, since the Mixe are extremely careful about their drinking water. They almost always obtain drinking water from springs and have a great horror of drinking water containing any foreign substance. Pneumonia is fairly common, from what I was told, and apparently diphtheria occurs but is not often epidemic. The great scourge of the western Mixe at present is typhus, owing to their lack of bodily cleanliness. Outside of a few of the more progressive towns practically everyone is badly infested with body lice and even in Ayutla during the drier and warmer part of the year there are usually two or three deaths a week from typhus. In the more eastern towns, which are at lower altitudes, I was told there was much *mal de pinto*. I saw many market visitors from eastern towns at Ayutla and nearly all showed some form of the disease.

---

[14] The figures given are from Starr (1902). His Mixe illustrations are highly typical, in my opinion. Starr notes that the variability of the Mixe stature is quite low. This might be interpreted as an effect of isolation and inbreeding, were it not that the other measurements show the highest variability in the region.

CHAPTER II

THE COMMUNITY OF AYUTLA

THE TOWN among the Mixe is primarily, if not wholly, a Spanish institution. The early references to the Mixe speak of them as dwelling in kinship groups in isolated and inaccessible rancherias. In the seventeenth century the Spanish crown decreed the "reduction" of the Indians of the New World into towns. Although there is no direct documentary evidence to show how this was carried out among the Mixe, there is good reason to believe that the towns were previously nonexistent.

Technically the community of Ayutla is a *municipio*. The use of the term "town" or "pueblo" is definitely misleading to most North American readers. A *municipio* is not a town or village in the sense in which most North Americans conceive such an entity: rather it is something like the township, county, or parish, although it is not exactly like any of these. It is a center of government and an area of land of variable size surrounding it. It may include a *cabecera* or head town, and various other centers such as villas, pueblos, haciendas, ranchos, and rancherias. Actually, Ayutla consists of a nuclear settlement, the town proper, surrounded at varying distances by individual ranches or clusters of ranches. These latter technically might be called rancherias; actually, they have no legal recognition.

Viewed from the Cerro Pelado across the canyon, Ayutla gives the appearance of a sizable settlement with well-defined streets. Close at hand it is revealed as no such thing. The streets turn out to be merely trails winding along a mountainside. What at a distance seem to be larger dwellings among less distinguishable structures are scattered one- or two-room houses separated by wide vacant spaces. Only the few public buildings about the plaza retain something of their first impressiveness on close inspection (pl. 7, *a*).

Since the formation of towns in many parts of Indian Mexico was a completely artificial device, they have not endured in their original form. Wherever strict control was lacking, the towns began very shortly to undergo a process of disintegration. The Mixe were no exception to this, and very few of their towns retain more than a semblance of Spanish form. The lack of adequate near-by lands made residence in the towns distinctly inconvenient and in most towns there has been a gradual drifting away from the artificial center.

Ayutla may be considered a typical town because the degree of drift away from the communal center is about average. The process may be visualized with some degree of probability. First, temporary residences were built on the farm lands for use during critical periods in the agricultural cycle when constant presence at the farm was essential. These were occupied for increasingly longer periods until the real home came to be on the farm, although a house was retained in the village. Later, most of the families gave up having any house in town at all. Ayutla, with a population of nearly twenty-five hundred, has now been reduced to some ninety residences, few of which are occupied permanently, and the drift away from the center seems still to continue.

Mixe towns vary widely in the extent to which this disintegrative process has taken place. Totontepec (pl. 8, *a*), Metaltepec, Zacatepec, Atitlan, and, to a somewhat lesser extent, Juquila, are fairly typical of the Spanish town. Practically everyone lives in or quite close to the center, houses are fairly close together, and most of the population can usually be found in the town. Totontepec, Metaltepec, and Zacatepec have large farming areas within easy reach of the town whereas Juquila is largely a village of traders. Tlahuitoltepec and Cacalotepec represent the second stage of development with practically everyone having a house in town but with relatively few living there all the year round. At the opposite extreme, Mixistlan has practically no houses in the town (pl. 9, *a*). There are actually eleven families living within a quarter-mile or so of the center of town, all of them incumbent offi-

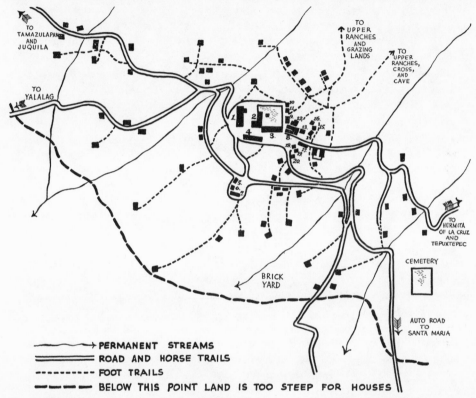

PERMANENT STREAMS
ROAD AND HORSE TRAILS
FOOT TRAILS
BELOW THIS POINT LAND IS TOO STEEP FOR HOUSES

Map 2. The Village of Ayutla, showing location of eighty-two of the houses and public buildings.

1. Church	5. Old *Municipio*	9. Colonel's storehouse
2. Vicarage	6. Jail	13. House of colonel's parents
3. School	7. *Municipio*	17. Public restaurant and inn
4. Market	8. House of Colonel	18. Schoolteacher's house

cials whose residence in the center is required. Ayutla and the other western towns represent an intermediate position with some families in permanent residence, others living transiently in the town, and the majority living on the rancherias or farms.

This distribution of population may be visualized by consulting map 2. This shows the location of the majority of the houses of Ayutla proper except a few which are too marginal to be included. Based on freehand sketches, the map gives a poor idea of the slope of the land. Corn fields occur in the very heart of the settlement. Few structures are on the same level, for the land is steeply sloping, and many rest on artificial terraces cut out of the hillside. Only the church, market, vicarage, schoolhouse, and schoolteacher's residence are on approximately the same level, clustered about a small plaza where the Sunday markets are held. It is with difficulty that a basketball court is squeezed into this space near the schoolhouse. The imposing two-story dwelling of the Colonel fronts on the plaza, but the lower floor and patio are five or six feet above the level of the plaza. The municipal building and the jail are on a slightly lower terrace west of the market.

The steeply sloping situation of Ayutla is also characteristic, though Ayutla is only moderately steep; few Mixe towns are situated in so favorable a spot. Ayutla is also favored by a number of springs and streams which provide abundance of pure water. Other towns either must carry water for a distance or bring it into the plaza through a series of hollow logs.

Officially the population of Ayutla is about twenty-five hundred persons. Obviously only a small portion reside in the official center. Indeed, the usual population is even smaller than the ninety-odd houses would indicate. Many of these houses belong to well-to-do people who occupy them only during part of the year or during fiestas and on Sundays. The rest of the time is spent on the farms, and at times not more than a fourth of the houses are occupied. As a result the settlement often has a very deserted appearance. The regular residences of many persons are as much as twenty miles away from the official center, although the majority live within a ten- to fifteen-mile radius. Most of these are to the northwest and west of the town, for in other directions the boundaries of neighboring towns are but a few miles away.

The semipermanent residents of the town are relatively few in number. They consist of the current public officials who must always be on duty. Since this group changes each year, there is a good deal of change in personnel. The Colonel and his close relatives nearly all live in town—his father and mother, two or three cousins, and a brother who runs the only tiny store. The postmaster (Ayutla boasts one of the two postoffices in Mixe territory), bandmaster, sextons, a few specialists, including a hatmaker and several butchers, and a few people who own land close to the center constitute almost the only residents who are truly permanent. Outsiders are also relatively permanent though few in number: these include the priest and three schoolteachers. The former is never in residence the entire year, and the schoolteachers are changed every two or three years.[1]

Despite the dispersal of its population, Ayutla seemed a very united community in 1933. Some towns occupying such a large territory have become divided and rancherias have split off to become new and independent *municipios* within recent times. No evidence of this tendency could be discerned at Ayutla. Probably several factors operate to maintain unity. To the west are Zapotec settlements with a tendency to encroach on Mixe lands, and a large united community is better able to resist this movement. A boundary dispute with Tlahuitoltepec a few years also contributed to solidarity. The influence of the Colonel is in the same direction. Furthermore, the community is a definite linguistic and cultural entity with numerous economic bonds centering about the weekly market.

More important than all these factors is the Mixe feeling that the village is the entity, aside from the family, to which they owe allegiance and loyalty above all

[1] With the establishment of a boarding school, this situation has probably changed somewhat.

else. A man can never really leave his town. Should a man be forced to flee elsewhere owing to some misconduct, the town in which he settles considers him a visitor. The visitor will be required to give service in the town, to be a policeman, give communal labor, and may be given communal lands to cultivate, but he is spoken of as "loaning his services." He must have the permission of the mayor before he is allowed to remain.

Thus at Totontepec I encountered a man from Ayutla serving as *mayor* (chief of police). He had shot a fellow townsman in a quarrel, seriously but not fatally. Now the mayor introduced him as "loaning his services temporarily here." The rest of his story I learned from my companion, Francisco, who had been secretary of Ayutla when the affair had happened. Francisco pointedly refused to shake hands with him when they first met, but after visiting a wedding and a funeral together, the mayor, Juan Chávez, persuaded them to shake hands, both being somewhat mellowed by aguardiente. Juan Chávez' argument that they were both away from home seemed potent. They discussed the matter at some length, agreeing that whatever might be in the past, here, where they were both far from home, they must remember primarily that they were fellow townsmen and had a common allegiance.

Another example is Antonio, personal servant of the priest at Ayutla. Antonio has been a resident of Ayutla since childhood; his mother is a native of Ayutla. Nevertheless, Antonio was always said to be of Tamazulapan, his birthplace.

Francisco had himself once been charged with treason to Ayutla and had spent several weeks in jail at the time he was secretary. Although he was an innocent victim, it cost him a fine to get out of jail. The story was a little involved and I heard only Francisco's version.

A quarrel over a boundary was brought before the *alcalde* or judge. One of the parties approached Francisco, then a youngster just out of school. By a long and plausible tale he persuaded Francisco to write a letter to the judge at Villa Alta, head of the district, and got Francisco to sign his own name to the letter. As a result, the judge at Villa Alta notified the *alcalde* at Ayutla that the cause was not to be settled in the local court but in Villa Alta. This immediately brought about inquiries, and no less a person than the Colonel discovered Francisco's responsibility and turned the information over to the Ayutla authorities. After his release from jail, Francisco was called a traitor to his pueblo and the officials suggested he should go to live in some other town as "one so young and who had started so badly would certainly do much harm to his town." Francisco has a stubborn streak in him and stayed, although he continues to be regarded with suspicion and is disliked. He has been given no other municipal office, although he is sent on small commissions by the Colonel.

Francisco's timidity outside his own town, unless supported by a letter from the Colonel, is remarkable. Although extremely confident of his abilities as a guide before leaving Ayutla, he became very nervous and practically useless in making arrangements when accompanying me to other towns. His confidence returned only in backward and "very humble" Yacoche and Tepuxtepec, where he was quite domineering. Natalio, the only other person to accompany me outside the borders of Ayutla, was likewise timid, so much so that all arrangements for food and lodging had to be made by myself. His attitude was somewhat more understandable because most of the time we were in Zapotec territory.

So strong are town loyalties that there is not any real tribal cohesion unless imposed by a powerful personality such as the Colonel. Quarrels between villages, usually over land titles, are not uncommon. Ayutla, for instance, carried on a three-year quarrel from 1912 to 1915 with Tlahuitoltepec over a strip of border lands. After several lives had been taken, the dispute was finally settled in favor of Ayutla by the intercession of the judge from Villa Alta. Eighteen years afterward, Ayutla men did not like to spend the night in Tlahuitoltepec, and vice versa.

This quarrel is interesting in the light of the old Spanish land titles given to the towns in 1721. The old manuscript title is in possession of the Colonel. In it a common title was granted to Ayutla, Tamazulapan, Tepantlali, Tlahuitoltepec, and Tepuxtepec. This must express a certain earlier unity between these five adjoining towns (see map 1). It may have been only linguistic, for the speech of these five towns is considered to be the same when contrasted with that of other Mixe towns. There are differences in speech, however, between Ayutla and its neighbors.

A somewhat different quarrel is now brewing between Tamazulapan and Cacalotepec on the one hand, and between Quetzaltepec and Cacalotepec on the other. It is said that Cacalotepec is a "new" town which "borrowed" its lands from the other two, and that the old boundary line between Tamazulapan and Quetzaltepec runs through the church of the town of Cacalotepec. Although Cacalotepec is new, no one seems to have any idea of the date of its founding and the town organization is certainly very archaic. So far the quarrel has not become acute, but, in telling of it, the informant remarked that now people from one town hesitated to visit the other.

The lack of unity among the Mixe must be ancient, even though there was sometimes effective coöperation. The isolated situation of the ancient settlements suggests that there was internecine warfare at times, although no part of Mixe territory is very far from other tribes who may have been the real enemies. It is asserted that the ancient site of Totontepec on a peak above the present town was for defense against neighboring Mixe. However, it was not more than five or six hours' travel from Zapotec villages and but a day from Chinantec villages so there may have been other enemies. As the Indians travel, there is no Mixe village which may not be reached in one or two days from a Zapotec or Chinantec town. That some unity existed among the Mixe at times is certain. It may have been no more than a unity of language and to some extent culture with vague connotations of relationship, to which powerful personalities such as the Colonel have temporarily given a deeper significance. Without some such unification the Mixe would have been unable to war with their more powerful Zapotec neighbors as they did in 1580. At that time the Mixe attacked the mountain Zapotec of the Cajones Valley so fiercely that it was necessary to send a Spanish expedition aided by two thousand Mixtec auxiliaries from Oaxaca.

It is possible that these speculations concerning tribal unity rest on a mistaken idea of the real tribal group. Actually, the ancient tribal unit may have been similar to the modern village community. If so, there is no great difference between ancient and modern conditions. Tribes in the past may have joined in common purposes or under unusual personalities as villages do today. The present strong village loyalties may then be but the extension of ancient tribal feelings.

Certainly today the horizon of Mixe interests is a limited one. A little group of officials I met in the plaza upon my arrival at Ayutla represented respectively the most important people of Ayutla. The *presidente*, or mayor, and the town council are all-powerful within their sphere and, practically speaking, their sphere is restricted only by custom and the personality of the Colonel. For the majority of the Mixe towns, this group is the government. Oaxaca, the state capital, is little more than a name. There is a governor of the state to whom a certain allegiance is felt and whom the mayors visit now and then, usually just after he takes office. But any interference by the state government with the affairs of the town is bitterly resented and usually effectually resisted. The organization and conduct of the affairs of the village is *costumbre*, "custom." Any effort to tamper with the *costumbre* by outsiders meets with a stubborn passive resistance. Only the village people, it is felt, have any right to change the customs of the town. With great difficulty the state has forced the recognition of tax collectors in some of the border towns, where they occasionally arrive to effect a somewhat hazardous levying of taxes on such established businesses as the making and selling of mescal and slaughtering of oxen. As for the federal government, it is an unknown, uncomprehended, unconsidered, and altogether vague entity whose organization and purposes are quite beyond the comprehension of most Mixe. Why it sends and pays for the unwanted schoolteachers is beyond the understanding of any. The Colonel explains that it is to reward the Mixe for their services in the revolution, but I doubt if even he understands the matter exactly.

Since there are many important personalities in Ayutla, it may be well at this point to describe some of the main characters who will appear in subsequent pages or who supplied information.

First and foremost must be mentioned the Colonel, Daniel Martínez. Scarcely over five feet, energetic, busy, progressive, sincerely interested in the welfare of his people, he represents the finest type of the local political bosses who are the real rulers of most of the Mexican people. I am proud to number him among my friends. He will be mentioned many times, for it is impossible to describe the present-day Mixe without discussing his work and influence. His cheerful and friendly wife, Doña Paulina, was almost equally important to whatever success I had. Eternally busy from morning to night, she cared for most of the administration of the Colonel's private affairs, which left him free to devote himself to the business of the tribe. She not only contributed much to my comfort but gave me much valuable information. She is one of the few persons in the town not a Mixe. Her father is the resident Catholic priest in Ayutla, Father Hernández, a simple, genial, witty old gentleman of seventy. Father Hernández has spent forty-six years in Mixe territory, twenty-five years in Juquila, where Doña Paulina was born, and seventeen years in Ayutla. He was a pleasant acquaintance who, although little interested in or familiar with native culture, told me many illuminating stories.

Living next door to the Colonel are his father and mother. Speaking only rudimentary Spanish, they figure little in this account. His cousin, Doña Sotera, acted as my cook and gave me some information on curing, for she is an herbal curer. Her brother, Gervasio, showed me secretly many of the sacred caves. A singer or *maestro* of the church as well as the town drunkard—if such a hard-drinking people as the Mixe may be said to have a town drunkard—Gervasio was of great assistance. The father of Doña Sotera and Gervasio, Tata Le, gave me most of my information on early customs in Ayutla. Nearly seventy, speaking little Spanish, he competes with his son for the title of town drunkard. Despite his age, he still performs his communal labor, acts as porter to bring such trifles as a sack of cement from Mitla, and supplies firewood to one of the little restaurants in Ayutla in return for his food and liquor.

Don Crescencio, brother of the Colonel, keeper of the one little store in Ayutla, acting *capillo* or chaplain of the band, singer in the church, clarinet player in the band, was also a great help, not only giving me much information himself but procuring for me my principal informant and interpreter, Francisco Reyes, then a servant working in his house. Francisco is responsible for most of the information in these pages, although it was almost entirely checked with one or more additional informants. He is a sober widower of some thirty-odd years, former secretary of the town council and one of the Colonel's men. His principal fault was that he never kept an appointment.

Of my other regular informants, Agapito Pérez, chairman of the school committee, was next most important. Most Mexicanized of the younger men, except the present secretary to the council, he has lived some years in Oaxaca and is an aggressive, not completely honest, person. Most of my formal work with him was done when he could scarcely escape me while I was curing him of a badly abcessed leg, the result of a neglected insect bite. Natalio, his cousin, was also an important informant, although he knew little of the earlier customs or of other towns. He was the most congenial of all, honest, willing, good-natured, and punctual. Nor was he given to drinking, a rare and desirable quality.

Among others who will appear in this account are the *presidente* or mayor and his *suplente* or alternate, Eustacio Chávez and Adolfo Galbán. Their sincere liking took the form of all-too-frequent efforts to persuade me to join in their almost daily libations, but I shall always remember with a certain poignancy the tall figure of the mayor praying whenever he became drunk and particularly that he wept as he kissed my hand and embraced me on my departure.

I will mention only briefly my informants outside Ayutla. In Tamazulapan the young secretary, a youth of little knowledge and less intelligence, gave some information. Most of my data on this near-by town came from Ayutla informants, although I made every effort to find a satisfactory worker there. In Yacoche the secretary was again my informant, the only Spanish-speaking person of the town. He was willing and informative, one of the few to speak freely about primitive practices. In Mixistlan the young secretary endeavored to prevent me from learning anything. He was again the only Spanish-speaking person I found. I did not get his name or the names of several others, for they are given with reluctance by the Mixe. A request for a name always suggests the possibility of some official and unpleasant reminder of the conversation at a later time.

In Tlahuitoltepec the various members of the town council gave data. In Totontepec the friendly mayor, Juan Chávez, and the only Mixe schoolmaster, Ismael Alcántaro, were my informants. The latter was the one really capable interpreter I found, and anyone planning a trip into Mixe territory should make every effort to secure his services through the ministry of education. He was guide, informant, and interpreter to Oscar Schmieder.[2] In Metaltepec my informant was the *alcalde*, or judge, and a young man designated by him, both prompted at intervals by the schoolmaster. In Juquila Mixes, Izekiel Ramírez was my informant, an intelligent and willing young man who refused any pay for his two days' services on the ground that it had been a pleasure. Doña Paulina, wife of the Colonel, also gave some data on this town, where she had spent her youth. In Tepuxtepec the mayor and the chairman of the school committee both acted as informants. They were naive and willing helpers for a limited time.

----

[2] Sr. Julio de la Fuente informed me in 1943 that Alcantaro was reported to have become a powerful local political boss.

CHAPTER III

MIXE GOVERNMENT

THE PHYSICAL CENTER of the Mixe town is the church and the *Municipio* or municipal building, usually built as nearly side by side as the terrain permits. This con-
tiguity symbolizes the union of church and state characteristic of Mixe government.
Even in so progressive a town as Ayutla contributions for the priest are collected
by municipal officials.

The town organization is primarily a Spanish creation which probably reflects as
closely as anywhere in Mexico the original Spanish concept of government for
Indian towns. It has undoubtedly assimilated certain native attitudes in the ideo-
logical complex which accompanies it. Thus for two of the officials native terms
exist, múdak, "judge," and némuk or "police chief." These two officials may represent transferences from aboriginal officers of analogous functions. The informal
position of the *principales*, "elders," unquestionably represents a carry-over of
native institutions since practically all native American Indian cultures have either
an express or implied control by the elder and more distinguished men.

Although minor differences exist from town to town, a few generalizations may
be made. The major officials are chosen by election at a *junta* or town meeting: the
minor officials then are chosen by the newly elected town council or the mayor. No
one is paid and the principal officials must give a fiesta to the townspeople. In theory,
every person is required to occupy every office before he is freed of the obligation to
serve the pueblo. In fact, this is impossible. There is a rigid line of succession to office
by which one advances from grade to grade, at each step enhancing one's prestige in
the town. When one's service is completed, one becomes an elder and no longer has
such duties as performing communal labor.

This office-holding system has become more than a discharge of duties to the
town. It is definitely the means of achieving social status and importance in the
community. Consequently, competition arises for the higher offices which not everyone may fill. Those who have ambition are eager to occupy one office after another
as rapidly as possible in order to gain prestige and influence. Particularly in the more
conservative towns, the elder has considerable authority and may even command
the mayor in certain circumstances.

An example of this authority of the elders was given me at Tepuxtepec, where
the chairman of the school committee served as my informant. One of the elders
wandered into the room and my interpreter and I began questioning him concerning
myths and tales. He flatly refused to admit to any knowledge, and when my interpreter made some allusion to the sacrificial rites practiced in the village, he said
rather hotly that they were none of our business and that in any case it was the duty
of the mayor to answer such questions. He went out hastily and returned almost
immediately with the mayor, who proffered his services. The mayor was obviously
bored and would have preferred to leave me with the young chairman of the school
committee, but under the sharp eyes of the old man he dared not leave. As he spoke
passable Spanish, which the elder did not understand, I secured information from
him which probably would have horrified the old man.

In general, ordinary election campaigns are unknown. In most towns anyone who resorts to open electioneering is despised and apt to be set aside. They have some hearsay knowledge that this sort of thing is done in the more Mexicanized Zapotec towns, and they have a profound contempt for it. Popularity should develop in a more subtle fashion without being obviously directed toward office holding. Thus one must be generous, particularly in the matter of providing liquor for everyone. Some of the young men in Ayutla say cynically that the conservative towns choose the mayor by the size of the mescal jugs a man brings to the town meetings.

The organization of Ayutla is typical of the Mixe villages. The officials are as follows, listed in the order of succession, the lowest grade first.

Twelve *topilillos*, servants of the church.
Sixteen *topiles*, policemen and messengers.[1]
Two *cabos*, or corporals, assistant police chiefs.
Two *tenientes*, or lieutenants, equal in rank to the *cabos*.
Two *mayores de vara*, police chiefs.
One *secretario*, secretary to the *alcalde* and *presidente*.
Five *regidores*, councilors.
One *suplente*, alternate to the *síndico*.
One *síndico*, administrator of the communal labor.
One *suplente*, or alternate to the *presidente*.
One *presidente*, or mayor.
One *suplente*, or alternate to the *alcalde*.
One *alcalde*, or judge.
Two *fiscales*, supervisors of the church.

In addition there is a *capillo* or chaplain of the church and five *sacristanes* or sextons.[2]

Manifestly, the occupation of each office by every man demanded by theory is impossible. If each *fiscal* must previously have occupied the office of judge, it would be impossible to have two *fiscales*. A man may become eligible by giving additional *mayordomías*. For other offices there are special services which enable one to omit various grades. The secretary, for instance, need not occupy any of the lower offices, or again, anyone who performs special services in connection with a major fiesta may skip certain intervening grades.

In Ayutla all offices above the grade of lieutenant or corporal in the preceding list and the office of chaplain are filled at a town meeting held December 1. Each man present is asked his choice, which is written down. The person most named for each office is declared elected. On December 24 each police chief appoints a corporal, lieutenant, half the police and "little police" or *topilillos*. No office, either elective or appointive, may be refused. The actual change of office is on January 1 and is symbolized by handing over the *varas* or canes of office. There is never any reëlection. In Ayutla only five officials have canes: the judge, mayor, their alternates, and the *síndico*. The *mayores de vara* or police chiefs, despite their name, have no canes, although in other towns they, and often the policemen, carry some sort of cane or staff.

To gain a clearer picture of the functioning of this system, each of these offices must be discussed in more detail. The sextons must immediately be set apart. They have little connection with the functioning of the municipal system. They alone of all the officials serve for life. When vacancies occur in their number, they fill the

---

[1] The term "topil" seems to be of Maya origin. See Roys, p. 40.
[2] The office-holding system is essentially the same in other towns. See Appendix II, p. 132.

place themselves from among a group of boys they have trained in the duties. They ring the church bells on all necessary occasions, assist the priest, and care for the church. They alternate, each serving one week. They receive no pay for their services nor any assistance from the community, but they are exempt from all communal service except the tekio or communal labor.

When a youth at Ayutla reaches the age of about seventeen, he is expected to begin to take a man's part in the community and he will be named *topilillo* of the church. Already he has probably been working in the tekio or communal labor since the age of twelve or even younger, if not by order, at least as a helper to his father. Now he will have to contribute maize to the church, one *almud* (about a quart and a half) a year.[3] As *topilillo* he will have to spend every other week in town, performing whatever service is required by the priest or *fiscales* in connection with the church and the priest's household. In the course of the year he first enters into the complex ceremonial life of the town when he, with his fellow *topilillos*, must serve atole ("corn gruel") to all the people one morning of Holy Week. Theoretically every young man must begin his service as a *topilillo* before reaching the rank of *topile*. Actually, as there are fewer places in the lowest grade, some youths of poorer families escape this appointment.

It is very unlikely that anyone will escape being named *topile* or policeman. Again, each alternate week must be spent in town under the orders of the chief of the division. The policemen arrest drunks and bring all those charged with offenses before the judge. They run errands, notify people to serve their communal labor, collect contributions levied by town councils, and do any other service required. If a policeman is sent as a guard to bring back some prisoner from another town, this is usually the first time he leaves his native village. But should a youth be fluent in speaking Spanish and apt at reading and writing, he may be named secretary and escape police service as well as all other services below the grade of alternate to the *síndico*.

If ambitious and not too poor, a young man soon will be named *mayor* or police chief, provided he has not been destined for the secretary's post. For a year he will command half the police and carry the keys to the jail on the weeks when his division is in charge. His service, again, will be performed on alternate weeks. He will name the assistants, corporal and lieutenant, the policemen or *topiles*, and the *topilillos* of his division. Those named corporal or lieutenant, though technically assistants, are considered to have given the same service as the police chiefs and do not have to fill the latter office.

A greater maturity and seriousness is required for the next office, that of the *regidor* or town councilor. These, five in number, are the advisors to the mayor and judge. Two are in charge of collecting the corn which is given to the priest. The other three assist in the administration of the communal labor in conjunction with the *síndico*. The councilors likewise spend only every other week in town at their duties.

If a youth aspires to higher offices, he must be prepared to serve the town an entire year at a time. No longer will he be able to return to his ranch every other week. An absence from town of more than a day on private affairs would be severely criticized and he might even be fined. If, as is probable, he is married when named

---

[3] This assessment is fairly common but is lacking at Juquila.

for a higher office, he must rent a house in the village, if he has none of his own. Formerly, by the time he had become *regidor*, a young man would have given at least one *mayordomía*, or fiesta to one of the saints. Today this is not necessary.

Following his service as councilor a man will become *suplente*, or alternate to the *síndico*, and then *síndico*. In this capacity he will become widely known, for he is a sort of straw boss of the men working at the communal labor and so has direct contact with every man of the village.

The next position of alternate to the mayor carries more responsibility than do most of the alternates' positions. The alternates of the *síndico* and judge serve only as substitutes in the event of illness or absence of the incumbents. The alternate, however, has occasion to gain valuable training against the time when he will hold the office. The alternate to the mayor, on the other hand, has certain definite functions, chief of which at Ayutla is the collection of the tax levied on the vendors at the weekly Sunday markets. This is the principal source of income to the municipality. The actual collection is done by *topiles*, or policemen, but the alternate keeps the records. If he cannot read or write he has the help of the secretary.

The mayor (*presidente*) is the guiding force of the administration. When a man has reached this office, he may be considered to have arrived socially. He is a personage in the community and within the customary limits has under his orders every man in the pueblo. Although he consults with the town council, he in fact makes most of the important decisions. The influence of the mayor fluctuates, naturally, with the personality of the man holding the office. Decision in the last analysis is made by him, however much talk may go on in the informal daily gatherings of the town council. He determines what improvements shall be undertaken through the tekio or communal labor. Work may include construction of new buildings, repair of roads and trails, and alterations and improvements of the church. He may send any man subject to service as far as Oaxaca to carry letters or supplies. He provides food for travelers and sees to their lodging. If necessary, he orders carriers to take their luggage. With his council he now passes on all cattle slaughtered in Ayutla to prevent the use of diseased or otherwise unfit beasts. This last, a relatively recent reform of the Colonel's, has made Ayutla the meat-producing center of the Mixe region.

In former times no one was eligible for the office of mayor who had not given two *mayordomías* or fiestas for a saint. Although this rule is now abrogated, two *mayordomías* are still required before a man finishes his service to the village. This is another of the links in the chain which binds together church and government.

Formerly, the mayors in Ayutla were always men fairly well along in years. This still is true in most towns. But with the rise of the progressive element in Ayutla the age has decreased. In 1933 Adolfo Galbán, the alternate to the mayor, was only twenty-nine.[4] In the normal course of events he became mayor in 1935 at the age of thirty-one. The year before, 1932, the mayor was a conservative. Unless there is a reversal from the present interest in progress, he was probably the last conservative mayor. This conservative was interested only in the church and spent his time work-

---

[4] The reduction in age was made possible by abrogation of the rule requiring two expensive *mayordomías* as a prerequisite, a change for which the Colonel was responsible. There is a lesson here for applied anthropologists. Only through intimate knowledge of the culture would it have been possible to know that abrogation of the *mayordomía* rule was a necessary prerequisite to attaining the desired end, namely, a reduction in the age of the higher officials of the community.

ing and praying there. The change in attitude is indicated by the fact that his concentration on the church so offended everyone that none of the other officials would help him. The only communal improvements accomplished that year were volunteer works undertaken at the suggestion of the Colonel and not through the formal machinery of the tekio. The mayor in 1933, Eustacio Chávez, was an ambitious although rather simple person. That year the town began the construction of a seven- or eight-room guesthouse and reroofed the church, both ambitious undertakings.

After a man has been mayor, he is in line for the posts of alternate to the judge and judge. Here, however, he may be superseded by one who has served as *capitán* in the town fiesta, for this office is considered the equivalent of that of mayor. As judge, a man hears all complaints and fixes fines for various offenses. He adjudicates property quarrels as well. Although his office is theoretically independent, he reaches no important decisions without lengthy discussion by the town council, often lasting for days. The judge in 1933 spoke no Spanish. Again he was probably the last non-Spanish-speaking person to hold this office. Four years before, he was mayor.

A man now well-advanced in years—provided he be noted, if not for piety, at least for good behavior—will next be named *fiscal*. In this office he administers the affairs of the church. At the close of this final year of service he will join the ranks of the principals or elders. Without official status, this group enjoys great influence in conservative towns. In Ayutla, with the rise of the Colonel and his progressive followers, the elders are little heeded. Their influential place in the town meetings has been taken by the five captains of the Colonel. They are still pointed out, however, as men who have finished all their service to the pueblo and are now free.

Although the chaplain is named at the town meeting with the other municipal officers, he is purely a church official. His service is considered equivalent to giving a *mayordomía*. For one year he "takes care" of the band. He summons it when needed, and it meets in his house. During the fiesta of San Pedro in June, he must feed the band at his house. This year, 1933, the chaplain is *"muy tonto,"* very stupid. He knows nothing. Consequently, with the ready adaptability which contrasts so strongly with Mixe attachment to custom, most of the functions are being discharged by Crescencio Martínez, brother of the Colonel. Crescencio is also a *maestro* or singer in the church and a player in the band.

The secretary in Ayutla occupies an enviable position compared with other towns. Not only is he excused from the lower grades of service, but he is not required to serve as *mayordomo* of a fiesta, or *mayordomía*. He is thus divorced from many of those functions which most fully reflect the conservative outlook. He must keep a record of all official business of the municipality, certify elections to the Mexican authorities at Villa Alta, and register all births, deaths, and marriages. He is held responsible by the Mexican authorities for all irregularities; but this means little in the Mixe towns. In some of the valley Zapotec towns a secretary is often fined for minor discrepancies in his reports. The next office open to the secretary of Ayutla is that of alternate to the mayor. It is a big jump, which I suspect the Colonel has arranged to insure the naming of a progressive mayor.[5]

In Zapotec towns, such as Mitla, there is often some church ceremonial connected

---

[5] Chinantec organization appears to be similar, although the account is sketchy. Bevan, pp. 71 ff.

with the transference of the canes when new officials take office.[6] Among the Mixe the ceremonial is entirely non-Christian in character. Although abandoned in Ayutla for some years, it is remembered by the older men. On December 31 the new members of the town government went to the cave above the town (see chap. vii, on "The Mountain Spirits") to perform sacrifices. They were required to bathe three times beforehand. Each man sacrificed a turkey by beheading it. Each left tepache, tamales, tortillas, and turkey and chicken eggs, "begging permission so that they might not die." They threw cigarettes into the water at the back of the cave. Afterward they gave a small fiesta in their houses, at which the flesh of the sacrificial turkey was served. The canes of office were given to them the following day. From the time they made the sacrifice until the fiesta of Espíritu Santo in June they might not cohabit with any woman. It was believed that violation of this taboo caused death.

These ceremonies are still observed by the people of Tamazulapan, who bathe in three different springs the night of December 31. (All the men of the town bathe three times in each of three different springs, according to the rather ignorant secretary of Tamazulapan.) After bathing they sacrifice turkeys, some in their own houses, some at Zempoaltepec, some on Cerro Pelado, the mountain behind the town. (This is a different mountain from that opposite Ayutla.) This is all done at night. The flesh of the turkeys is eaten at the houses the following day, but there is no fiesta. The secretary, although but a youth, had sacrificed a turkey upon taking office. The same period of chastity is required as was formerly observed at Ayutla. The canes of office are transferred on January 1 after the sacrifices.

Probably the officials of Yacoche have a period of chastity to undergo, but I did not know of this custom when I was in the pueblo and so did not make inquiries. At Yacoche, from January 1 until the middle of March, the mayor and judge call out at intervals from the municipal building every morning for an hour or more, beginning about five. This was said to be to let people know they were on duty. There is no tekio or communal labor during this period. After March, if there is to be tekio, the police chief calls from the municipal building.

At Mixistlan there is a period of "penitence," *penitencia*, for all officials. For an indefinite period of fifteen or twenty days they observe chastity and avoid any contact with women. During this period they cannot make any journey. They speak very little, remaining in a state of "monotony," occupying themselves by collecting pulque for the tepache to be served at the house of the mayor at the end of the period. To this celebration the *principales* or elders are invited, the only formal recognition of the *principales* I encountered. The elders drink tepache and eat tutteke tokshr (literally "turkey leg"), a stew of turkey flavored with *yerba santo* and chile. Before eating, a person called the néku kashr, usually the oldest man, speaks for the happiness and well-being of the community. He recommends especially that the authorities be lenient with the sons of the pueblo who commit some fault through genuine necessity. Afterward there are drinking, songs in Mixe, dancing, and usually some fighting.

On the first Saturday after the New Year both incoming and outgoing officials at Tupuxtepec take turkeys to kill on the mountain above the town. They are accompanied by the elders. They leave tepache, corn meal, and tamales with beans.

---

[6] Parsons, pp. 168 ff.

Either three or thirteen tamales are left according to individual inclination. Both numbers are characteristic of old Mexican rituals. It is said that blood is put on the corn meal but that the latter is neither buried nor sprinkled. Nevertheless, the bushes behind the sacrificial altar were covered with corn meal when I saw the place. It was also said that the sacrificial turkeys were plucked at the house. Again, however, when I saw the shrines, the ground was littered with turkey feathers, although there was no sign of their ceremonial usage.

It is possible that these elaborate rites may be a form of New Year's observance in which the officials play a prominent part. However, I do not incline to this view. The individual nature of the observances in most towns and their general lack of any communal character hardly suggest a communal New Year's rite. Moreover, in at least one conservative town, there are reports of definite New Year's rites which are quite apart from those described for the incoming officials.

In most if not all towns the incoming officials must make a *gasto*, "an expense," which always means that they must give a feast. In Ayutla this is done January 6. The new mayor sends his *topiles*, or policemen, with corn to all the unmarried girls. They grind it for the atole, or corn gruel, to be served by the town council. The *topiles* may take maize only to girls of their own division, or *barrio*: should they take it to a girl of the opposite group, she would send it back to the mayor without grinding it.

In Juquila the *gasto* of the new officials is on Ash Wednesday, in Yacoche, February 22, in Metaltepec, March with no fixed day, in Tlahuitoltepec, February 23. The expense is usually borne by the mayor and judge jointly. In some towns the *fiscales*, or churchwardens, must also make a *gasto* or feast. In Tlahuitoltepec this is February 26 when the *fiscales* invite the people to their houses. In view of the dates, the *gasto* seems more likely to be a New Year ritual than do the ceremonies of induction into office. The date of the ancient Mixe New Year is not known, but the beginning of the Mixtec and Zapotec New Year seems to have been in the neighborhood of March, probably fluctuating a good deal in different localities.

The governmental system outlined is far from efficient. The large group of officials for communities which never have more than twenty-five hundred inhabitants is utterly unnecessary. The requirement that all the important officials spend all their time in the town proper, particularly when, as at Ayutla, most of the people live in scattered ranches, is burdensome and unnecessary. Only the endless conversations which accompany every act require this constant attendance to duties. Even so, except for those actively engaged in supervising the tekio, or communal labor, the officials of Ayutla probably do not average an hour a day at community business. When the tekio is close to the village, all the officials are much in evidence, but they do little, if any, actual work. Much of their time is passed in endless and pointless conversation accompanied by a great deal of drinking. However, at an earlier time when written records were lacking, the conversation may have served a purpose.

Drunkenness is common among town officials. The director of the school at Ayutla was greatly annoyed by the habit of the mayor and some of the officials of sitting on a bench on the plaza and passing a bottle of mescal in full sight of the school. This usually happened about the time the director was supposed to give the pupils a short lecture on the evils of alcohol. When I first visited Yacoche it was the day the officials gave their *gasto*, and all were drunk.

Cumbersome and inefficient as the governmental system is, the Mixe are strongly attached to it. Any attempt by outside authorities to modify it would probably meet with the same bitter opposition as has happened in the Zapotec towns near the capital. Even the Colonel with all his influence does not attempt to tamper with the organization, although he subtly directs it at times. The linked church-state organization with its elaborate prestige mechanisms is the core of Mixe society. With the church rituals related to the organization, it is the primary force integrating the community. With all its faults, the system works, because it has behind it the full force of community approval and support.

Some incidents may illustrate the inadequacies of the system and its often capricious administration of justice. On the road out of Atitlan early one morning, I encountered the mayor and most of his council drunk. This arose out of the following situation:

A captain serving the Colonel, while visiting ranches to assemble men for work on the highway, encountered a woman and boy from Juquila selling mescal from two large jars at a trail junction. He assumed there was something wrong about the situation, since they had not asked permission of the mayor of Atitlan, and tried to take them to town. The woman and one jar of mescal disappeared somehow, but he arrived at Atitlan after dark with the boy and the other jar of mescal. The boy was deposited in the jail, foodless and blanketless on a cold, rainy, and foggy night, while the mescal found its way to the mayor. The latter insisted that it was necessary to sample the contents of the jar to discover if it was really mescal. Each time a member of the council arrived, the process was repeated. After that, they apparently decided they might as well finish the jar before going to the fiesta at Cacalotepec. What happened to the boy I never found out, but as I left the town, the mayor urged me to delay and have a drink, after which we would all go to the fiesta together; I declined. The mayor and the council had not arrived at Cacalotepec when I left there two days later. My companion, Francisco Reyes, was highly incensed at the entire proceeding and announced his intention of notifying the authorities at Juquila. This threat he did not carry out.

Apparently any means of keeping out of jail is justified. Once one is in jail, some sort of punishment is certain. If one manages to stay outside the doors, there is still a chance. In Totontepec a Yalalag Zapotec buying coffee was accused of using abusive and insulting language to a local woman. One of the *topiles* was all for putting him into jail, but he resisted violently. Upon the arrival of other officials, the effort to put him in jail was abandoned, the matter finally talked out, and the man released. The principal difficulty seemed to be calming the zealous *topile*.

Fidel, houseboy of the Colonel in Ayutla, got into trouble with a drunk during a Sunday market. His antagonist was dragged off to jail. Then a *topile* and the police chief tried to take Fidel to jail. He resisted so vigorously that he was dragged most of the way to jail by one foot while the rest of his anatomy made irregular contacts with the ground. After the jail door had been opened, he broke loose and fled across the fields, pursued by an excited and shouting crowd. Fifteen minutes later Fidel was back in the plaza and was presented with his hat by the police chief as if nothing had happened. In the excitement the jail door had been left open, but the inmates were apparently too drunk to take advantage of the situation. Later the town council in a body waited on the Colonel about the affair. The Colonel wisely refused to take part and Fidel eventually paid a small fine.

Agapito, one of the Colonel's men who was assigned to my service and who acted as informant at times, once became drunk and started home for his gun, saying he was going to kill people. His gun was taken from him and there was some talk of jail. Agapito is the only Mixe I ever saw reach for a weapon or threaten to use one. Such behavior is probably the result of several years spent in school at Oaxaca. Agapito fancies himself as "very Mexican." He is rather ashamed of his Indian environment and this also probably adds to his aggressiveness. On the other hand, mere residence in Oaxaca is not a sufficient explanation; for another of my informants, Antonio, personal servant to the priest, has spent even more time in the state capital, and he is never aggressive or quarrelsome, although well able to take care of himself and his interests. Probably the explanation lies not only in the fact of residence in Oaxaca but in the difference in the basic temperaments and the detailed histories of the two individuals.

Agapito is well aware of the consequences of fighting and is ready to take advantage of another's misfortune. He makes a modest addition to his income by always having cash to buy maize at bargain rates from individuals who must raise money to pay fines in order to get out of jail.

The Mixe indulge in frequent fist fights, especially while drunk. Although I probably saw several hundred fights, I saw no weapon used, although nearly all men carried machetes and many carried rifles. Most fights start with a drunken quarrel. When the pitch of the voices reaches a certain point, everyone expects a fight. The men hold out their weapons to the onlookers, and then begin to fight with their fists, swinging wildly until one falls down. The victor helps his opponent to his feet and usually they embrace each other. The loser usually says that his opponent is a good fellow; probably he could have hit much harder. Then they have a drink together. Sometimes, however, when one of the men is hurt by falling on a rock, or the fight threatens to become too serious, both men are put in jail overnight.

A few of the towns have means of raising communal revenue aside from special assessments voted at the town meeting. Ayutla gets some money from the fees of the Sunday market. Juquila has a tax system based on landholding and Jayacastepec has a per capita assessment. A few other towns have communally owned lands which are cultivated coöperatively and whose produce is sold for the benefit of the town treasury.[7] Funds so raised might be used to improve the church, but there is no direct connection. Metaltepec has communal lands, and the produce is stored in the municipal building. Totontepec also has communal land belonging to the town. In 1933 I heard a lengthy discussion in which it was decided that all the town officials would plant these lands for the benefit of the municipal treasury.[8] From the talk this was evidently an innovation. The land previously had either been left fallow or planted by only part of the officials, usually those belonging to a single *barrio* or ward. This had led to jealousies and the feeling by some that the *barrio* had perhaps misappropriated funds by making off with part of the product. Some of the municipal lands were rented, the income going to the town treasury.

The complete lack of communal funds in some towns and the very inadequate resources in all means that only through the tekio or communal labor system are any improvements accomplished. The tekio is voluntary in the sense of having the approval of the majority of the people. Although it is contrary to the Mexican constitution, the tekio is so deeply rooted in all the towns of Oaxaca that state and federal officials wink at its use, realizing that even the federal school system depends upon it. Only at Jayacastepec has the tekio been supplanted by a tax system and paid labor.

The firm position of the tekio results at least partly from the individual's identification of himself with the community. It succeeds for much the same reasons the governmental system as a whole succeeds. Its results are part of the individual's

---

[7] These fields seem never to be called the "lands of the Saint" as they are among the Zapotec. Parsons, p. 4.

[8] The discussion was mostly in Spanish. I gained the impression the use of Spanish was to impress me with how "civilized" the town is.

community interest and he feels personal satisfaction in witnessing the material achievements. Consequently, a man will do for the tekio what he would be unwilling to do for pay. For example, he will carry a stranger's baggage or act as guide without pay if ordered to do so by the mayor, but he will refuse to do it for pay. This attitude is reinforced by the nonacquisitive habits of the Mixe. Although they use money as a means of exchange, it does not represent wealth to be sought or hoarded by the individual.

Despite its firm hold on the Mixe, it is probable that the whole tekio system was a post-Spanish introduction. What little is known of pre-Spanish settlements and the absence of pyramids or other large public works suggests the absence of any communal labor. Neither could any Mixe word for the system be secured. Tekio is an Aztec word and was probably introduced along with the system, perhaps by Tlascalans from the garrison of Villa Alta.

In most towns the mayor orders what work is to be done by the tekio. In Ayutla a *junta* decides the number of days' service each year, usually three days for the municipality and three days for the church, but the mayor still decides the purposes. The only check upon him is the question of funds. If extra money is to be expended on a project, he must have the authority of a town meeting to levy a special assessment for the purpose. In most towns the mayor, shortly after taking office, makes a formal announcement in which he indicates the projects he wishes to complete. This is looked on as part of his duties and some of his reputation will depend upon the effectiveness and amount of labor undertaken.

Some of the labor is the improvement of trails or the opening of new ones, but in pueblos like Ayutla, where a new order is in the making, much of the labor is devoted to construction projects. For the church bricks must be made, floors laid, walls whitewashed, and roofs repaired. The schoolhouse, homes for the teachers, and new municipal buildings must all be built or repaired. Toward this work each man must contributed a *fanega* of lime, roughly a bushel. At Ayutla under the influence of the Colonel a long-range project is planned. It will create a modern, more or less conventional plaza about which will be grouped the new municipal buildings, the market, the schoolhouse, and the church.

Certain persons are exempt from working in the tekio. These include the mayor and all the officials, although some of the minor officials may do some work in connection with the supervision of the tasks. The mayor, however, should do nothing. My informant was quite shocked at the idea he should perform any work. Some ten or twelve of the Colonel's men, the captains and a group of young men who run errands and work for him, are also exempt from tekio. So are the sextons and elders. Those who must serve are notified by *topiles* a week in advance of the time when their services are required. If they have not appeared by the end of the week, they are arrested and fined or made to do ten or fifteen days' additional labor as punishment. The councilors have the tekio under their particular charge, while the *síndico* serves as foreman.

In addition to the tekio, in Ayutla and some other towns a man may be called on for service as *mozo* at any time. This means that he may be expected to go on a journey of several days' duration without pay to bring supplies for some municipal enterprise, to carry messages, or to act as porter for some traveler. Few exceptions are made, and old Tata Le, seventy or more, went the long trail to Mitla to carry back a sack of cement on his back. However, those who are exempt from the tekio are also exempt as *mozos*. In addition, the musicians are excused. A considerable discussion arose one Sunday morning on this very point. A young man, who had been practicing with the band for some time and was about to become a regular member, was ordered to go to Mitla. The band immediately rose to the defense of what it considered an infringement of its prerogatives.

One interesting feature of the tekio is the daily call to work. At Ayutla each morning and evening the *regidores* call from the plaza or the brickyard below the town to remind people to come to work. The call, shouted in unison, floats musically along the mountainside and echoes in the gorge below.

> *Atsók miókch, atsók miókch, atsók miókch, yatsók yung yagabáda.*
> Hurry, hurry, hurry, that the work may be finished.

At Tlahuitoltepec the drum and flute are played every evening to notify the people of tekio the following day. The drum is an ordinary two-headed instrument of Spanish type, twelve to fourteen inches in diameter and fifteen inches deep. The flute is really a whistle about twelve inches long with seven or eight stops near the lower end. Both instruments are known only by the Spanish names. They are kept in the office of the mayor. These instruments were formerly in use in Ayutla but the people "didn't like them."[9] At Yacoche it is the police chiefs who call from the plaza while at Totontepec the councilors formerly called as at Ayutla. At present, the church bell is rung. The drum and flute are used at Totontepec, not with the tekio, but with the church fiestas and *mayordomías*. This reminds one of the practice at faraway Tepoztlan near Mexico City.[10] I know of it nowhere else in Oaxaca. At Juquila the police chiefs call the *topiles* by shouting. At Metaltepec everyone works at the same time, the word being carried by the policemen or *topiles*. Tamazulapan uses the drum during the day and at night the flute. While work is going on, the drum and flute are also played softly. At Tepuxtepec the entire city government calls from the plaza on Saturday and Sunday when there is to be tekio the following week.

One of the most puzzling features of Mixe town organization is the presence in many of the towns of two or more divisions called barrios. Barrio is a word of Spanish origin referring originally to a political division more or less equivalent to a ward. The Spanish applied the term in Mexico to native divisions within towns. The nature of these early "wards" has been the subject of much inconclusive argument. The barrio is still found in many Mexican and Indian communities and in the Indian villages it has many elements which are reputed to be of Indian origin, although some students have vigorously denied an aboriginal basis.

The most puzzling fact about the barrio among the Mixe is that there is no logical reason for its existence. The frequency of two barrios in Mixe towns with their accompanying organization and certain functional aspects suggests a survival of an aboriginal division of the people into two divisions or moieties. It seems unlikely that they were introduced by the missionaries, because none of the towns is large enough to make this a warrantable administrative device. On the other hand, the lack of any native term for the unit argues against its aboriginal origin.

---

[9] This is probably part of a reaction against anything "primitive" or "uncivilized," which is a frequent occurrence when progressive forces operate in a town in Mexico.
[10] Redfield, p. 152.

Membership in the barrios of Ayutla is inherited from the father. The lands are not divided specifically between the barrios, although the town proper is geographically partitioned. That part above the plaza is considered the barrio of San Pedro, while that below is of San Pablo, the two titular saints of the village. However, the people live without regard for these geographic divisions, and membership in the barrio is unaffected by residence. There are no nicknames for the barrios, nor could I discover any tendency to marry either within one's own barrio or outside it. It was stated repeatedly by Francisco Reyes that land owned by a person in one barrio could not pass to another barrio, but concrete instances contradicted the assertion. It seems clear that marriage places a woman in her husband's barrio. Since a woman may inherit land from a member of her father's barrio and pass it on to her children, obviously land ownership can pass from one barrio to another. If a woman is widowed, she remains a member of her husband's barrio unless she remarries a man of the opposite barrio. In this event, it is said that the children do not go with their mother but are kept by relatives of the father. If she should marry a man of the same barrio as her former husband, she would keep the children. It was in this connection that Francisco first volunteered the statement that lands must not leave the barrio. I was unable to resolve the contradictions in statements.

It seems significant that the mayor and judge, the two most important officials, must always be of different barrios. The offices rotate annually. Thus, if this year the mayor is of the barrio of San Pedro, the judge will be of the barrio of San Pablo. Next year the offices will be reversed. Somewhat similarly, the *regidores*, or councilors, *mayores*, or police chiefs, and the police themselves will be divided equally between the two barrios. They rotate in office on alternate weeks, so that the barrio of San Pablo is in charge one week, that of San Pedro the next.

The pueblos where I inquired about barrios were Ayutla, Totontepec, Metaltepec, Atitlan, Cacalotepec, Juquila, and Tepuxtepec. Of these, only Metaltepec lacks barrios. At Totontepec the barrios have no geographical localization. Membership is inherited from the father, but there are no marriage rules. The mayor and judge are supposed to rotate as at Ayutla. If they do not, there is hard feeling. There is a distinct impression that a mayor favors those of his own barrio. This came out practically in the discussion noted above about the communal lands of the village (see p. 29). The lack of any geographical localization for the barrio at Totontepec is interesting because it is one of the few Mixe villages which is compact and where such localization would serve an administrative purpose. It is here one would expect localization to survive, if the barrio were primarily a Spanish administrative device.

Juquila, another relatively compact village, has a geographical limit to the barrios. Barrio San Ildefonso lies east of the river through the town, Barrio San Juan west of the river. However, residence is, as usual, indiscriminate, and membership is entirely through inheritance from the father. Atitlan and Tepuxtepec have barrios, but I could learn of no function whatever for them. Officials in these towns do not rotate in office. Of the two, only Atitlan has any geographical division, the two barrios forming almost separate villages about half a mile apart. At Cacalotepec the officials rotate by barrio, and the interesting assertion was made by the secretary that a man moving from one barrio to the other would change his barrio affiliations. My time in Cacalotepec was not sufficient to verify this statement properly.

Functionally the barrio at the present time serves little purpose, although it is a rallying point for a slight degree of community feeling. As such, it is very feeble. A man does, however, usually know the barrio affiliation of his friends and neighbors, and there seems to be some feeling of closer ties with a person of one's own barrio than with one of the opposite barrio.

On the whole, there seems a strong probability that the Mixe barrio is an altered remnant of some pre-Spanish institution. Although our knowledge of the village organization of sixteenth- and seventeenth-century Spain is deficient, I know of no suggestion of a Spanish institution of this character with membership determined by inheritance rather than by residence. Neither does there ever seem to have been any administrative purpose which would have led the Dominican missionaries to have introduced a ward organization in the towns or to have led them almost always to form two divisions. Although early writers assert that aboriginal Mixe settlements were always of related families and hence exogamic, there is no evidence in the kinship system of formalized exogamic divisions such as clans or moieties. A dual organization in which the wife changes membership at marriage, which shows no trace of exogamy, and in which property apparently passes from one division to the other certainly does not conform to the traditional definition of a moiety organization. Consequently, it seems as difficult to derive the Mixe barrios from a previous moiety organization as it is to imagine a Spanish introduction.

These difficulties are lessened if we imagine the aboriginal groupings to have been primarily or wholly for ceremonial and political purposes. We know that elsewhere in America there were barrio divisions with administrative and ceremonial functions. The Aztec calpolli, whatever its origins, primarily served functions of this type at the time of the conquest. References to native barrios are numerous in early Spanish literature and much ink has been spilled in arguments over their nature. It is possible that the whole problem of barrio and moiety in America has been unwittingly and unnecessarily complicated by the longstanding preoccupation of most anthropologists with exogamic institutions, a legacy from the early evolutionary theorists. It is quite possible that, just as offices rotate between Mixe barrios today, various offices or functions may have rotated between some aboriginal dual divisions. A parallel case is afforded in some of the Rio Grande pueblos in the United States where offices and functions rotate between dual groups which are persistently miscalled moieties although they no more deserve this title than do Mixe barrios. Even though to say so is highly speculative if not downright heretical, I venture the suggestion that the effort to consider moieties and clans as historically linked problems in much of America has badly obscured the real history of the two institutions. Actually, the two may have almost wholly independent histories. Clans probably originated as exogamic institutions centering around kinship groups. The moiety is possibly related historically to the barrio, both originating as nonexogamic institutions concerned with ceremonial and political problems and little or not at all with kinship. It may even be that where the moiety today is found in America as an exogamic institution, exogamy is frequently a late addition through the influence of exogamic clans. This, I know, is treason, but, although I am not prepared to defend myself to the death, I strongly suspect that a whole generation of antievolutionist anthropologists has been misled by an evolutionist dogma with respect to moieties in the Americas.

To round out a discussion of the Mixe community, one must also consider the church briefly. This is not the place to discuss the church as a religious institution, but it has certain social functions which intimately relate it to parts of the civil organization. The civil officials have functions in connection with the church, while the officials of the church, with the exception of the *maestros*, or singers and sextons, are named in the same manner as civil officials.

The physical upkeep of the church is performed by the officials of the town. Likewise, town officials provide the care and subsistence of the priest in such towns as Ayutla where one is resident. In Ayutla each adult male must give a measure of corn to the support of the priest. We have already discussed the duties of such civil officials as the *topilillos* or "little policemen" and the chaplain in this respect.

Another group which has been mentioned but not discussed is composed of the *mayordomos*, or majordomos. A more detailed account of their functions will be given later. Every Mixe town has its majordomos, varying in number from Yacoche with one to Juquila with seventy. Each one is in charge of a saint for from one year to three, the latter being the term of office in Ayutla. In this post the majordomo cares for the saint and his candles, collects and accounts for alms, and so on. In addition he must make certain expenditures from his own pocket. These may vary from approximately seventy pesos to nearly five hundred pesos for the *mayordomo* of San Juan, the titular saint of Juquila.

The office of *mayordomo* is usually filled from the ranks of the more wealthy citizens of the community. Although every man is expected to conduct two *mayordomías* or fiestas in the course of his life, a man who manifestly could not make the necessary expenditures would not be appointed to the office. The appointments are made by the mayor. In some towns the approval of the *regidores* or councilors is also required. The mayor audits the accounts of the saint and is present when the funds are transferred from the old *mayordomo* to the new.

The funds in the hands of the *mayordomos* ordinarily constitute the largest collections of ready cash in a Mixe town. In fairly prosperous and progressive communities like Ayutla levies upon these funds are sometimes made for nonchurch purposes. The schoolhouse at Ayutla was constructed partly with funds taken from the *mayordomos*. In a conservative town this procedure would be unthinkable; even at Ayutla it caused great argument.

The majordomo's office is another tie which integrates the individual with the community. As *mayordomo* he is serving the town as a whole, both providing an entertainment for his townsfolk and contributing, through his care of the saint, to the spiritual welfare of the community. A certain redistribution of wealth is also accomplished by the *mayordomía* system through the tendency to pick wealthy individuals for the office.

No description of the Mixe villages could be complete without a discussion of the Colonel, already mentioned many times. Although in a larger sense the Colonel and his influence are an example of the *caciquismo* or bossism common throughout Mexico, he is at the same time the principal expression of what little tribal unity exists among the Mixe and the principal influence for progress among the Western Mixe.[11]

The antecedents of the Colonel are somewhat obscure. He is a full-blooded Mixe, native of Ayutla, about forty years of age. His father, who still speaks no Spanish, was a *viajero* or traveling trader. This no doubt provided a somewhat wider back-

[11] This is perhaps less true today than in 1933. Rival bosses now control some of the towns.

ground for the Colonel's youth than that possessed by most Mixe, for traders are rare among them. At some time in his youth the Colonel left Mixe territory for a number of years and became thoroughly *ladino* in most respects. The reasons for this departure and what he did during this time I never succeeded in discovering. It may have had something to do with a family quarrel. He has living in Ayutla one brother, Crescencio, with whom he is on friendly but far from intimate terms. Another brother lives in Oaxaca. With him the Colonel's relations are definitely distant. A fourth brother lives in Quetzaltepec in the region of the central Mixe and of him the Colonel never speaks.

On his return to Mixe territory the Colonel immediately assumed a position of some importance. At that time he probably was one of the few Mixe who spoke Spanish and had a technique for dealing with the problems of the outside world. Mexico was in a turmoil of revolution at that time. Although it scarcely affected the Mixe, it may have caused them to turn with some relief to a person of their own tribe who could in some measure interpret and deal with the problems arising from their few outside contacts.

In 1914 a letter was sent to all the Mixe pueblos from some official in Mexico City, ordering them to name for the region a *Jefe de Defensa*, chief of defense. In accordance with this letter, a meeting of all the Mixe pueblos was held and the Colonel was named to the office "because of the confidence he had inspired."

There is again a period of obscurity during which the Colonel began building up his influence. At first this must have been very little outside Ayutla. He was first named a captain, but at a later meeting the towns elevated him to the position of colonel.

The achievement of his present eminence has not been without opposition. The Nexapa Mixe have consistently remained apart under the leadership of another local *cacique*. The town of Isquintepec was for some time divided on the question of its allegiance, so much so that federal troops had to be sent there to put a stop to the internecine warfare which developed. It now obeys the Colonel. Before 1923 even near-by Juquila flouted the Colonel's authority under the leadership of a captain. Like most Mixe towns, its people were armed, and, unlike most Mixe towns, it was noted for its disorderliness. In 1923 the Colonel raised a force of some four hundred men from Juquila, Tamazulapan, and other near-by pueblos, including a few from Zapotec Yalalag, and marched to the Isthmus to assist in the suppression of the revolt of García Vigil. On the way the force descended upon Juquila early in the morning and disarmed the population. Now there is a captain in Juquila who obeys the Colonel.[12]

The telephone system was the next step in the extension of the Colonel's influence. This was bought and installed by the villages, and has put the Colonel in much closer touch with many of the towns. Within a year or two it is expected to reach the Isthmus and also to be extended to Oaxaca with government help.

Another consolidation of his influence was the formation of a *Junta Regional* or

---

[12] I am told by Sr. Julio de la Fuente and others that the influence of the Colonel is now much less, owing to the rise of a rival cacique at Zacatepec. A Zacatepec leader was annoying in 1933. Incidentally, Sr. de la Fuente, who has studied the Zapotec of the Cajones Valley over a period of years, has a very low opinion of the Colonel, considering him ruthless and brutal in his methods. I can only record what I saw and heard in Ayutla and other Mixe towns in 1933. Obviously, he was not without enemies and many feared him. I found no one who considered him dishonest or self-seeking and many who loved him greatly.

regional council for the construction of roads. In 1930 this *junta* of nearly all the Mixe villages raised thirty-five hundred pesos to buy a Chevrolet *camión*, to serve as a combination truck and stage. It was brought to Ayutla by unbelievable labor. Since then work has gone forward steadily. Sixteen kilometers of road have been built from Ayutla toward Mitla, through the worst of the country to be traversed. Another three years were expected to see its conclusion, but the Colonel wrote me that the summer rains of 1933 had been unusually heavy and had washed out all the bridges and culverts.[13] This disaster will probably set the work back nearly a year. Every adult male in the villages under the Colonel's jurisdiction must give three days' work a year in the construction of the road. Inasmuch as several towns are two, three, and more days from the road, the actual time involved may be nine to twelve days. The villages have also raised money to buy tools and dynamite, and to pay the foremen.

These external evidences of the way in which the Colonel has reached his present position and influence do not tell the entire story. They do not account for the admiration amounting almost to veneration in which he is held. The veranda outside the Colonel's office in Ayutla is occupied almost day and night by a motley group of people from all over Mixe territory. Hundreds of disputes are brought to him to be settled instead of being taken before the regular authorities. People come to appeal against the decisions of authorities in the towns; authorities come to ask advice upon problems with which they do not know how to cope. Thus the mayor of Mixistlan asked for help against an armed robber whom his people were afraid to arrest. The Colonel sent his soldiers to seize the man. When the Colonel went to Mexico City, he was accompanied by an armed guard as far as Mitla. When he returned, he was met by a force of fifty men from Ayutla with ten porters to carry his belongings. They scoured every rock and tree within gunshot of the trail. These guards, who try to accompany the Colonel whenever he stirs out of town, are voluntary. The Colonel frequently goes out alone and is roundly scolded by his followers. Not only does he sometimes go alone but only once in three months did he ever carry a gun himself.[14]

The love which the majority of the people evidently bear the Colonel is due to his character. His disposition is mild though determined. He is thoroughly appreciative of the way the native mind works. And more than all, he appears to be thoroughly honest. For all his services he is paid nothing. (But when he planted his corn crop, over seventy people appeared to help.) For each of his various activities he keeps careful books, which he shows to anyone who wishes to see them. He shapes his improvements as far as possible to native habits and operates through native institutions.

When work on the road was started, the Colonel conceived the idea of buying the truck. Before it appeared, work on the road was most desultory. When the people saw the truck, it became possible to organize the labor and push it ahead rapidly. When local improvements are under way, the Colonel always sees that they are started before demands are made on the people for labor and materials. He explained this technique to me by saying that the people resented being asked to do things for

[13] Actually the road has not been completed. Instead, the Mixe are trying to have it form part of the national highway from Oaxaca to the Isthmus.

[14] This is personal observation, not hearsay. I leave it to those who know the Mexican temperament well to say whether the Colonel would have been still alive and in good health in 1940, when I last saw him, if he had been as ruthless a tyrant as outsiders have depicted him. I may add that he has no bodyguard in Ayutla.

a project only planned, but that once they saw work begun, they became eager to see it finished—sound psychology, particularly with the Mixe.

The Colonel is never overbearing in his attitude. His own story of the raising of the money for the purchase of a corrugated cement roofing for the school is instructive. Money was lacking, so a town meeting was called. The Colonel summoned his five local captains and explained the situation, asking their support. At the town meeting he proposed to take the funds out of the money in the hands of the *mayordomos*. This aroused a great deal of discussion and was violently opposed by the older men. The Colonel then pointed out that money taken in by the municipality at the market had gone into work on the church.[15] "We are all of one party here," he said. "There is no party of the church and another for the school. We are united." Evidently this is always a powerful appeal to the Mixe. With the support of the captains, the project was put through. *"Callete viejo!"* ("Be still, old man!"), the young said to the old ones. "You are old now. What do you know of these things?" At the next town meeting an old man arose to say he was still not reconciled to the use of sacred things for profane ends. No one answered him; he was simply ignored.

At the present time, the Colonel has five groups of soldiers in Ayutla, each under a captain. He also has soldiers in the other towns. These men are usually of the more progressive element and include practically all the Spanish-speaking people. They are enlisted with the Mexican government as irregular troops, a sort of national guard. Though the Colonel renders reports to higher officials, actually, the little army is his and his alone. It is a highly personal following.

In the Colonel and his closest followers, not only is the unity of the Mixe expressed, but also within this group lie the major aspirations for the future. Willingly or unwillingly, the majority of the Mixe are dragged for better or worse into an effort to improve their living standard and to bring about some degree of incorporation in the life of the larger community of Oaxaca and Mexico. Telephones and the road are two of the measures imposed by the progressive group. Schools are another. Owing in large part to the Colonel's influence, there are federal schools in nearly every Mixe town. That they remain is almost entirely because of his efforts. Undaunted by economic disabilities and obstacles which may well prove insuperable, since they are inherent in the geographic environment, the Colonel is earnestly endeavoring to give his people better houses, better clothes, and better food.[16]

---

[15] The first improvement for which the Colonel was responsible was building a new church.
[16] Some further details of the Colonel and his projects are given in Appendix II. The aboriginal political structure is also treated in the same place.

CHAPTER IV

THE FAMILY AND MARRIAGE

FAMILY RELATIONSHIPS loom large in the life of the Mixe. That they are not of even
greater importance is perhaps owing to the enveloping character of community
interests. But if the average man or woman's interest and knowledge extend little
beyond the limits of the town, his friendships, his personal relationships, reach little
beyond the range of the family in its more extended sense.

In pre-Hispanic times, the family among the Mixe was probably a more important
unit in society than at present. What slender documentary evidence exists for the
Mixe points to a relationship grouping which was also the community unit. These
units were undoubtedly much smaller than the present villages, probably mere
rancherias.[1]

It is possible that these restricted groupings of relatives represented something
approaching a localized clan unit in the technical sense, but there is no evidence that
they actually limited marriage between the real or putative relatives. They may
represent no more than a lineage clustering about the oldest man, somewhat in the
manner of the modern Lacandones of near-by Chiapas. On this point the kinship
system gives no assistance. The present barrio system throws little light on the
the situation either. The probabilities, however, seem to favor the idea that these
early settlements were localized kinship groups which were, in effect, clans.

The kinship system, on the other hand, is definitely opposed to any suggestion
of clan organization. It is substantially a generation system today. Grandparents of
maternal and paternal lines are merged and are distinguished only by sex. Parents
are distinguished from their siblings, but there is again merging of the two lines.
Nephews and nieces are distinguished only by sex. However, Quintana's data suggest
greater differentiation formerly. In the generation of the speaker, older brother and
older sister appear to have been distinguished, but younger siblings were merged
without even distinguishing sex. Both cross and parallel cousins are merged with
the siblings. Of perhaps some significance is the rather large number of terms for
relatives by marriage. All these facts are in agreement with the present importance
of the bilateral family and the rather close and friendly attitudes toward relatives
by marriage.

It should be remarked that the Mixe seem little interested in kinship terms. It was
only with extreme difficulty that the interest of informants could be held to detailed
genealogical investigation and I was unable to resolve the considerable variations
which appear in the following list. My time in other towns did not permit the collection of full lists of kinship terms, but I present some terms from Totontepec, Metaltepec, and Juquila. These suggest the degree of dialectic variation in the western
area. I am also giving the terms recorded by Father Quintana for Juquila. If it be
remembered that Quintana uses c where I have used k following a vowel and x for
an sh sound, the terms may easily be approximately equated with my own. The
Quintana data suggest that there has been some merging of terms or else that
Juquila is somewhat divergent from Ayutla. Not only are avuncular-nepotic terms
more elaborate, but sex of speaker is frequently indicated in the Quintana terms.

[1] Burgoa, 2:305.

	Ayutla	Totontepec	Metaltepec	Juquila	Quintana (Juquila, eighteenth century)
Father	dáta, dátits	te, táta	te·ech	táta	teit
Mother	dágits, nána	tak, nána	tetchniyañ, nana	nana	taac
Child	utsüñ, unk, mank	únuk	unk		
Blood child	tuigüitsu				
Son	mánguts			unk	unk, manc
Daughter	nú·shits			toshúnk	nôx
Father's brother and mother's brother	tságum, tsúgum	em	u'	tsugú·	
Father's sister and mother's sister	tsúgu, tsugúk	túkuk	um	tsukúm	
Father's brother					tzucumteit
Mother's brother					haim
Father's sister					tzucuu
Mother's sister					tzucuutaac
Brother's son	tzukmánk		hamyúñ	sopmánk	tzocmank
Sister's son	tzukmánk		hamyúñ	sopmánk	haim
Brother's daughter	tzuknísh		hamyúñ	soknúsh	tzocnôx
Sister's daughter	tzuknísh		hamyúñ	soknúsh	haim
Grandfather	tetmeái, tetchmiái	ap	tetchniyáñ		ap, apteit
Grandmother	dokmoíis, takmái	ok	takamuk		oc, octaac
Grandchild	ápmets, ap		ok	ok	apunk (m. sp.)
Grandson	utsu ap	ap			ocunc, ocmanc (w. sp.)
Granddaughter	apas	ok			ocnox (w. sp.)
Brother	mögúktsua			mugúk	motuucqueex
Sister	dashchük			mugúk	cotoix
Older brother	atsh, nókshits	atch	atch		aitch (m. sp.) ay (w. sp.)
Younger brother	itch, údshits	uts	utch		vich (m. sp.) ay (w. sp.)
Older sister	tzu, tzuu	tsäü	sü		tzôô (m. sp.) coyai (w. sp.)
Younger sister	itch, údshits	uts	utch		vich (m. sp.) coyai (w. sp.)

Cousins are called by sibling terms. Distant relatives for whom no regular term exists may be called by the same term as a nearer relative of the same general category. For example, a cousin of an uncle would be called by the same term as the uncle.

Wife	nédó'shits
Husband	neyékwits
Husband's mother, son's wife (w. sp.)	shrékshits, sheks
Husband's father, son's wife (m. sp.)	tzut, chú'u
Wife's mother, daughter's husband (w. sp.)	múktak
Daughter's husband (m. sp.)	míu't
Wife's father	múkteit
Sister's husband, wife's brother	hui
Brother's wife (m. sp.), husband's brother	ingópis, kop
Husband's sister, brother's wife (w. sp.)	ókits, ohi'

Wife's sister, sister's husband (w. sp.)	gop
Husband's brother's wife	tzúesna, míu't (?)
Wife's sister's husband	mwé·ai
Co-father (*compadre*)	yap
Co-mother (*comadre*)	yoké
A distant relative of any sort	pamagúk

The modern family group is undoubtedly considerably changed from the aboriginal pattern, yet in large measure the people living on privately owned rancherias in towns such as Ayutla actually do come pretty close to the old system. A man holds his land until his death, and his grown sons bring their wives home, build their houses near by, and cultivate the family lands held by the father. We may surmise that the extended family of the aboriginal Mixe comprised the blood relatives and the relatives by marriage, words for both father's relatives and mother's relatives being found in Mixe. (Techchanikiyók, all relatives of the father: takchanikiyók, all relatives of the mother. These names are obvious compounds.) The alteration created by the Spanish in the extended family consists primarily in the many close relationships established by the adoption of the Catholic godparent and co-father and co-mother concept. Throughout Mexico the Latin extremity to which these relationships are carried has profoundly altered family relationships. The Mixe are no exception, although they do not go so far as the neighboring Zapotec. The Mixe have godparents for baptism, confirmation, and marriage. The same individual never serves in more than one capacity. These godparents are regarded in a peculiarly intimate sense. In certain crucial functions they supersede the parents, and their children are regarded by the godchildren as being practically the same as brothers and sisters. Furthermore, the godparents of one's children, the co-father and the co-mother, have claims upon one which approach those of consanguineous family obligations. Consequently, one has, in addition to the bilateral blood relationships with their feeling of solidarity, a group of co-fathers, co-mothers, godparents, and godchildren which extends this solidarity far beyond the limits of consanguinity and weaves a network of relationships over the whole community. That these relationships contribute immeasurably to community solidarity needs scarcely be stressed. Thus persons of influence and prestige, such as the Colonel and his wife, will have a peculiarly intimate relationship with the people through having been godparents to one child of practically every important family of the community. In addition, these pseudo relationships extend far beyond the community limits and are a means of tying important people of other towns to a common set of interests.[2] These interfamily bonds are made further important by being of genuine functional value and are rendered doubly significant by being called into play particularly in times of difficulty and emotional disturbance. As an example, the godparents arrange the funeral of a small child.

The family is theoretically brought into existence by marriage, which has more extended meanings than the conventional viewpoint would give it. Financial reasons and the small number of priests in Mixe territory combine to make church marriage merely a matter of ostentation. Civil marriage is usually observed only when the church marriage is undertaken, although in some towns it is observed where church

[2] The influence of these relationships may be remarkably important even in non-Indian Mexico. A godfather of the Colonel's only child is a former minister of education. This fact affected the whole course of federal educational programs in the Mixe region for a number of years; possibly it may still be significant.

marriage is almost unknown. Church and civil marriages have little validity beyond that possessed by the informal sanctions already recognized by the Mixe. Marriage for the Mixe is really a business of living together, having children, and working out a common set of economic interests. To be recognized as legitimate it must be semi-permanent, but this legitimacy springs from a sense of community recognition resting on a vaguely defined set of values which is entirely apart from the conventional church or civil marriage. Evidence of serious intention on the part of the principals themselves is chief of these values, and performance of certain ceremonies having no relation to the church or civil ceremonies supplies this evidence immediately. If one gives the proper preliminary feasts, unites with the woman of one's choice with the consent and aid of the parents on both sides, and particularly if the marriage is arranged with the help of the parents, it is immediately of the best standing. On the other hand, a marriage by elopement under various circumstances must prove itself by the subsequent conduct of the principals.

Under these conditions, church marriage becomes merely the expression of the economic status of the couple. It rarely precedes the actual consummation of the marriage and usually it occurs a year or often many years after the consummation. It is an ostentatious affirmation, first of the satisfaction of the principals with the arrangement and the belief of the husband in his wife's virtue, and second, and far more importantly, of the superior economic status of the family. In some towns, where church marriage is almost impossible, the civil marriage has to some extent taken its place for the first of these functions.[3]

A real social disability attaches to only one type of sex union, that which is nonpermanent. People who habitually form unions of but a few months' duration are called bachelors (*solteras* and *solteros*). The male of this type is but a shade more respectable than the female. In a town the size of Ayutla there are perhaps a dozen men and an equal number of women who are notorious for forming these temporary unions. The likelihood of their forming a permanent or semipermanent union is considered very small. Although an unattached person may live with one of them for a while, most people would hesitate to do so because there is always the danger that, should the union prove temporary, they would find themselves in the bachelor class. Then only with great difficulty could they form a permanent union, however much they might wish to.

In addition to these more or less open irregular sex relationships, there are, of course, frequent extramarital or premarital relationships of a more transitory nature. These will be dealt with later.

Marriage as a family affair varies considerably in different towns. It is common to find some sort of public sanction of the union. Ayutla, however, presents the typical situation of the disrupted culture. Perhaps owing to the presence of a priest and to the more sophisticated character of the population, the church marriage is more frequent, and the nonchurch union more often without any form of public announcement. Where in other towns a technically unofficial union (in the eyes of church or state) would commonly be publicly announced with certain prescribed ceremonies, in Ayutla such a union is entered into far more casually. Here, usually, it is purely a matter of living together.

The reasons for the decline in marriage ceremonial at Ayutla are easily discerned.

---

[3] See Beals, 1936, for a discussion of some problems raised by Mixe marriage customs.

The priest in residence has naturally frowned upon the unorthodox type of ceremony which, in a measure, competes with his lucrative business of marrying couples. Consequently, the more devout look down upon these marriages to some extent. Since most couples cannot afford the expense of a church wedding and since the civil wedding has acquired no real significance, there seems little point in going to the expense of presents and feasts for a ceremony which will give no general community standing to the marriage. Once the ceremonial accompaniment is abandoned, there seems little reason to solicit the intervention of the parents which a ceremonial marriage would require. The majority of the unions therefore have become extremely informal and the very informality seems to have led to an increasing brittleness in the ties.

The age of marriage has a wide range, from eighteen to thirty years. Most people live together before a church marriage, the majority without even informing their parents of their intention. Some, however, still observe the traditional forms. Traditionally, a man goes with his father to ask the parents of the girl for her. They take a present of mescal. Occasionally, the girl will delay a year before making a decision, and her wishes are invariably deferred to everywhere among the Mixe. Generally, however, the man and the girl will have reached an understanding beforehand, for there is a good deal of unobtrusive courting. The only direct evidence of this I saw, besides whispered conversations on the trails, occurred when I consented to take photographs for some young men. It developed they did not want their own pictures but each one had some girl whose picture he wished me to take. These were quite young people, many of whom I had never seen together before.

At any rate tradition prescribes at least two, or preferably three, visits before final consent is given. If the parents of the groom are dead, he asks an older man to accompany him, "one who knows how to manage." When the matter is decided, the prospective groom gives a small fiesta (often called the *gasto* or expense), serving tepache, atole, tamales, chocolate, and mescal, and with stringed music for dancing. Those without money for expenditure may put in a year or more working for the girl's parents. Sometimes the groom gives tamales and tepache to the girl's parents before the fiesta. The fiesta is really the wedding ceremony and properly lasts for three nights. At the end of the third night the parents go home, leaving the girl behind. Formerly there were other elaborations resembling those in Totontepec (described below).

A man customarily will have built his own house before the ceremony, and the fiesta is held there. If he should not have his own home, it is held in his father's, where the couple will live. This is rare. Residence in the bride's house is held to be unknown. The bridal couple receive no gifts, although the man's relatives will help him with his expenses. The man buys all the household equipment.

For a church marriage at Ayutla there is one set of godparents, not two as in some of the Zapotec towns.[4] Certain parts of the ceremony are stereotyped, such as the use of *las aras*. The sexton pours seven pieces of money from a plate into the man's hands. He, in turn, lets them fall through his hands into those of the bride. The money is returned to the priest after the ceremony. At the same time, a chain of silver is put about the necks of the couple by the priest. This is removed at the end of the mass, not worn for three days as at Zapotec Mitla.[5] After the marriage, the

---

[4] Parsons, p. 103.   [5] Parsons, p. 104.

godparents come to the house of the groom and there is a two- or three-day fiesta at which tepache and mescal flow freely.

Formerly a turkey would have been sacrificed in connection with a wedding, but whether this applied to the church ceremony or to the more informal type of wedding is not remembered.

The purely ostentatious character of church marriage is indicated by the fact that separations occur as freely after a church marriage as before. Separations are usually caused by excessive drunkenness or mistreatment by the man, by inattention to household duties on the part of the woman, or by some variant of the triangle situation. After a separation, the children are divided, "like chickens" according to one informant, and the wife returns to her parents. Just what would happen to the normal inheritance of property in such cases I did not ascertain.

At Totontepec I had the fortune to witness a marriage in the old style. Here, as at Ayutla, the youth goes with his father and mother to the house of the girl. They go as many times as are necessary to arrange the affair, which will be much talked over by relatives and godparents. Even the mayor may be consulted. When everything has been arranged, the *prenda* is held. At Totontepec this is frequently referred to as the wedding, and civil and religious marriages are often delayed or never celebrated, as in other towns. After the *prenda* the couple begins *de facto* married life.

I could secure no native equivalent for *prenda*. The Spanish word *prenda* appears to have been applied with its somewhat unusual meaning of "gift," for a gift seems to be an important part of the ceremony. Nevertheless, the ceremony is not Spanish, although it may be a post-Spanish borrowing from the Zapotecs, a hypothesis which might account for its Spanish name among the Mixe. The Mitla betrothal ceremony,[6] with which that of the Mixe may be equated, is clearly related to the upper-class wedding described by Burgoa for the Mixtec town of Tilantongo.[7]

At a modern *prenda* witnessed in Totontepec, the mayor and town council, together with most of the guests, assembled at the municipal offices. Led by the officials, the group first went to the house of the groom, where a small glass of aguardiente and cigarettes were given to each guest by the groom's father. The more important people were seated inside the house and served personally by the father. The rest grouped themselves around the yard of the house and were served by helpers, friends, and relatives. The party then went to the house of the bride's parents, wandering along cheerfully despite the fine rain which was falling as dusk came on. The groom entered the house first, bearing a basket of bread on his back. He was a little late and the accompanying party paused some hundred yards from the house until he had gone in. After this, the principal men of the groom's family entered and stood just inside the door. The principal men of the bride's family received them, standing in a line on the opposite side of the room. The groom's relatives chanted a formal speech and were answered by the bride's relatives in the same fashion. These rather lengthy formal speeches are called the *parangón*. They are supposed to be known by the *regidores*, or town councilors, who teach them to those who must officiate at a wedding. The mayor then entered and greeted the party. After the greetings he asked the bride and groom in turn, "Do you accept each other as husband and wife, willingly and with

---

[6] Parsons, pp. 98 ff.

[7] Burgoa, 2:76. "En sus casamientos eran combidados de sus vasallos, de otros Reynos, los Señores, y Grādes caziques, para esplendidos combites, y todos contribuiàn de los frutos regalos, y animales, que se dabā en sus provincias, y venia prevenidos de sus mayores galas de vestidos, y joyas, para los bayles, y mitotes." After the baptism of the cacique of Tilantongo, a powerful personage with towns rendering him tribute, he married his son to the richest and most powerful chieftainess of the Mixtec, Dona Iñes de Guzmán of Yanguitlan. At this time there assembled "2,000 Caziques, Principales, y hombres de quenta, y lucimiento, y tuuo tanto la fiesta, banquetes, saroas, y bayles, q̄ todos à competencia salieron al mitote del Teponaztla con tantas galas, y joyas de oro, y piedras de estima."

pleasure? No one compels you or forces you?" Each answered in turn, "Yes." The mayor then said, "It is good. It is for this the council has come, to be sure. The authority does not lightly leave its place to come to private houses." He then spoke at length, urging them not to delay the religious marriage called for by the law of the Church nor the civil marriage demanded by the law of the Republic. He continued, expressing his pleasure at the arrangement and counseling the couple not to allow the inevitable small difficulties which would arise between man and wife to disturb them.[8] During the speech, the bride covered her face with her hands while her mother sobbed audibly and wept visibly. This, I was told, was unusual, but the bride's mother was notably emotional.

The groom now asked permission of all present to take the girl as his bride. No one objected, and he handed her an envelope. Normally, he would give her a ring of silver, earrings, and other gifts. Since the families were too poor to do this, the formality was complied with by passing the envelope.

A table was now laid at one end of the room beside the house altar and the mayor, three members of the council, my guide, Francisco, and I were served coffee and bread interspersed with several drinks of aguardiente. Had the families been better off, there would have been chocolate and more elaborate food. When he had finished, while the other members of the town council and various important people were being served, the mayor made another lengthy speech on the advantage of completing the formal marriage at once to avoid any difficulties which might arise. He pointed out that the priest would be available in a few days and that he himself would be at the town offices the following morning and would be glad to perform the civil ceremony without charge. He added that it was pleasing to him to "see a man speak up and ask for the woman he wishes, not just take her as so many do, causing great grief and pain to the parents who have labored so hard to raise the girl." Finally, he was gratified by the fact that the parents were so fully in agreement. The father of the girl meanwhile plied the guests with drink after drink of aguardiente, the acceptance of which was practically obligatory. Indeed, the mayor had asked me if I could drink aguardiente before he took me to the wedding, assuring me that it was a necessary part of being a guest.

The bandmaster and his wife came in and were served at the third or fourth table. They had been delayed because they were arranging the funeral of one of their godchildren who had died that afternoon. They invited me to attend the funeral. Outside had begun the monotonous Oaxaca fandango which would continue all night. Everyone would get rousingly drunk. We left shortly to escape the same fate.

Francisco remarked that not many years ago the Totontepec custom had been followed in his home town of Ayutla. It is now much abbreviated, if observed at all. At Totontepec a smaller fiesta is usually given at the time of the church wedding.

Customs at other towns differ. Metaltepec occasionally observes the *prenda* but the town council does not attend the ceremony. The church wedding comes later and is not observed with any sort of household ceremony.

Marriage at primitive Yacoche is a civil affair so far as it consists of registering the fact with the secretary. Accompanied by his parents, the man goes to the girl's house and asks for her hand. When the girl has given her consent, he brings her a gift of tamales. The marriage may be delayed from a month to a year, according to the wishes of the girl's parents. There is sometimes a form of church marriage observed in which the chaplain "prays like a priest." After this church wedding there is a fiesta at which tamales and tepache are served. The bride's parents come to the groom's house for this. The fiesta lasts one day and one night and includes a formal eating ceremony in which the bride and groom and their mothers sit together. The bridal couple eats first, then their mothers and fathers, then the godparents for the wedding. The man gives the girl a collar of beads and a ring, but there is no use of a

---

[8] The mayor's speeches were always in Spanish. As a progressive he felt it his duty not to talk Mixe, especially before a visitor.

chain or *las aras* (the money symbolically given the bride by the groom). Flowers are brought from the woods especially for this occasion, but I could learn of no offerings of food and drink, as is the custom at Zapotec Mitla.[9] At some point in the ceremonies a turkey is killed outside the house and the blood poured over pinole or corn meal. I could obtain no more specific data.

At Tepuxtepec the man sends his father to the parents of the girl. He must make a second visit because the parents will not give a girl away at once. When consent is given, the man goes to work at the house of the girl's parents, sometimes for as long as a year. If the girl is to be given at the second visit, the man takes a collar and a ring. This is considered the *prenda*. When he reaches the house, the girl is grinding corn and making tortillas. The man and his parents have also brought tamales and tepache, but they eat no food at the house. The food is distributed among the godparents and relatives of the girl. After this ceremony the man comes for the girl and they live together. If they have lived together before the *prenda*, the ceremony is not held. "Who would make the *prenda* after having joined with the girl?" says the native. There is no sacrifice of a turkey, because at Tepuxtepec a man may not sacrifice until he has married.

Weddings at Juquila are more elaborate than anywhere else. The girl marries at fifteen to eighteen years, the man at twenty-one or twenty-two. The father of the man goes to the house of the girl to ask for her. The father of the girl sets a period of at least fifteen or twenty days for an answer. At the end of this time, the groom's father takes two or three cartons of Monarca brand cigarettes, five or six pesos' worth of bread, chocolate, and sugar, a large olla of *tamales delgados*, and an olla of atole, the latter well made with brown sugar. These gifts are divided among the relatives of the girl's parents but there is no fiesta. Another term of five or six months is set during which the boy goes every day to the house of the girl and works there for her parents. He cuts wood, carries water, works in the fields, or does whatever else is asked of him. He does not sleep at the house but is fed there. On every saint's fiesta he gives two or three pesos of meat as a present.

The night before the marriage there is a fiesta. There is dancing to the music of stringed instruments at the house of the godparents for the wedding, at the house of the bride, and at the house of the groom. Everyone drinks and smokes except the bride and groom. In the early morning the bride is taken to the house of the godparents and dressed. The party then goes to church where the bride and groom kneel during the mass, their heads covered by one cloth. After mass they dance again at the homes of the godparents, of the bride, and of the groom. At the groom's house the party finally breaks up, leaving the bride with her new husband. Before marriage, the groom has prepared his own home. Very rarely he may live a time with the parents of his wife, but he will never take his wife into the house of his own parents to live. This reverses the custom in most Mixe towns.

From my informants in Juquila I could obtain no suggestion of the informal marriage. Such relationships probably exist, however, for I distinctly got the impression my informants were interested in establishing the good reputation of the town. The word *prenda* is known but it is applied to a gift of chickens and corn which the groom gives to the priest at the time of the wedding. The groom also pays for the mass.

Elaborate as this marriage is, compared with the practice in other towns, it is

---

[9] Parsons, p. 101.

much simplified from older customs described by Doña Paulina, wife of the Colonel, who spent most of her early life in Juquila. The early preliminary arrangements described by Doña Paulina were similar to those already given. After the marriage had been agreed upon, the man worked for the girl's parents, not five or six months, but for one or two years. Moreover, he was expected never to come to the house without a present of some sort. This seems an extraordinarily onerous requirement, but Doña Paulina was positive that this was so. Should a man arrive at the house without a present, the girl would send him away with "words of scorn." Otherwise, during this period, she pretended to ignore his existence.

For the wedding proper, the groom and his parents went to the neighbors with cigarettes, asking them to come and help grind corn. This asking with tobacco is an old form of almost compulsory request and is probably the only survival of aboriginal usages of tobacco. The grinding of the corn dough continued for three days, a ceremonial period through much of Mexico. When the corn was first put on to cook, preparatory to grinding, a *camarazo*, a piece of lead pipe charged with powder, was exploded. Another was exploded when the corn was taken off the fire, and a third when the grinding actually started. Tortillas, atole or corn gruel, and the famous flat Juquila tamales of turkey mole wrapped in banana leaves were made. The day before the wedding there was dancing in the houses of the godmother, the bride, and the groom. Then the party went again to the house of the godmother. In the early morning the bride was dressed in one corner of the room while the guests were dancing. Every article of clothing she had on was changed for a new garment given by the godmother.

Before this dressing was done, there was a certain amount of ceremony. The bride and her party entered the house first, and there was about a half-hour of speech-making between the bride's party inside and the others outside. This suggests the *parangón* and *prenda* of other towns. Before the dressing actually started, there was a symbolical handing on of the bride. The godmother of baptism gave her to the godmother of confirmation and the latter gave her to the godmother for the wedding. This was regarded as an indication that the first two had now completed their responsibilities.

After the dressing, the party awaited the sound of the church bell for a very early mass. If the godmother were wealthy, she not only had the band present but also an orchestra of stringed instruments. Not only did friends and relatives of the bride and groom attend, but the friends and relatives of the godmother, who stands most of the often considerable expense. The costs when Doña Paulina's aunt was godmother for a wedding included the killing of two steers and three pigs.

Further ceremonies followed the mass at church. The groom's parents, seated on a fine mat, awaited the party at the door of the house. All the livestock the groom owned—chickens, dogs, horses, burros, pigs, and sheep—were tethered before the house. The bride and groom knelt on the mat at the door. The mother of the groom raised the bride and led her into the house. The father did the same for his son. They knelt on a mat inside, and an old man "took the word" and gave them advice. The godmother then formally gave the bride to the groom. There was evidently no ceremonial eating. Food was served to the guests, however, and dancing continued until about four in the afternoon.

The groom always had his own house, and everything in it, including the clothing of the bride (except that given by the godmother for the wedding), was purchased by him. The bride brought nothing whatever to the house. Afterward, when they quarreled, it was common for the groom to say, "I brought you here with nothing. What have you to complain of?"

These Juquila weddings have several interesting aspects which require further investigation. It is apparent that there is far greater formality than elsewhere and that the church wedding and ceremony have merged with the *prenda* of other towns. The Juquila wedding in particular is closely similar to the wedding ceremonies at Zapotec Mitla.[10]

The long period of bride-service at Juquila is unusual. Although it occurs at some other Mixe towns, it is neither as long nor as universal. It is interesting that my reports, although possibly incomplete, indicate bride-service only for those towns which border on Zapotec territory closest to Mitla and the valley of Oaxaca. Interesting, too, is the fact that residence, if it is not independent, is always matrilocal, whereas in the other Mixe towns it is always patrilocal. Again, the fact that the bride brings nothing whatever to the new establishment suggests that possibly land is not inherited by her, either, although on this point I did not obtain definite data.

In Ayutla, which was the only town where I had an opportunity to make observations on the nature of family life, although two persons have been married and live in their own house, the family as a unit does not lead an independent existence. Assuming a couple to have all the parents living, the chances are that the groom has no economic resources which are, strictly speaking, his own. Land, the only real source of wealth in Ayutla, is all held by individual ownership save for a few tracts used for municipal purposes. Normally, it remains in the hands of the head of the family until his death. When a young man wishes to marry, the only money or property he has is acquired through presents from his parents or through working for some wealthy person. In the latter circumstance, he would have very little. Consequently, his brothers and his father help him with the expenses involved in the wedding. Very likely his godparents also assist.

If, as is usual, he builds his own house before the wedding, the house stands, not on his own lands, but on those of his father. Thus Francisco and all his married brothers have their own houses, but they are all built on their father's lands. As a matter of fact, he always spoke of these lands as belonging to the family as a whole. They were always "our" lands, never "my father's" lands, but when asked specifically regarding title he always said it was in the hands of his father. On these lands Francisco might and sometimes did plant his own crops, from which he received all the product even though he did not own the land.

Francisco had a church wedding when he was married. I suspect, although he would not admit it, that he had been living with his wife before the marriage. Part of the expense of the church wedding must have been borne by the rest of the family. Again, Francisco would not admit this, but his financial status was such that he could not possibly have paid all the expenses himself. He made it clear also in his manner of speech that a church wedding was a family affair. His references were always in the plural. "We spent" so much for this or "we did" that, never "I."

The only complete economic independence, then, which could be secured by

---

[10] Parsons, pp. 100 ff.

Francisco, was either through purchase of other lands with the profits he made from farming his father's lands, or through his father's death. This may be slightly modified by the fact that his house was considered his own, even on his father's lands, and his father might make him a present of livestock. Francisco had purchased a small tract of land within the town proper by profits from his farming. Since he had no livestock of his own, he planted it in partnership with Crescencio, an arrangement which, he somewhat proudly explained, most Mixe could not understand. On his father's death Francisco will obtain a portion of his father's lands and important personal property and livestock. In all probability he will know which are to be his long before the death of his father; customarily the necessary papers are drawn up to give title, since wills are unknown.

Economically, then, the family is a unit knit closely together in an interdependent group. This would seem for the most part to be reflected in personal relations. Agapito, whose service for the Colonel kept him much in town, lived at the house of his brother-in-law, Adolfo Galbán, alternate to the mayor. When sick, for greater quiet he moved next door to a house owned by his aunt. His relationship with a girl cousin, but little younger than himself, was entirely that of an older brother. She waited on him; he gave her orders, and even criticized her housekeeping. He did not, however, depend on the family financially. He brought corn when occasion offered and, while sick, gave his cousin money to buy food for the household.

This close integration of the family works fairly well. Despite the dependence of the children, there is usually little apparent interference or resentment. At times, however, difficulties arise. One dispute which came before the Colonel was a case in which a mother and daughter had each a half-interest in a cow. The arrangement had endured amicably for sixteen years, although what the daughter received for her ownership I could not see. The latter was married and away from home; the mother cared for the cow and kept all the calves. Finally the daughter suggested she should have one of the calves; the mother refused, and the quarrel was on.

On other occasions more unfortunate results follow parental interference. The Colonel's own niece, Lydia, daughter of Don Crescencio, wished to marry. Her parents refused to approve of the match, forbidding her even to see the suitor. "Why should she want to leave home?" rhetorically demanded her mother, María, "Here she has a good house, all the food she wishes, good clothes, and not much work" (for Crescencio is wealthy enough to have servants). But despite all this, Lydia, in appropriate time, gave birth to a child. It is rumored in the village that she still sees the father secretly.

If Crescencio were not so influential, Lydia would probably have left home and lived with the man. But probably her lover does not wish to incur open hostilities with Crescencio, while quite possibly Lydia does not wish to forego the economic advantages inherent in her present situation. If her parents can be reconciled to the man of her choice, she may both have her cake and eat it. Indeed, she very nearly does; for, though there may be inconvenience in seeing her lover secretly, she has lost little standing at home and the grandparents are quite foolishly fond of the child.

In general, the Mixe have a tolerant attitude toward all sexual relationships. Casual sex relations are evidently quite common before marriage and are not particularly frowned upon. In Ayutla unmarried mothers are frequent and apparently still have a good chance of getting a fair husband, although it is extremely unlikely that any man will think well enough of such women to go to the expense of a church ceremony. It is only when a girl or woman gets the reputation of making frequent changes in her lovers that she is really held in disrepute. Once this reputation attaches to a girl, her chances of entering upon a permanent union are very slight. She is held up to a certain amount of ridicule, being forced to sit with others of her kind at the house of the captain of the fiesta of the titular saint, San Pablo, and subjected to rather jeering advances on the part of various men.[11]

The general sexual attitudes extend to a certain hospitality toward strangers, though frequently it is not the sexual aspect which is important. An unmarried male who is resident for some time becomes an intolerable nuisance in the majority of Mixe towns. It becomes necessary for the officials to force some woman who already has a family of her own to care for, to provide food for another person. With the exception of Ayutla, Juquila, and Totontepec, the most progressive towns, bachelor schoolteachers are almost always provided with a native woman. Their existence would otherwise be almost impossible. The new schoolteacher at Alotepec told me he was forced to leave his post because he refused to enter into such an arrangement. When he refused, the civil authorities simply cut off his food supply.

Even in Ayutla, where there is no economic necessity for such an arrangement because several women are sophisticated enough to be willing to take a boarder for pay, bachelor schoolteachers are frequently offered a companion. One of the more prominent women of the town offered one of the schoolteachers her own daughter for the duration of his appointment to Ayutla. "It would be nice to have new blood in the town," she remarked.

The evidence seems to indicate that there is a reasonable amount of faithfulness after marriage. There are, of course, postmarital relations of an irregular kind, but most husbands and wives seem to get on quite well. Should there be flagrant unfaithfulness by either, the marriage would ordinarily split up, a result to be avoided by both parties unless there is an incompatibility of temperament which makes the union impossible. Both are apt to suffer in their reputations and to have difficulty in making a satisfactory remarriage if they separate without obvious reasons.

One point which is significant of the lack of intrusion of Mexican standards is that women travel alone on the trails freely. They have little shyness toward strangers of their own tribe. I have seen an Ayutla woman stop a group of men from another town who were returning from Mitla. She wished to purchase some onions. They had onions, so they sold them. It was a perfectly ordinary event, apparently, and the woman had no fear of making the request even on a lonely section of trail. Even attractive young girls go about alone a good deal, and I saw little in the attitude of the men to indicate that they would be molested. Men will ordinarily make little effort to approach a woman unless she has a reputation for irregular sexual relations. In conversations among themselves even the most *ladino* of the men are not very broad in their remarks about the opposite sex, and conversation in mixed groups is about as free. Women and men both will discuss the sexual activities of others rather openly and sometimes broadly; the only difference is that the women will sometimes profess to be shocked by very broad statements. Alone, men may make some remarks about the sexual attractiveness of a woman, or exchange notes concerning women who are sexually promiscuous, in a way they would not do before women.

---

[11] At Mitla *solteras* must make a paper lantern for the town fiesta. Parsons, pp. 112, 240–241.

I also suspect men of being willing to arrange an irregular sexual affair for others, although it was naturally difficult to secure specific information. If this is so, probably women, too, are equally willing to act as go-betweens.

Most of these sexual attitudes, so far as they deviate from Catholic morality, would appear to be of very long standing. The *Confessonario* of Father Quintana, published first in 1733, makes numerous references to sexual irregularities of this sort and particularly to men and women acting as procurers. However, it also makes many references to homosexual and other abnormal sexual practices which would suggest that they were very common. Probably there is homosexuality present in a group of this size, but I could learn absolutely nothing about it. It is certain that the more or less licensed sexual invert is completely lacking. Very likely many of the specific questions of Father Quintana sprang from an overdeveloped sexual imagination, but on the other hand, the data on homosexual practices in non-Aztec Mexico indicate clearly that they were developed to an amazing degree both north and south of the Mixe. Consequently, they possibly existed aboriginally among the Mixe.

Most of the simple data on inheritance have been mentioned already but, before the end of this chapter on the family, they should be summarized briefly. The most important items inherited are land, livestock, clothing, and household equipment. Although a few presents of personal property may be made by a man to his children, he apparently never surrenders title to his land until his death. Wills are unknown, but the father usually makes a division of the land among his children before death, preparing the necessary papers to establish their title. When he dies, these are placed on record with the municipal authorities. Occasionally he may actually have parceled his lands out to his children for their use, but he will not have given them title.

Should the father die suddenly without making provision for the division, this is made by the eldest son. Should he be too young, the nearest male relative makes the division. Personal property is divided in the same way. An attempt is made to distribute all the property equitably between all the children, both male and female. If there are not enough oxen to go around, one will take a gun, another something else.

At Juquila exactly the same practice is followed. In those towns where land is held communally, individual rights enduring only so long as the land is in use, only personal property is inherited.

CHAPTER V

THE CYCLE OF LIFE

AMONG THE MIXE the beginning and ending of the cycle of life, birth and death, represent two important points of contact between the individual and his social surroundings. These two events of which he is least conscious make him the passive center of a series of observances by the society which he is entering or leaving. Paradoxically, he is perhaps never more a part of society than when he is unaware of its existence. His marriage, which to him probably looms much more importantly, has far less formal social recognition, as a rule, although this depends on many contingent circumstances such as the type of marriage and the standing of the families. The individual may not marry, or his marriage may be completely unorthodox or without social recognition, but societal action at the time of his birth and death is inescapable. Mixe culture prescribes a certain minimal response in terms of social activity and recognition of these events. Should those responsible not respond to this minimum extent, Mixe public opinion would be violently upset. A breach of etiquette is often far more disturbing than the breaking of a law. In fact, for the Mixe, failure to make this proper minimum recognition of the events of birth and death is an inconceivable notion. One cannot accurately gauge the degree of horror which would be aroused, because it has never happened, and no Mixe can be sufficiently objective about the situation to estimate his feelings should such a thing occur.

Of the two extremities of the life cycle, birth is perhaps less important than death in the degree of social recognition which it receives. Anciently it was perhaps conceived of as a more important life crisis than at present. The entire complex of events and observances before baptism still seems almost entirely aboriginal.

Long before birth occurs, the individual begins affecting the lives of others through a series of customs which partake of the nature of social regulations. When conception is known to have occurred, the mother goes to the sweat bath once.[1] From this time on, the husband no longer cohabits with his wife. There seems no definite rule to this effect. Informants merely thought its violation an amusing idea when I asked if sometimes a husband did not continue to have intercourse. It was clear that in their opinion he did not, or, if he did, he would be a very queer fellow.

The Mixe regard pregnancy and childbirth as a perfectly natural occurrence. I never saw anything to indicate that there was the slightest distaste for pregnancy on the part of women; on the other hand, it does not seem to arouse any great emotion, and young children are treated rather casually but usually rather well. Consequently, there is probably only rarely an attempt at abortion. My informants denied it entirely. That anciently abortions may have been attempted is suggested by the *Confessonario* of Father Quintana.

Father Quintana includes several questions, asking if herbs, blows, or application of pressure to the abdomen (a common Indian method) have been used to cause abortion or herbs taken to prevent pregnancy. He also asks concerning the killing of a new-born child. It is questionable how seriously Father Quintana is to be taken, for he appears to be almost morbid on the subject of sexual irregularities.[2] Still, such

---

[1] At Juquila the mother never goes to the temescal before birth.
[2] See Quintana, esp. pp. 48–49.

customs are often reported for Indian communities elsewhere, just as similar practices are not unknown in our own culture.

At the present time, the frequency with which women have a child before marriage suggests that abortions are rare. Infanticide would also certainly be regarded with horror now, and contraceptive knowledge is completely lacking, unless my informants misled me.

The lack of any attempt at abortion is the more striking in that there is a general belief in a quite easy method of accomplishing it, namely, using the temescal unduly. Women use it once and no more. "A woman will never go oftener because the child would be lost," insisted informants. In other words, there is a definite feeling that no woman would be so foolish as to lose her child deliberately. Why should she, indeed? Except for what the Mixe consider as the rather slight physical inconvenience of the period of pregnancy, there are no social disabilities to having a child. It will little affect a woman's chances of marriage, her family will be delighted with the child, even though they may scold her a little for not getting married, and it immediately and beyond question establishes the fact that she is not barren, although this last consideration seems less important among the Mixe than among most primitives. The amount of psychological disturbance caused by pregnancy in even the most abnormal circumstances must be slight indeed.

When confinement begins, no men are present. The Mixe have no midwives or doctors. The neighbor women are sent for and volunteer their services. Delivery is in a kneeling position. If there is difficulty, a woman sits on the ground behind the kneeling mother and squeezes the abdomen with her arms. The cord is cut with scissors, and the woman and child are washed at once with warm water. The afterbirth is also washed and then buried outside the house. The infant is nursed as soon as possible. No herbs or medicines are administered to either mother or child. After birth the mother uses the temescal every day until the flow of blood stops.[3]

Interesting is the survival of a salt taboo for the mother following birth. Her first food, given about the second day, is atole or corn gruel prepared without salt. For two or three days she is fed only this. Then other more solid food is gradually given her in increasing quantities and salt is added to the food in the same way. This diet, it will be noted, also excludes fats and meats for a time, a common Indian taboo. Normal diet is given in about ten days. There are no restrictions whatever on the husband, but he does not cohabit with his wife for from five to six months after the birth of the child.

The lactation period is about a year and a half ordinarily, but some women nurse the child up to three years, or rarely, longer. This is not well thought of, however. There is no belief that prolonged lactation delays another pregnancy. The first solid food is a special tamale of finely ground corn wrapped in leaves (not husks) of the plant and baked in the ashes of the fire for from one to two days. The center only is fed to the infant, rolled in small pellets and pushed into the mouth. Water is also given. If the mother's milk is inadequate, tamale may be fed at about fifteen days. I saw a rather healthy-looking and plump infant of six months said to have been raised on this diet from birth. The more usual time to begin the feeding of solids is from six to eight months, depending on the mother's milk supply. At about one year

---

[3] At Juquila she uses the temescal only once or twice. At Tepuxtepec the temescal is used daily for from fifteen to twenty days "until the mother is cured." Other towns use the temescal as does Ayutla.

the usual child's diet consists of a little specially prepared tortilla with a touch of ground chile (!), atole, meat broth, bean broth, and coffee.

Formerly a young cockerel was killed at the cave above Ayutla on the occasion of a birth. The afterbirth was buried in the graveyard. For other sacrifices in connection with birth, see chapter vii on "The Mountain Spirits." Other towns present few differences in birth customs except for the greater prevalence of sacrificial rites.

Baptism normally takes place very shortly after birth. At Ayutla the godparents take the child to the church. They give clothing to the child for the baptism and afterward take it to their home, where they serve tepache to all visitors. At Yacoche the godparents are accompanied by the mother to the church on the third day after birth. Twenty days after birth the godparents sacrifice a turkey for the child. Of course, baptism is usually not orthodox, for there are no priests in most towns. The rite is performed by any person asked by the parents who thinks he knows how, usually a singer or chanter.

Names were formerly given to the child by a shaman or native priest, to judge by the *Confessonario*, for Quintana says, "When your sons were born, did you send for the wizard, that he might give a name to the infant, and so that he might do as the Ancients did in antiquity?"[4] Native names were in use up to very recent times, but I learned of none at present. Bishop Gillow mentions Tastahen as a masculine name and Xaxahen as a feminine name.[5] The *Confessonario* indicates that the first son or daughter was known as Cob, "rabbit," the second, Puu, "deer," the third and subsequent sons as Octz, "lion or puma," and the third and subsequent daughters as Oic, "armadillo." These were archaic words for these animals, according to Quintana.[6] At Totontepec I was told the eldest son is still called Kop, which is clearly the dialectic equivalent of Quintana's Cob (pronounced Kob), "rabbit," for Juquila. Names used contemporaneously are saints' names, which for practical purposes are abbreviated into forms easier for the Mixe to pronounce. Unlike the "nicknames" used at Zapotec Mitla, none of these abbreviated forms appear to be survivals of aboriginal names. A few of these altered names are as follows:

Mele, Ismael	Shuan, Juan
Pancho or Chico, Francisco	Pat, Pedro
(a straight Mexican nickname)	Shaf, José
Mani, María	Lencho, Lorenzo
Andum, Antonio	Anas, Ignacio

The surname of the father is used only by a small percentage of the Mixe. Instead, a second name which appeals to the parents or godparents is usually given. Thus in one of my genealogies the children of Andrés Domingo and Bernabel Antonia are named respectively Francisco Reyes, Vidal Antonio, Emilia Petrona, Demetrio Historia, Juana Modesta, and Emilia Guadalupe. Not one of these names appears elsewhere in the genealogy.

Yacoche alone retains a hair-cutting ceremonial. The boy's hair is cut at the age of one year, and the godparents give a necklace which is worn through life. The same day all go to church. At the same age, a girl is also given a necklace, although the hair is not cut. The girl's necklace forms the beginning of the accumulation of bead strings, often many pounds in weight, which characterizes the women of Yacoche and near-by Mixistlan.

[4] Quintana, p. 25.　　[5] Gillow, p. 212.　　[6] Quintana, pp. 89–90.

Nowhere could I learn of any adolescent ceremonies. Neither male nor female children have this life crisis called to their attention. Girls are not isolated nor are they taken to the sweathouse. The process of maturity on the surface appears to be as naturally handled as growth. What psychological problems may arise beneath the surface I could not learn in the time available. I doubt if there are many. Like the other physiological changes, the Mixe treat it as a natural, unextraordinary event concerning which one is fully informed long before its occurrence.

Few people have so little entertainment for their children as do the Mixe. Tales, which once must have formed a part of the background of every Mixe child, have been reduced to fragments known only to a few. Spanish folk stories are practically unknown, as well. There are no games except those introduced in the past five years by the federal schoolteachers.

The life of the Mixe child is entirely a preparation for adulthood. From earliest youth the child constantly accompanies its mother and later, a boy, his father. In Ayutla the child is carried in the rebozo, in Tamazulapan in the length of white cloth serving as a shawl. The mother leans forward until her back is nearly horizontal, pushes the child into position diagonally across her back just below the shoulders, places the rebozo over it and ties the ends in front, one end passing over the right shoulder (usually), the other under the opposite arm. Thus the child goes to the fields for planting or harvesting, to market, or fiesta. To nurse the child, the rebozo or cloth is slipped around to bring the child in front. Nursing is done with no regard for privacy: I have seen it done in church and in the midst of the market. At market the child may pass almost the whole day in this sling while its mother squats behind a jar of pulque. When it frets, the mother pats it gently on the rump. Usually it is completely invisible except as a lumpy bundle on the mother's back, but if a little older and awake, it may be drawn up a little higher and its head allowed to protrude behind its mother's shoulder.

In the house a child may occasionally be allowed to sit on a mat. Cradle boards of any sort are unknown but a boxlike cradle is commonly used, generally suspended from a rope. When a child is old enough to sit up, it may be given some object to play with, but there are no playthings as such.

Children's clothes are simply a copy of adult clothing, although frequently a bit of finery or some grotesquely elaborate garment or headdress, knitted cap, sweater, or other unusual garment is purchased for the child. In the progressive towns very small children are frequently better dressed than their parents. Elsewhere, there is no difference.

At an incredibly early age children begin assisting in the activities of their parents. Boys accompany their fathers to the fields, on woodcutting trips, or on journeys, as soon as they are able to walk. Girls go to the spring with their mothers. A boy who goes with his father woodcutting brings back wood, even though only a tiny piece, slung on his back with a tumpline in adult fashion. Girls have their little jar with which to bring water from the spring. The nearest approach to spontaneous play I saw was small girls dabbling in the waste water or stream while their mothers washed clothes.

By the time a child is nine or ten it has entered fully into all the economic activities of the household. Girls are working at the metate or grinding stone, bringing water, cooking, washing, learning to sew. Boys are cutting and carrying wood, driving oxen, taking their place in the planting or harvesting. Other education until recently was completely lacking. Although children go to church, there is no effort to teach them prayers or ritual.

Reverence for the aged was formerly inculcated very strongly. An elderly person was always to be saluted respectfully (probably by hand-kissing), even though the man was a stranger encountered on the road. If the salutation were omitted, old people became very angry.

Ridicule is also a strongly conservative force. One of my very helpful aids, Antonio, had been reared by the priest, Father Hernández. Several years of his life had been spent in Oaxaca and he normally wore "city" clothes. Nevertheless, on Sunday, market day, when the village was crowded, Antonio always wore the traditional white "pyjama" trousers and shirt. The dress of many others was also notably more conservative on Sunday than at other times. When I teased Antonio and urged him to wear his "city" clothes on Sunday, he was quite adamant. To wear other than conventional clothes on Sunday meant ridicule. People would say, "Who are you? It looks as if you didn't belong here. It looks as if you were from Oaxaca, from somewhere else." Such ridicule Antonio feared much more than he did mine.

Since the establishment of schools, this picture has changed somewhat. There are both games and education, but they are entirely outside the home and lack any integration with the tribal life. Children as young as four go into the school, where they are put into a preparatory class to spend a year learning Spanish. It is rare for a child, even in a progressive town such as Ayutla, to know any Spanish when it first reaches school. Even in the rare family in which both parents know Spanish, they never speak it in the home.

Some of the schools offer no more than one grade of schoolwork after the preparatory class, but most of them have two to four grades. Even so, there is little effective instruction because often there is but one schoolteacher with from thirty to seventy or eighty children. Since the single schoolteacher is male, except at the state school in Ocotepec, girls do not attend school in most towns. Parents will not send girls unless a woman is on the staff of the school, even though they do not object to men instructing the girls.

Formal education is limited to reading, writing, elementary arithmetic (at its best worked out in practical problems of mensuration), Mexican history, a suggestion of geography; and that is all. A great deal of time is spent on presumably practical subjects, the care of rabbits, fowls, school gardens, or bees. Usually some carpentering, tanning, or shoemaking is taught, according to the abilities of the teachers and their success in raising money to buy equipment. Efforts are made to develop coöperatives to raise funds by selling products produced in school, but they have rarely been successful so far. Often there is a plot of land which is sown to corn for the benefit of the school or, on rare occasions, for the benefit of the schoolmaster's private purse. The teachers are also supposed to teach improved agricultural methods. Actually they have all been sensible enough to realize that Mixe agriculture is adapted to such highly specialized conditions that they dare not tamper with it and to confine their advice to such things as fumigation of seed. Girls are taught sewing and sometimes a little cooking or baking if there are resources and sufficient ambition on the part of the schoolmistress. Usually the sheer inertia of dealing with a group speaking Spanish inadequately tends to reduce these efforts to futility. Little if anything sticks to make a change in the routine life of the individual after he leaves school.

The younger children are also taught some amusements. Simple nursery games are performed under the supervision of the schoolmistress, if there is one. Songs, occasionally a folk dance, sometimes a little pageant, are taught. For the older boys, or in schools where there are only boys, basketball is the only amusement. None of these games or amusements are ordinarily performed spontaneously outside of school hours. Unsupervised play consists of shoving and pummeling one another. Even this does not appear on other occasions, such as fiestas, when groups of boys and girls are apt to assemble. Some of the boys now finished with school do occasionally play basketball. At Ayutla, impromptu teams usually play after the Sunday market. Sometimes the Colonel or a visiting ethnologist takes part.

Not all the children go to school, even in so progressive a town as Ayutla. The scattered habitations of the people make the problem enormously difficult. Unless the authorities, the mayor in particular, will coöperate by arresting and fining parents for not sending children to school, there is no means of forcing attendance. Few mayors will court unpopularity by wholesale arrests and at best a few examples are made. In Ayutla there are children whose homes are as much as twenty-five kilometers from the school. These children must be given enough food for a week and allowed to sleep around at the houses of friends or relatives, a gypsy sort of existence without any supervision in their time out of school. They arrive about noon Monday and leave for home at noon on Friday. If they are very small, one of the parents must make the trip with them. However, and it is a commentary on the settled conditions of Mixe life, I have seen children not over seven carrying their week's provisions (which consist entirely of tortillas) entirely alone a distance of sixteen or seventeen miles through sparsely inhabited, ruggedly mountainous country in all sorts of weather to reach school. Considering all the factors, the under-nourished condition of such children and the underpaid and not very competent teachers, it is small wonder that the educational program has so far had relatively unsatisfactory results.

Those children at Ayutla who continue through the four grades offered in addition to the preparatory grade are rarely over twelve by the time they have finished. Their education completed, they sink back into the tribal life. Their reading and writing are for the most part forgotten, as they have no opportunity to use them. Books are almost unknown, and no newspapers reach Mixe territory except one taken by the Colonel. Even if books and papers were generally available, knowledge of outside affairs is so slight that there would be no interest in reading about them. Thus, the child is little better equipped for life than before the school training. A boy's agricultural knowledge has not been improved by a contact with school-teachers who have little practical knowledge and who are completely unfamiliar with the peculiar conditions of Mixe agriculture. He does not continue growing the various vegetables introduced in the school gardens because he has not acquired any taste for them. He has little opportunity to put into use the handicrafts he has learned. He goes back into the routine of helping his family in farming the family lands; commonly, his life pattern is unchanged.

Manifestly this is an unfair judgment when it is considered that the federal schools had been in existence only five years in 1933. The school training is causing changes.

Children who have been to school lose the painful shyness of the Mixe. Their social contacts are greatly improved. They have learned to speak some Spanish. They are more cleanly, a symptom of a personal pride which is lacking in most of the Mixe. The young men of twenty to thirty who were among the first products of the very inadequate municipal school started by the Colonel in 1922 can be distinguished almost unerringly from their confreres who did not attend the school. They dress better, speak Spanish, and are friendly and open with strangers. When they marry, they tend to pick *ladino* women, and the children of such marriages will probably have some knowledge of Spanish when they arrive at school. The results of school training may be judged more fairly with the arrival of the second generation at school.

Certain interests and desires are also evident. The sewing machine in particular has made a great impression, although it is economically an impossible acquisition for most Mixe. A desire for progress, for appearing civilized, has been developed. So far, it is largely expressed in externals, in the wish for better clothes, buildings for the town plaza, and machinery, but it will eventually reach deeper.

Such success as the schools have had emphasizes a serious problem. The school is widening the gulf between the progressive *ladino* and the conservative. It is creating for old institutions a contempt which will increase with time, and it has not yet created an understanding for the institutions which will take their place. The conservative Mixe has a certain orientation toward his world which leads to a psychological adjustment, far away though it may be from our own. The progressive has acquired little but a dissatisfaction, the cause of which he does not know. He compensates by seizing avidly everything new he can get hold of, though he is unable to adapt it to his needs because he has not acquired the cultural setting into which it fits.

This shows up clearly in Mixe attitudes toward clothing. All over Mexico the introduction of Spanish clothing for women was unaccompanied by the introduction of any European attitudes toward the care and treatment of the garments. The Indian woman early adopted the long dust-collecting skirt of the Spanish woman, but instead of sitting in a chair and keeping her clothes out of the dirt, she still squats by the hearth on the dirt floor just as she did in less ill-adapted garments. Similarly, men among the Mixe are now making a maladjustment. They have discovered shoes and, some of them, socks, but they have not learned how to care for shoe leather or that socks should be clean. They wear the shoes about town and soften up their feet. Then, because shoes are quickly cut to pieces on the mountain trails, they go back to sandals for a journey and find their feet blistered and cut. Worse, I have seen Agapito wear socks with his sandals, with the most unfortunate results imaginable. The socks were immediately filthy and remained so, and were quickly worn out. In similar fashion the Mixe have bought a truck and are building a road, but they have made no effort to acquire steel plows or vary their diet.

The period of adult life may be passed over in this chapter. Marriage, the family, the achievement of social position, and most of the personal development of the adult period are given in the sections on the family, the community, and religious rites and festivals. Only a few supplementary remarks may be added. When one has passed through the period of active life as described in these chapters, the individual generally declines into a patriarchal old age. The man keeps control of his property until his death and so is assured of his support by his children. Few Mixe reach great age, but those I saw seem to retain their vigor and vitality until late in life. Consider Tata Le, at least seventy, who is still hale enough to carry a bag of cement on his back from Mitla to Ayutla. Rather than a slow decrepitude, his end will more likely come suddenly as the aftermath of some drinking bout or exposure. He is unlikely to succumb to disease, for any Mixe who has reached his age must possess a remarkable set of natural immunities. Yet death does come and often with tragic suddenness and frequency.

The day of my arrival in Ayutla, the great bass bell of the church began a mournful and solemn tolling which I came to know with more and more sad frequency as the almost annual spring scourge of typhus gradually spread through the community. At considerable intervals the sacristan sounded the bell all afternoon, an undertone to the increasingly animated preparations for the fiesta of the patron saint to be held on the morrow. About four in the afternoon the band went to the edge of town to meet the visiting band of Tamazulapan, invited for the fiesta. Later about a dozen band members went to a house below the municipal building. After about half an hour spent in drinking mescal, they returned to the church followed by the mourners with the corpse. The body was wrapped in a mat and carried on a crude litter of two poles with crosspieces bound on with bark. After a few prayers in the church, the procession continued through the town to wind up the hillside to the graveyard on the summit of a flattish shoulder near by (pl. 15, *b*). At dusk as we sat in the house of the captain of the fiesta, eating the first fiesta meal, we saw them return, no longer a procession, but a straggling group of disorganized people.

The dead are always buried in the graveyard, formerly located about the church but now always on the edge of town. If a death occurs away from town, the body is laid on a stretcher and brought to the church. A small child may be carried to the house of some relative in town on the back of its father or some male relative, slung in a rebozo tied over one shoulder as it would have been carried in life. An exception is the custom at Mixistlan, where adults are tied in a flexed position and carried to the church on a man's back, supported by the regular carrying band across the forehead. Even here the body is extended in the church and carried the short distance to the graveyard on a stretcher. The grave in Mixistlan is particularly shallow, rarely over a meter in depth. Interestingly enough, the grave opening here is relatively small, the excavation being larger below, so that to insert the body it must again be flexed and extended in the large space below. There is a vague possibility that this is reminiscent of earlier practices. Nowhere does there appear to be any particular orientation of the body, although all the bodies in each graveyard lie in the same direction. At the conservative towns the individual graves are not marked in any way, there being but a single large cross in the center of the graveyard. At Mixistlan, particularly, care is taken to obliterate all signs of a new grave. The day after an interment at Mixistlan I was unable to locate the grave. At all towns the body is wrapped in a mat, which is sewed up just before the burial, although at Ayutla and elsewhere some of the more wealthy and progressive are beginning to use coffins.

At Ayutla and probably in other towns the body is washed before burial. It is dressed in new or at least good clothing if possible, and the old clothing is thrown away. At Ayutla, for some reason, the progressives object violently to the washing of the body, but so far they have made little progress in stopping the practice.

Everywhere except at Mixistlan the funeral rites for adults differ from those for children. Children under the age of seven or eight are considered *angelitos*, "angels," as almost everywhere in Mexico, and the funeral rites are in the nature of a rejoicing rather than mourning. Mourners and friends dance at the *velorio* or wake. However, practices for both children and adults vary in detail from village to village.

At Ayutla, those living on the ranches sometimes kill a rooster before taking the body to town for interment. If the family can afford it, all or part of the band is hired to accompany the body, as well as a singer or chanter to say prayers. The drunken Gervasio usually officiates. The band is paid twelve centavos each, the singer fifty centavos. Mescal is always given to the band and to those who carry the body. If possible—that is, if it can be afforded—food is served also, usually tamales and coffee. The body is taken to the church first, then to the graveyard, the singer reading prayers at each place and also as the body is being carried along. If the priest is in town, a burial service, *vigilia*, is paid for by those who can afford it. The priest may also accompany the body to the grave and read *responsos*. Copal, aboriginal pine-gum incense, is burned in the house and church.

Nine days after the burial the novena is celebrated. Those who helped at the burial are summoned and given food and tepache. There is no dancing or music, but the visitors pray. If wealthy, the family may have another *vigilia* by the priest on the novena.

The full elaborate ceremony with priest, *vigilia*, and *responsos*, is expensive. Francisco Reyes, on the occasion of his wife's death, paid out in the neighborhood of sixty pesos. It is interesting to note that his family felt that, as his wife had been good enough to marry in the church, they had a certain duty to give her an elaborate church funeral.

For a child the Ayutla ceremonies are similar to those for adults except that there is dancing at the wake, usually with a stringed orchestra of guitar, mandolin, and violin. The only food served is corn gruel (atole), and everyone gets drunk. For a child brought from the ranches, it may be necessary to hold the *velorio* and the dancing the second night. One child died late in the afternoon. About eleven the following morning the father brought the corpse to the house of relatives in town. The dancing began toward evening, this time with the band, and the burial did not take place until nearly three in the morning.

This distortion, as it evidently is, of the customary procedure, is an effort to comply with the spirit of the law requiring burial within twenty-four hours. In some pueblos, notably at Mixistlan, this law is ignored, and the body is kept in the house until the third day. Mixistlan also has no *velorio* or wake with dancing nor does it observe the novena. These are obviously Spanish institutions which have taken no root in conservative Mixistlan.

The practice of the novena at Ayutla requires some elaboration. It is customary to pray in the house each night for the nine days of the novena. On the ninth day, the mourners go to the graveyard and pray there. Then they return to the house and each one takes three drinks of mescal, followed by a breakfast of beef or turkey stew, coffee, and tortillas. The wealthier have music and dancing. This is the progressive upper-crust practice.

The conservatives have similar rites but in addition they kill a turkey either in the cave above the town or in the house. Also offerings are evidently made at the graveyard. In the brush at the rear I observed hidden bowls and gourds of tepache, baskets of tamales, and a large number of pieces of pottery. Pottery is apparently deliberately "killed" by breaking a rather small hole in the side or bottom (pls. 15, *b*; 16, *a*). I did not succeed in getting a satisfactory explanation of the beliefs which accompany this practice. Most informants denied that offerings were made. Others admitted them but said they knew nothing about them and that the progressive town dwellers became "very angry" whenever they discovered them. The offerings were evidently made at night, as partly burned fragments of ocote or pitch-pine torches were to be found in the brush and along a hidden trail leading up to the graveyard from the rear.

Natalio, who knew nothing of the purpose of the offerings (he had seen them but not at Ayutla; such things are always known for some other village), had seen the same offerings while passing by the graveyard of Tepantlali early in the morning. Tata Le added the amusing comment that when he was a boy, if a dog was found eating the offerings, it was shut up in the jail.

One of the most curious offerings was a mat in which were twenty or thirty bundles of needles of the long-needled ocote pine tied with palm-leaf strips. Natalio had also seen them at Tepantlali. I came upon them at a number of shrines near Ayutla and in other towns. The only informant who had any idea about these offerings was old Tata Le, who called them "the house of the dead." He said that formerly they had always been left in the cave above the town and represented physically and actually the house in which the dead dwelt. Ocote pine needles are left at many shrines, but the more elaborate offerings are usually at shrines connected with the dead and with weather control. I shall refer to this later.

Owing to the many deaths from typhus at Ayutla during my stay there, I did not make any attempt to see funerals at close range in this town. At Juquila I saw part of an adult funeral and at Totontepec participated in a child's funeral ceremonies.

At Juquila the body is laid before the house altar on a stretcher and a mat. Candles are burned all night and until the burial, while friends and relatives say prayers constantly. Everyone who enters the house sprinkles the body with holy water and prays. In the morning the neighbors bring their grinding stones and the women grind corn for tamales to be made in the early afternoon. These are the famous Oaxaca tamales of turkey mole wrapped in a banana leaf, and they are served with coffee to all the visitors about the middle of the afternoon. A bowl of tamales is given to each neighbor who has helped when the grinding stones are taken home. About five o'clock a part of the band assembles and is fed tamales and coffee. The body is brought out of the house. The *capillo* or chaplain of the band prays and the sexton sprinkles the body with holy water. The women weep while the body is arranged on the stretcher. Money previously laid on the dead person's chest is given to the chaplain and sexton for their services, twenty-five cents for each *responso* and fifty cents for each *salvo* they are expected to read. The leader of the band is given two pesos. Branches of yiyíai, an herb, which had been tied to the house posts by the door, are torn down and laid under the head and feet of the corpse. The band plays again, and the body is then taken to the church. The band leads the procession, followed by the women mourners with candles and then the corpse. After a few minutes of prayers in the church, the body is carried to the graveyard, the band still playing. The band plays once in the graveyard and most of it then departs. The chaplain prays again and the sexton sprinkles the body with holy water. The sexton and others sew the body into the mat and arrange ropes at the head and feet while the chaplain prays. The women go into a stereotyped wailing while this is done and repeat it again when the sexton throws the first handful of earth into the grave and sprinkles holy water.

During the interment, most of the women who had accompanied the body, paying no attention to the ceremonies, burn candles, place flowers, and kneel beside the graves of their own dead. The following morning the chief mourners pray again at the grave.

For a small child the observances are said to be the same except that the band plays all night, there is dancing, and the men all get drunk. Corpses of both child and adult are dressed entirely in new clothing.

At Totontepec the wake or *velorio* is omitted if the disease which caused the death is known to be contagious. There is no dancing for adults. The band always accompanies the corpse from house to church and then to the graveyard.

In company with the mayor of Totontepec I attended the wake of an infant of three years. Here, as in most towns, the godparents have complete charge of the wake of an infant, and the elaborateness depends on the amount they are able and willing to spend. The godparents of this child were the bandmaster and his wife, and the wake was elaborate.

The wake was held in the house of the parents of the child, a large house with wattled and plastered walls and a high-peaked thatched roof. The corpse lay on a table which served as the house altar, and one or the other of the godparents sat near by nearly all night. The body was dressed in a red garment with a flowing cape of dark blue, both decorated with pasted-on designs cut out of gold paper. A red cap, with similar decoration, and white stockings completed the dress. The hands were tied up to hold a huge bunch of flowers on the chest. A portable organ provided the music, mostly waltzes and fox trots (Totontepec is the most sophisticated Mixe town in many ways), and there was dancing of a sort on the hard earthen floor. Both the godparents danced occasionally, as did the mayor. As a foreign visitor I was particularly urged to dance, a most difficult procedure on an earthen floor with hobnailed boots and bare-footed partners. The local assistant schoolmaster, a Mixe, played the organ most of the time and sang several songs. The godparents also sang an exceptionally sentimental song, "Niño con ojos de amante," composed by the godfather. The godfather, his very composed young daughter, and the father of the dead child, passed drinks occasionally, but there was none of the insistence on drinking observable at a wedding we had left shortly before.

As each of the guests arrived, he greeted the parents of the child with a little speech of sympathy and generally made a gift of a few centavos, rarely as much as fifty cents. The mayor, both on arriving and departing, made a rather formal little speech to the father, expressing his sympathy and exhorting him not to feel his sorrow too deeply.

The dancing lasted all night. Late the following afternoon the band arrived and played a couple of *jarabes*, then led the procession to the church and thence to the graveyard. The corpse was carried in a flower-decorated wooden coffin covered with colored paper and with a bunch of dyed feathers upright in the center.

Yacoche has some different customs. A man who has lost his wife or a wife who has lost her husband kills a turkey in the house before the body is removed. On the novena, tamales and tepache are taken to the church and left. These are eaten by the chaplain, the two *fiscales*, and the two *topilillos* of the church, who then go to the graveyard and pray. On Monday of Easter Week prayers for the dead are said in church. Those who wish prayers said take tepache and tamales to the *fiscales*.

Some of the beliefs and practices concerning the dead vary widely. At Ayutla all informants insisted that nothing is buried with the dead, but at Juquila a cane is filled with holy water and buried with the corpse. At Totontepec crowns are sometimes put upon the dead and frequently a little money, corn, cigarettes, and coffee are buried also. At Yacoche a pouch containing thirteen miniature tamales and corn meal is hung on the belt, but no water is buried.

Ideas of a journey after death are almost completely lacking but crop up in the more conservative towns. At Yacoche the dead are said to go to heaven if good, to the inferno if bad. At Tepuxtepec I encountered a version of a widespread Mexican story.

The dead travel eastward for three years to a lake across which they are carried by a black dog. There are white dogs, too, but they will not carry anyone across. For this reason black dogs are not beaten; if one steals, it will be forgiven.[7] After crossing the lake, the soul travels for three years more to the house of Jesus Christ. There is a man at the door who tells the soul to wait. It waits until the sun comes up. Then it is given a letter to return to this world. What it does in this world I do not know. If an *angelito* [small child] dies, it goes to heaven.

At Tepuxtepec, atole is served when the body is about to be removed from the house and is drunk by the helpers and neighbors. Some is thrown on the ground beside the corpse instead of holy water. Only a few people in Tepuxtepec have a special dance for the small child. Neither do the godparents arrange a small child's funeral; all the details are attended to by the parents. There is no turkey sacrifice and for the novena only prayers are said.

Metaltepec sacrifices a turkey in the house for the dead, the blood being thrown on the ground outside. There is a dance for the *angelitos* or small children as elsewhere, but for the adult dead there is no music at all. For the novena only prayers are said.

At Ayutla it is believed that the soul goes to heaven "to see where it is going" unless there are no prayers said for it. If there are no prayers, the dead come out of inferno to molest their families. The soul generally is believed to return to earth on All Saints' Night. Some people will not sleep in the house where a death has occurred until after the novena, fearing that until the novena the dead may return to the house. Some say they have seen ghosts, others attribute strange noises in the house to the dead. The drinking of tepache at the novena is believed to "lay" the ghost. Some fumigate the house after death by burning creosote or the leaves of a plant unknown to my informant. The principal mourners also enter the house to be fumigated. This fumigation or purification may well have aboriginal antecedents.

Tata Le's account of earlier customs in connection with the novena contains many implications of aboriginal practice. On the ninth day after death, tepache, *posole* (tepache with partly ground hominy), tortillas, tamales, and corn meal were formerly taken to a sacred cave, together with pine needles of the ocote pine wrapped in a mat. These were all for the dead person, who would thereafter live in the cave. The feathers left in the cave were also left for the dead, according to Tata Le, although he could give no use to which the dead person might put them, nor could he remember that any fixed number of any of the offerings was left.

On All Saints' Eve, offerings of food are generally left between candles on house altars. At Ayutla the food includes cooked green corn ears, oranges, bananas, apples, tamales, atole, coffee, tepache, and mescal. The household prays for the dead for about two hours between seven and nine. In the town proper, in the evening and morning the musicians go out after the services in the church and pray at the house altars. Half the food on the altars is left all night, and it may never be eaten by people of the house. It is not, however, given to the band or those who accompany it (one informant contradicted this). Neither are band members paid. They may be given a little tepache at the house, but they do not drink much. This abstinence is striking. The priest goes to the graveyard during the day and says prayers for the dead of those who pay the requisite fee. There is no food taken to the graveyard, although the custom is familiar from Santa María, the nearest Zapotec town.

---

[7] Parsons, p. 152, mentions several instances of similar beliefs.

Bunches of *cemposuchil* (a yellow flower associated with death) are tied to the crosses.

At Tamazulapan, the nearest Mixe town to Ayutla, food is also taken to the grave-yard, mostly tamales and tepache. People go to the graveyard and cry beside the single big cross to be found in the cemetery of this town. Food is also put on the house altars and is later collected by the sextons, *fiscales*, and others. At Tepux-tepec, tamales and tepache are put on the house altar. A few people here sacrifice a turkey, but the majority do not.

The observances on All Saints' Eve mark the last social recognition received in the normal life cycle. Even this is generalized, prayers for specific individuals being made for a varying but usually short interval after death. At the same time, the dead are still important to the community and probably anciently were deified. This will be discussed in the chapter on "The Mountain Spirits."

CHAPTER VI

CATHOLIC RITES AND FESTIVALS

MANY FOOLISH and baseless things have been written about "idols behind altars" in Mexico. In extensive regions of Mexico it may not be uncommon to find idols associated with Christian altars, but to demonstrate that they are endowed with specific esoteric meaning is another thing entirely. I suspect they often have about as much religious significance as do the slightly indecent postcards of voluptuous women or highly colored pictures clipped from advertisements which are often found on the walls beside house altars in Mexico. Among the Mixe, however, idols are not only behind altars, they have a life and worship of their own. Moreover, they have been known to move right onto the church altar itself on terms of equality. In certain Mixe towns which lack resident priests and where the church is kept perpetually locked to strangers, I suspect they still hold places of honor.

Archbishop Gillow tells of finding a wooden idol on the altar with the saints during a visit to Mixistlan. The inhabitants were so incensed by the removal of the idol that the visiting party barely escaped violent treatment.[1] The church of Mixistlan today is always locked, and I was not permitted to enter. Offerings, ceremonies, and sacrifices of a pagan nature are still made inside the church, as they were until very recently in most Mixe villages.

To the Mixe the church is but another shrine, as its name, "tsápteig," implies. Teig is the term for hilltop and cave shrines where sacrifices are made to the memory of the pre-Christian mountain spirits. Tsap is a general prefix to indicate a new form, something wonderful or unusual. It also means sky.[2]

The coexisting religions and rare contact with priests in most towns lead one to expect that Catholic rites would be shot through with pagan practices. They are not. The Mixe makes the same sacrifices to the Christian God that he makes to his older supernaturals. But he does not combine them with specialized Catholic rites. The important thing to the Mixe is, I suspect, the careful performance of ceremonialism. Consequently, it is natural that the ceremonials of new deities should not be corrupted. Similarly, the elements of the relatively new Catholic rituals have been transferred to the pagan ceremonies only to a slight degree. Particularly is this true in towns with resident priests like Ayutla. There the Catholic rites and rituals are performed with less admixture of local *costumbre* than appears in more civilized Zapotec Mitla. There are certain local variations in the way some of the festivals are celebrated and the incense used in church is the ancient copal incense. Little offerings of corn and flowers are made on the altars for a variety of occasions.[3] But there is no dancing in the church as among the more northerly Yaqui and Mayo in connection with purely church rites. In more backward towns, as suggested, offerings and sacrifices are made in the church, but they are not made in conjunction with Christian rites.

---

[1] Gillow, chap. 10. A translation was published by Frederick Starr in *The Open Court*, July, 1899, pp. 387–391. Starr gives a picture of this idol in his *Indians of Southern Mexico*, pl. xcvii, *b*, and a description in his *Notes upon the Ethnography of Southern Mexico*, p. 56. It apparently was connected with water in some way.

[2] Compare Quintana, p. 95.

[3] Corn ears, shelled corn and beans—often mixed with rose petals,—flowers, and candles are the most frequent offerings. Iris is the most common flower in spring, but marigolds, roses, daisies, and wildflowers are also used.

The church organization has already been dealt with in chapter iii. The salient feature there brought out was the intertwining of religious and secular duties in connection with the village authorities. The maintenance of the church building is a major responsibility of the mayor and town officials and is usually taken very seriously. In Ayutla the priest is partly supported by an *almud* of maize collected from every adult male. Failure to pay would be punished. In a few towns, lands are cultivated or cattle kept for the support of the church. Cacalotepec has a herd of saints' cattle, *ganado del Santo*, kept below the town. The fiesta of San Isidro on May 15 is celebrated at the corral.

The only purely religious authorities are the *fiscales*, the sextons, and the *mayordomos*. The chaplain is also practically a religious official (see p. 25).[4] The band is also essentially a religious institution. It performs at every church service without pay. This is generally true throughout Oaxaca. The service may be rather onerous at times, for matins and vespers as a minimum are celebrated every Sunday and on some special saints' days. At Totontepec the drum and flute, used in some towns in connection with the tekio, are also played before all church services, during any procession, and after the services in front of the church. Later, they are played for a time under the arcade of the municipal building.

In each town there are also two or three men who are known as *maestros*. These are men who have the ability and willingness to read the services for vespers, matins, funerals, and various other occasions. They are resorted to when there is no priest available or when it is not desired to pay the price for a mass. These men do not attempt to perform mass, it should be noted, confining themselves to reading the services. Even in Ayutla, when the priest was in residence, the church services were more commonly conducted by one of the *maestros* than by the priest. The *maestros* are not paid for regular services but are paid for *mayordomías*, funerals, and other special services.

The *maestros* are evidently expected to have no other qualifications besides the ability to read the services. Gervasio is one of the most popular *maestros* in Ayutla and he is notorious as a worthless drunkard. He is said to have buried more people than anyone in Ayutla, although he is not an elderly man. The first time I met him he was striding longleggedly uphill ahead of a corpse, mumbling services out of a dog-eared book. As he passed, he winked at me solemnly and drew a long face without missing a word of his prayer.

If there is no priest present, the *maestro* performs the services for the *mayordomías*. Much of the active participation of the Mixe in the church is bound up with this institution. The number of *mayordomías* varies from town to town. In some there may be only one for the patron saint, as at Yacoche (where the *mayordomo* is called a captain), whereas Juquila has approximately seventy.

At Ayutla are the following saints who have *mayordomos* and for whom *mayordomías* are celebrated: San José, Corazón de Jesús, Jesús Nazarene, New Year (Sagrario Familia), Señora de Dolores, La Soledad, San Antonio, Santa Cruz, San Pablo, San Pedro, Santo Entierro, Corazón de María, San Isidro, and Guadalupe. In addition masses are paid for Rosario and Corpus Cristi by the *Regidor de los Gastos* (see p. 76).

In Ayutla the *mayordomos* are named by the town meeting which names the

---

[4] In 1933, Crescencio, brother of the Colonel, acted as chaplain, "because the present *capillo* is stupid and doesn't know anything." Crescencio is also a *maestro*.

secular officials. The mayor speaks first, suggesting candidates. Service is obligatory and for three years, but only those who can afford the service are named. For those who can afford it, two *mayordomías* are required. Formerly two *mayordomías* were a prerequisite to holding the office of mayor. The prerequisite still exists in many towns.

The expenses of the *mayordomo* are heavy. Out of his own pocket he is expected to pay for one or more masses, usually fifteen pesos each, pay ten pesos to the band, and provide food for all comers. However, for a major fiesta, like that for the patron saint of the town, he will have some assistance. At Ayutla two captains are named for the major fiesta. Each of them must provide food. The *mayordomo* provides three meals. One of the captains also provides three meals and the fireworks for the fiesta. The other captain gives food to the band and to anyone else who may come. This may mean meals for two or three days. If a band from elsewhere is invited to assist, a third captain is named to provide their entertainment.

These captains are named for one year only. Their expenses are somewhat more than those of the *mayordomo* but these occur only once, whereas the *mayordomo* has to repeat his expense three times. Nevertheless, the captains' services are considered equal to those of the *mayordomos* and they may in this way escape once the onerous service of acting as *mayordomo*. Or they may give two *mayordomías* as well and be relieved of the position of mayor. One of the present *fiscales* never was mayor. On the other hand, there can be no doubt that the service of *mayordomo* has more prestige and involves in the native mind somewhat greater spiritual rewards than does service as a captain. Moreover, the *mayordomo*, if clever, can make a good thing of his position in ways which are regarded as perfectly legitimate, provided they succeed and the funds of the saint are unimpaired.

The *mayordomo* has in his charge rather large funds, which he acquires in three ways: first, from funds which are passed on to him by his predecessor; second, from profits made by the sale of candles from the wax belonging to the saint; and third, by sale of gifts of corn and beans which are left before the particular saint of which the *mayordomo* has charge. Ultimately, surplus funds are used for church improvements and repairs. Although it is possible that a certain amount of "graft" can be collected by the *mayordomo*, most Mixe are so horrified at the idea that I doubt if it often occurs. There are occasions, however, when *mayordomos* are careless and lose the money entrusted to them. These, when their term has expired, have been forced to make restitution and have submitted to heavy fines which often ruined them. But with all honesty it is evidently possible for a profit to be made by using the saint's capital in small business enterprises. One man in Ayutla has voluntarily kept the *mayordomía* of Dolores for a number of years because of the advantage of using the capital for buying coffee and maize. Not only has he kept the saintly treasury in excellent condition, but he recently presented the church with a brand-new image costing some eleven hundred pesos. He is exceedingly prosperous and his use of the capital of the saint is not in any way criticized; rather, it is admired.

The ordinary *mayordomía* starts with a mass paid for by the *mayordomo*. After this, the band plays for a time in the plaza, then goes to the house of the *mayordomo*, where it plays intermittently all day and usually all night. The *mayordomo* provides tepache, mescal, and food. He also purchases the few fireworks, mostely *cohetes* (explosive rockets), used for an ordinary *mayordomía*. The saint is never taken to any private house, either on this or on any other occasion (except Christmas Eve).[5] The visitors drink, eat, and dance. Women dance at the *mayordomías*, but they never dance in the fiestas, where there are many more people present and drunkenness is more evident. This prohibition is peculiar to Ayutla, so far as I know.

Another public event is the transference of the position of *mayordomo*, called the *entrega*. In 1933 the *entrega* of the *mayordomía* of Santa Cruz was held on Saturday, February 4. The band met at the new *mayordomo's* house and played. Then the retiring *mayordomo*, a young man, paid over the money in his keeping, reading a statement of receipts and expenditures. The wax and the candles were weighed. There was some discussion. Evidently the wax and the candles had previously been weighed together, and it was decided that henceforth they should be weighed separately. There were both partly burned and unused candles. The mayor supervised everything, and all receipts and expenditures bore the municipal seal. Before and after the weighing tepache was served to everyone. Afterward the band played again, and three women and one young man, the new *mayordomo* and his feminine relatives, danced a fandango until the noon bell at church (pl. 12, *a*). The band and a few women then went to the church. After a short service, the cross was carried out. Only women carried it, using a rebozo passed under the cross and tied about the back of the neck. It was heavy and, particularly where the trail was steep, the bearers changed frequently. There was a good deal of eagerness to carry the cross and women pushed their daughters forward when the latter were bashful. More and more people joined the procession as it went along. A young man carried a little silver plate on which a few placed alms. The group went out the trail toward Tepuxtepec, the women singing and the band playing alternately. About half a mile from the church everyone knelt and prayed, and after that the band struck up a lively tune and there was no more singing.

About two and a half miles from town the party approached the *hermita*, or trailside shrine, where the cross stays until the fiesta of La Cruz on May 3. Near it the singing and playing began again. By now nearly everyone was carrying lighted candles. When they reached the *hermita*, the cross was taken in and lengthy prayers and services were read by a *maestro*. Afterward the *mayordomo* served tepache and mescal. The band played at intervals as the people sat about under the trees in the shade, drinking. Later there was dancing on the narrow trail. The group did not return until about six, when it went to the house of the *mayordomo*, where there was dancing until late at night.

The *hermita* is a square adobe structure about twelve by twelve feet, with a thatch roof. The door was decorated with a rope of miscellaneous greenery intertwined with yellow roses and marigolds. The cross is a massive wooden affair about two feet high with a figure of Christ on it. There are other *hermitas* for other saints, but this is the only one on a main trail.

The Day of the Cross, May 3, is celebrated by most Mixe by making a special large tamale with beans. At Ayutla there is a further special celebration. If the priest is in town, he and some of the townspeople go to the great cross high on the mountain overlooking the town and there hold services. The people spend the day

---

[5] Apparently only pictures are placed on household altars at Ayutla, but elsewhere some households possess images. A man at Tamazulapan sold a pair of oxen to buy an image of San Isidro Labrador, patron of farmers, for forty pesos. Two days after the arrival of the saint he gave a fiesta or *gasto* at his house with music and served beef stew and tepache. A week later he repeated this on a smaller scale, the novena.

there, drinking tepache. The same thing is done on the occasion of prolonged droughts. Significantly, the cross is at the brow of a cliff directly over the sacred sacrificial cave.

There are a few other special features of the *mayordomías* at Ayutla. For Christmas Eve the infant Christ is taken from house to house. A godmother and godfather are appointed to give a feast. After the Rosary, or evening prayers, the band and most of the worshipers go to the house of the godparents for food. The godparents must pay for the mass also.

When the tamales are put on to cook for a *mayordomía*, a *cohete* is fired. Another is fired when the tamales are tried to see if they are done, a third when they are taken off the fire.

No dancing accompanies *mayordomías* which occur during Lent. The *mayordomía* of the Virgin of Dolores (Our Lady of Sorrows) on the fifth Friday of Lent is marked by a procession around the church in the morning with the Sacred Heart. On Palm Sunday there is a procession inside the church. Afterward and again on Monday the village patron, San Pablo, is taken outside in procession.

Whether the New Year is a true *mayordomía* or not, I could not learn. There is no making of offerings, or *pedimentos*, as at Mitla, at any special shrine.[6] Maize, candles, flowers, and similar offerings are usually left before the saints in the church.

At Ayutla there is also a special society of the Sacred Heart of Jesus, composed of young people. They hold frequent evening services in the church, usually with Gervasio as *maestro*. Afterward they carry the picture of the Sacred Heart in a procession about the church. The organization is probably rather recent in Ayutla and has a different flavor in its rites from those of the *mayordomías*.

A fiesta is also a *mayordomía*, but it is more elaborate; a *mayordomía* is not necessarily a fiesta. At Ayutla, the three big fiestas are San Pablo, San Pedro, and Easter. The time of the principal fiesta, that of San Pablo, is really January 25, but the fiesta proper always is held on a Sunday. If the date falls on a Wednesday, as it did in 1933, only the proper masses are held on that day. Few people come into town to attend them. The ceremonies really began on Friday. It was early on this Friday afternoon that I arrived in Ayutla, and my first contact with Mixe ritual was the fiesta of San Pablo. The band was already playing desultorily, going from house to house.

About four in the afternoon the band marched down one of the trails and out toward the edge of town, playing. There they met the band of Tamazulapan, invited, together with the *fiscales* of the church, to coöperate in the fiesta. I inquired about photographs and was told I could take all I wished. The band returned, still playing, the band of Tamazulapan silent behind, led by the two aged *fiscales* from Tamazulapan bearing dark mahogany staffs with red ribbons attached. I took a picture as they wound up the trail toward the plaza. Each member of the Ayutla band greeted me as he passed. One member dropped out, a young trader I had encountered briefly in Mitla. He chatted for a few minutes and excused himself. He had an engagement; there was a funeral that afternoon. About half the Ayutla band went to a house a few hundred yards below the plaza while the rest dispersed (see p. 58). The band from Tamazulapan entered the church, where it played and held services with the chaplain and a *maestro*. No one else attended.

⁶ Parsons, p. 233.

The mayor and some of the town council were drinking from a bottle behind the market building. After a long consultation, the mayor came to me and invited me very formally to accompany them on the *calenda*. Delighted that I had been received so readily, I innocently accepted the invitation for what turned out to be a prolonged drinking bout.

When the band from Tamazulapan came out of the church, we went to the upper inside balcony of the Colonel's house. The principal people were invited into his office (temporarily my room), while a bottle passed outside among the band and the followers. We then went to the house of the captain for the band of Tamazulapan. The mayor entered first, then I was invited inside under the portico and given a chair; my Mitla guide and Agapito, to whom the Colonel had given special charge of me, were also asked in. The band played. Mats were spread on the ground for their instruments and the men were seated on benches around the little patio before the house. Tepache and cigarettes were passed. After great scurrying, two metal enamel cups were produced for me and my Mitla guide, and we were also served tepache; the others had gourd cups, the regular drinking receptacle for tepache. Then we were fed black beans, tortillas, and coffee. After we had eaten, the band played again. The Ayutla band and the burial party could be seen filing down the hill from the graveyard.

Agapito invited my guide and me to visit his house, a log cabin. His father is a *palenquero*, a maker of mescal. Mescal and cigarettes were served. We talked awhile about Mexico, about the United States, and about similar topics. After a while we left. It was quite dark but Agapito had a coal-oil lantern. We found the Ayutla band in the court of the Colonel's house. His big gasoline lamp was hung in the center, the band playing and the mescal bottle passing. Other bottles circulated among the onlookers. The Colonel's monkey provided great sport until it bit several of its tormentors or tore their blankets; then it was left alone. The band of Tamazulapan arrived and played. The bottle was passed some more. After a time, headed by the mayor, his alternate, Agapito, myself, and my Mitleño guide, we began a round of visits to the house of the mayor, the alternate, Agapito, the captains, and *mayordomos*, in fact, to the house of anyone of importance in the town.

For this tour great pitch-pine torches had been lighted, together with huge paper lanterns on bamboo frames. Globes, human figures, an airplane, and various other forms were represented. These went at the head of the procession with the bands behind. Only men were in the procession but there were perhaps two or three hundred, a colorful and picturesque sight as we went from house to house along the narrow trails on the hillside. Agapito had slipped a poncho over my head. Everyone watched me to see that I did not stumble or fall. In rough places I thought everyone within reaching distance had hold of my hands and arms.

The procedure at each house was similar. With the principal men, I was invited inside, where a few chairs and a table, spread with a dingy cloth, were ready. The band and the others stayed outside and were passed mescal and tepache. *Copitas*, small ounce glasses, were usually used inside to serve the mescal. At one house there were no glasses, and the mayor indignantly made the host send to another house for them. An honored guest from outside must not drink from the bottle. It was practically obligatory to drink one *copita* of mescal in each house. Subsequent ones could be refused with sufficient formality. After the mescal, a bowl of tepache usually was offered. There was lengthy talk at each house about my journey, my country, the cost of my travels, and the time they took. Later in the evening men began to make speeches, particularly the postmaster, Don Honorato, and Agapito, telling me how welcome I was, how much they appreciated my condescension in coming to visit their poor, despised, lowly, ignorant people. They, who rarely could see the outside world, were grateful for visitors, so much more so when they came not from the immediate outside world which they knew, but had the kindness to come from foreign parts, from far, far away. And so on *ad infinitum*. There was dancing outside, the Oaxaca fandango but much more vigorous than among the Zapotecs of Mitla. I was implored to dance and did so to applause. The dance is easy to learn.

Everyone became befuddled, but the only quarrel was between Agapito and the postmaster, the two most *catrín* (citified) of the younger men. Agapito tried to take a claspknife from his pocket, and the room suddenly filled with men who surged quietly between the antagonists until they were well separated. There were several unsuccessful attempts to get Agapito's knife from him. The mayor stood fingering a police whistle, but did not blow it despite the urgings of an excited companion of Agapito. The two were spoken to gently. Some said, "Don't quarrel before visitors." Agapito's father, a great hulk of a man, although shorter than Agapito, came and took him home. Agapito would not leave without me, so I went also, helping him up the trail. I left him at his house and was accompanied by another of the Colonel's young men back to my room. The house-to-house visiting continued all night.

Next morning at six-thirty all was quiet. I went for a walk down the road. A mass was held while I was away. After, I entered the church. There were heaps of flowers and piles of corn ears before all the saints, offerings to be gathered up later by the *mayordomos*. The mayor and his group were standing in the plaza, still passing the inevitable bottle. I stayed away from them.

After a while the bands began to play. I went with them to the house of the *mayordomo del castillo*.[7] It was about eleven. The Negritos (masked dancers, see p. 80) emerged from behind the church following the band and straggled into the court of the captain's house, some still arranging their costumes. There was mescal and tepache, then we were served tamales, huge affairs with a little very hot sauce inside, bread, and coffee, and afterward *agua de caña*, a mildly fermented drink of the juice of the sugar cane. After the meal, the host insisted I take the several tamales remaining. When I begged off, on the grounds I could not carry them, he sent them to the house of the Colonel. We sat talking and drinking tepache. The mayor blessed his, making the sign of the cross over it by holding his hand, the palm vertical, in two directions at right angles successively. The older men usually lift their hats while drinking and sometimes pour a little liquor on the ground, saying "Pun yetnašrín matunsún bektsh." My informant translated this as "May God give us this Holy Trinity." We talked. The noon hour came. We took off our hats—at least the others, who had not removed them in the house, did so. The mayor prayed. We greeted each other, "Good afternoon, ešnásh." After, all went out before the market building.

Three old men from Tamazulapan stood before the church making the day hideous with wailings on three long buglelike trumpets, such as one sees in the illustrations of medieval tournaments. They finally went off with the Tamazulapan band to the

---

[7] The captain who provides the fireworks is sometimes called a *mayordomo*.

house of their captain. The Negritos danced in front of the market without their sticks for perhaps half or three-quarters of an hour. Later they danced with their sticks (see below). From every direction people were arriving with their bundles of food and their blankets.

During the afternoon Gervasio appeared dressed as a *tiznado* (a variety of clown) and mounted upon a white horse. Charcoal had been rubbed over the horse's head and shoulders. Gervasio's face had been blackened with charcoal and decorated with red spots and lines. He wore a cape of ocelot or tigerskin. He had no stirrups and the horse was led. His assistant pulled him from the saddle. A broken frame for a fireworks bull was produced and he carried it over his head, charging back and forth amid the crowd with wild hilarity. A man with a lasso roped him and was chased by the "bull." This went on for some time, the helper removing the rope when a cast was successful and being chased for his pains. This continued until the framework disintegrated completely. They then started on a round of visits. As he passed the Colonel's house where I stood with Doña Paulina, Gervasio shouted as he reeled in his saddle, "I am lord of the world. No one will have the advantage of me." Doña Paulina told me that the night before he was thought to be dying and his family had come seeking medicine. Truly a remarkable recovery, but also a remarkable man—clown, town drunkard, and *maestro* of the church. Later, he was part of an informal procession accompanied by a man in a domino who made, in Spanish, a typical carnival proclamation.

Since noon the mayor had been busy supervising the erection of the tightwire and the ladder and swing for the acrobats. A place had been leveled off for the *castillo*, or fireworks castle, on the low spot below the plaza. The *castillo* had been brought up from the municipal building and placed in the marketplace before the *tiznado* appeared, while the fireworks maker and his assistants worked feverishly putting on the finishing touches. At dusk, while church services went on, it was erected with much heaving and straining. The proposal to face the most elaborate side toward the church was vetoed promptly: it was faced toward the Colonel's house. A fence of canes surmounted by bombs was made about it, and two small sets were placed on poles on either side of the *castillo*.

About four-thirty the band had gone to the *mayordomo's* house for mescal and tepache. Then the *mayordomo* candles were escorted to the church, where services began about five. During the day, the outside of the church had been decorated with a rope of pine needles and a series of rosettes made of the leaves of a wild agave (century plant). The leaves were interwoven with the shiny white broad butts exposed (pl. 15, *a*). Inside, the church had been swept and two ropes of pine needles suspended from the ceiling, cross-fashion, while more rosettes decorated the lower walls. The priest—not the regular Ayutla priest, who was ill, but a visitor from Zacatepec—sat in a chair on a mat facing the altar. The *mayordomo* lighted the candles, tall, fat, yellow ones, before the altar and before all the saints lining the walls. Many small candles were also burning and many of the worshipers had lighted candles. Two gasoline lanterns belonging to the Colonel gave added light. The Ayutla band played music for a long time. The mass was long, lasting until nearly eight. By that time there was a crowd of kneeling people before the church door as far as the cross. The band of Tamazulapan meantime was at the house of its captain.

After the church services I went by special invitation with the Colonel, Doña

Paulina, and the priest, to the house of the *mayordomo*. It was a larger house than most, with a cement floor, a fact upon which the priest commented. The band was also invited inside. Mescal, black beans, tortillas, bread, coffee, and then a bowl of tepache were served. The priest drank both his mescal and tepache. We returned to the Colonel's house, where he hung a large gasoline lantern on a pole erected at the edge of the plaza. The priest, Colonel, and I sat on a beam on the edge of the plaza overlooking the low spot where the fireworks were. First came five fireworks bulls. These "bulls" are frames of fireworks which a man carries over his shoulders; when the fireworks are lighted, he charges into the crowd, which scatters delightedly, pursued by the bull. Often injuries result, but this time all were very well run. Only one fall occurred and it did not damage the framework. Each bull was succeeded by a large rocket, a bomb, and a shuttlelike piece that ran back and forth on a wire behind the *castillo*. Following the bulls two pairs of *gigantes* (huge fireworks figures worn by a man) danced. They were excellent, and there were shouts of "Viva el *cohetero!*" ("Long live the fireworks maker!"). The crowd was working up to a pitch of excitement. A small set piece was hung on the wire and burned, then the two side pieces. All was ready for the *castillo*, which dragged a bit and had to be lighted again every few minutes since it was made in sections. The Mixe *castillo* is not like those of the Mayo, where everything goes from one lighting and there is a tremendous, though shorter, blaze of glory. The finale provided a bit of amusement. After all else was dark, a fountain high up burned interminably, interspersed with explosions. A drunk decided each explosion was the last and began to shout "Viva el *cohetero!*" only to have the fountain begin again. By the time it finished, everyone was laughing. Applause came when the top was illuminated, revealing a figure of San Pablo.

The acrobats and tightrope walkers now began, the scene illuminated by five or six great pitch-pine torches. The Colonel's lamp became clogged and there was no other light. The man in the domino acted as master of ceremonies for the tightrope walkers. Some were dressed as women. The bands alternated playing fandangos and *jarabes*. The walkers on the wire danced to the music, the domino dancing on the ground below them. Hour after hour it went on, while the Colonel worked at cleaning his lamp and repairing it. Finally, we swung it on a beam projecting from the porch of the house and the scene stood out vividly. On the outskirts of the crowd, scores danced in maudlin drunkenness, sometimes with partners, more often in staggering isolation. The bands played until after six in the morning.

A little later there was a procession and a mass. During this the Tamazulapan band was at the house of its captain. After mass, the *mayordomos* busily gathered up the remnants of candles and the ears of corn from before the saints and the altars. More and more people gathered in the marketplace, for this was Sunday, market day, as well as fiesta.

After mass the priest, the Colonel, and I went again to the *mayordomo's* house to be served mescal, cigarettes, tepache, then a broth, *caldo*, of strips of dried meat stewed with cabbage, frightfully piquante. "Qué sabroso!" ("How tasty!"), I heard a member of the band say. There were stacks of tortillas and big bowls of black coffee, frequently replenished. Then more tepache. One of the band members made a little speech of thanks, and the host, the *mayordomo*, responded. The band, accompanied by the dancers, filed out and the band of Tamazulapan came in to be fed. Men were dozing off occasionally where they sat; they had not slept in forty-eight hours.

Activities shifted back to the plaza. The Negrito dancers performed again, this time before the Colonel's house. They were now accompanied by a *viejo*, old man, in a wooden mask who policed the crowd and danced drunkenly about them (pls. 11, 13, *b*). While the dancers rested the *tiznado* entered the circle and bandied jests with the *viejo*, who responded in a high falsetto voice. They improvised songs. Both songs and jokes were frequently indecent, to judge from the gestures and occasional Spanish words. The *tiznado* came off worst in the exchange. Two men covered with a blanket pretended to be a bull and charged about the crowd with a small boy riding on their backs. The Tamazulapan band, a short distance away at the south end of the market place, played *jarabes* and there was a drunken group dancing the fandango about them.

The Ayutla band played a couple of "concert" pieces to which some of the drunks tried to dance, unsuccessfully. The *tiznado* appeared on his white horse and attempted to ride into the circle of the band but was dissuaded. More and more people showed signs of drunkenness. A couple from Zapotec Yalalag amused the crowd. The woman was very drunk, staggering. Her husband tried to get her away. He would entice her to the end of the plaza, sometimes dragging her. There she would break away and stagger back to the band. The women of Tamazulapan were mostly drunk and dancing solemnly by themselves, their full blue skirts circling out gracefully, their heads lolling from side to side as they occasionally staggered. The Tamazulapan men seemed a little less drunk; at least they carried their liquor better. The Ayutla women mostly sat at the sides of the plaza.

There were various couples who entertained the crowd, husbands trying to get their wives home, wives trying to get their husbands home. One man took a firm grip of his wife's hair and dragged her off, fighting like a cat. His face was scratched and bloody.

In the midafternoon a basketball game was staged by the *ladinos*. The band played and the drunks kept encroaching on the ball ground in the middle of the plaza. The priest and I had seats of honor in the shade. Five of the prettiest girls sat behind us as godmothers to the winners, a very interesting bit of acculturation. At the end of the game they pinned little rosettes of ribbon on the winning players, who knelt before them in the center of the plaza. The Negritos then danced in the basketball court before the market. Most of the more drunken element were with the Tamazulapan band south of the plaza. This band was now showing the effects of the fiesta. Small in numbers to begin with, some members had apparently dropped out. "Blue" notes were frequent. A new *tiznado* appeared, Gervasio having "passed out." After the dancers performed, both bands played awhile. There was a short Rosary in the church, after which the bands went to the houses of the captains. Most of the visitors had left. In the gathering dusk I played an improvised game of basketball with the Colonel and others.

After dark the bands returned. The domino again directed the tightrope walkers. There was a much smaller crowd, mostly of town dwellers and a few Tamazulapan residents, too drunk to go home. Many, including women from Tamazulapan, were dancing a fandango. The entertainment again continued all night.

In the morning, Monday, there was another mass. Afterward, the Ayutla band sat before the market. Few people were about, most of them eating around fires in the marketplace. Bottles were still passing. After breakfast, the priest left for his home parish of Zacatepec. The band led the way to the cross at the edge of town on the trail to Tamazulapan. The Colonel and I accompanied the priest on foot. The band members all kissed the priest's hand, the mayor gave him a peso and a bundle of food. The priest appeared reluctant to accept the money. He had already been paid. Then the leader of the band gave him two pesos. He rode off on his mule, the band playing until he was out of sight. He was followed by a boy of fifteen or sixteen carrying his belongings in a pack. Then we returned, stumbling across the rocky places while the band played. The mayor went to the municipal building, the local band to the house of the captain. The Tamazulapan band played feebly at the south of the marketplace. After a while it rather unceremoniously departed for home. The plaza was littered with sleeping drunks, lying where they had fallen. The remains of the *castillo* were removed to the municipal building, for salvage of usable parts.

About midday the Negritos danced again in the plaza. The police functions of the *viejos*—there were now several of them—were more evident and more necessary. There was much pantomime with a chicken leg, which amused the crowd vastly. A *tiznado* appeared with another "bull." He had a fur cap and someone tied a tail of horsehair to his belt. The *viejos* acted as bullfighters (pl. 14, *b*). About four in the afternoon the band played again in the plaza and the drunks danced.

During the afternoon the *viejos* and several men, dressed as women, their faces covered with veils, burlesqued the Negrito dance. The band played a tune said to be different from that played for the Negrito dance proper. The *tiznado* took the part of the *viejo*, policing the crowd, one burlesquer burlesquing the other. Part of the time the group danced to the music of guitar, violin, and mandolin. When they tired, there was a game of basketball. The band went to the captain's house and played until about nine.

At ten o'clock the stringed music with a half-dozen followers came to the balcony of the Colonel's house and serenaded him. He brought a bottle. Part of the time he played the mandolin himself; a few danced. When the bottle was finished, his brother, Crescencio, member of the stringed orchestra as well as acting chaplain of the band, announced that the fiesta was over. They departed.

Next morning, Tuesday, at about ten the bass drum was beaten in front of the house of Crescencio, the chaplain. People slowly began to gather there. Meanwhile, the police whistles also blew and a considerable gathering formed at the municipal building while the council considered what to do with the various prisoners resulting from the fiesta. After a short walk, I returned to the house of Crescencio. The band and the Negritos had gathered, and mescal and tepache were being passed. A Spanish-English dictionary was produced and I was asked to pronounce the English equivalents of various phrases. It produced a great deal of laughter, but eventually Crescencio saw that I was bored and stopped the performance. The noonday bell rang in the church. Everyone uncovered and crossed himself. *Cohetes* were fired. Evidently the crowd had been awaiting this, for immediately after, the dancers began in the patio. In the intervals, Gervasio, his face now whitened, and another similarly decorated clown, staged elaborate fights with resounding Spanish oaths. They were soon dirty from rolling on the ground, and cut and bleeding. The "women" appeared; one was placed beside me "to see if I like her," at which there was much laughter. Another intermission, and the *viejo* danced with my companion. There was much vulgarity. The "woman's" chest was padded to resemble breasts, at which the *viejo* pretended to suckle. Later the *viejos* and *tiznados* and the men dressed as women burlesqued the Negrito dancers.

In the afternoon the Negritos danced in front of the market. Afterward, all went to the house of a captain. *Jarabes* were danced to the sound of the string orchestra and the band. Beans, tortillas, and coffee were served at sundown with tepache; apparently there was no mescal left. One man with a handkerchief over his face was acting the clown in the patio, using a small dead bird which he tried to wipe across the faces of unsuspecting bystanders. There was also more play with the chicken leg, all but the claws being wrapped in paper.

Seven or eight young women with babies were seated on a log under the veranda of the rather large house. They were the *solteras*, women of loose morals. It is said they are compelled to attend. Everyone pressed tepache upon them and they were rather drunk. All the rest of the women were in the large kitchen, making tortillas on enormous *comales*, grinding corn, or looking on from some distance. They did not associate with the *solteras*. Dancing went on until late.

The following morning, Wednesday, the pueblo was practically deserted. There was the usual morning conference at the municipal buildings. I strolled by, and a stranger asked politely if I had business in the *Municipio*. At a house near-by I was invited in. I chatted a while. My host was going to Atitlan. Saturday there was to be a fiesta there. He was going to see what it was like. We chatted about our respective countries. Were there mescal, fiestas, priests, cattle in my country? What religion was there? Did I think wheat would grow in Ayutla?

Next Sunday was the novena. It would have begun on Saturday, but the *entrega*, the changing of the *mayordomos* of the Santa Cruz, took place then, and the band was occupied until late at night by the accompanying festivities. There was a service in the church in the morning, although the market was already well under way. About eleven the band played east of the market. After noon the Negritos danced again. There were only six, and the figures went very badly. The *viejo* was present and after the dancing two more *viejos* appeared with a *tiznado*. After a time they went to the captain's house. In the evening there was another service in church and a procession with the picture of the Sacred Heart of Jesus. Later, the band returned and the tightrope walkers performed again, the domino likewise appearing to act as master of ceremonies.

About nine some energetic soul started a round of vivas. "For our Holy Patron San Pablo y San Pedro," "for our Father Hernández," "for our Colonel," "for those in charge of the fiesta," "for the band," "for the acrobats." The band played briefly and all the vivas were repeated. The band played again, and again the vivas were given. The band then went to the house of the Captain and played a fandango before disbanding. The fiesta was now really over. Nothing more remained but clearing away the tightrope and trapezes the following morning.

The other big fiesta of Ayutla is Holy Week. It is relatively a much less unrestrained event. There is less drunkenness and there can be no dancing until after Easter Saturday. People generally are in an elevated frame of mind, possessed with a certain mystical enthusiasm as well as a suppressed excitement. Several special features mark the final week of Lent. There is no "justice" all week. The officers of the town leave their canes of office in church from Palm Sunday until Easter Saturday, a symbol that they abandon all authority. The various organized groups all have special functions to prepare for. The priest (this time the regular priest, Father Hernández) feeds all his *topilillos* and sacristans during the week and they sleep on the porch of the *curato* (vicarage). The *topilillos* must feed atole to all the people the morning of Holy Friday. On the day before, the *topiles*, or police, have prepared the elaborate meal for the Apostles, and on Easter Saturday the remaining members of the civic administration must feed atole to the townsfolk.

Every morning and evening during Lent there are services in the church. On Wednesday evening of Holy Week are observed the *tinieblas*, a ceremony in which all the candles in the church are gradually extinguished and later relighted in the same way, one at a time.[8] Thursday morning there are two services, one about five, the second at seven. At the later mass the priest led a procession inside the church. Rose petals were strewn before him. After mass until noon people were praying constantly in the church.

At noon were sounded the *metracas*, mechanical noise-making instruments used to call people to church during Holy Week when bells are forbidden. The principal *metraca* at Ayutla is a large wooden sound box on top of which a cylinder, turned by a hand crank, lifts a series of wooden hammers on long pieces of flexible wood which slip off the camlike projections on the cylinder and strike sharply on top of the resonator. Almost at once the *topiles* began carrying food for the dinner of the Apostles.

The preparations for the dinner of the Apostles are extremely elaborate and are entirely in the hands of the *topiles*. Several days before they make a round of all the households in the town and its outlying ranches. Each family gives half an *almud* (about a quart) of corn, beans, or the equivalent in eggs. Twenty-five centavos are also collected from each family and entrusted to a man known as the *Regidor de los Gastos*, to be spent for necessary supplies, fish, rice, and so on, the total amounting to about eighty pesos.

Theoretically, each person should be served twelve different dishes plus twelve tortillas. Actually, latecomers may get less or nothing. The list of twelve dishes actually turns out to be thirteen. Whether this is the fault of my informants, or Mixe failure to follow theory in favor of the old ritual number thirteen, I do not know. This is the list:

Fried eggs	*Frijol del campo* (beans), átsuan
Fried black beans, shük	Rice, *arroz*
White beans, pokmukshü'k	Fish, aksh
String beans, petshü'k	Dried peas, popshíp
Chilecayote (squash)	Greens of tips of squash vines, akshashü'f
Fried *pepitos* (undeveloped squash), šebák	*Frijol delgado* ("thin" beans), mutskshík

Habas (pealike vegetable of a Spanish origin), tsapshík

The preparation of this meal took all Wednesday night and Thursday morning. A dozen or more fires burned all night in the open space in front of the municipal buildings, and the *topiles* with various woman assistants scurried about under the direction of my cook, Doña Sotera. My own meals were decidedly irregular these two days.

Formerly, the Apostles were twelve old men, but, owing to their propensity for getting drunk, they have been replaced by boys of eight or ten who are picked out

---

[8] At Yacoche new fire is kindled in the church to relight the candles. At Ayutla one candle is concealed behind the altar.

by a sexton at the door of the church Thursday morning. While the *topiles* were still carrying up food, the boys chosen were scurrying about collecting flowers for their mothers to weave into circlets for the Apostles to wear on their heads.

When the meal was nearly ready, the *metracas* sounded repeatedly and people began to gather. After a short service in church, a procession came out headed by a numerous group with portable *metracas*, then the band, followed by the Apostles with wreaths of flowers on their heads, and last the Christ image, Jesús Nazareno. Men and women wearing red ribbons formed a file on each side. The priest also was present in his vestments. Canes and pine trees had previously been set in the ground before the door of the main theater of the school. Everyone went inside. The image was placed at the head of the table. The Apostles washed their feet, the priest prayed, then the band played while the Apostles ate. The Apostles then went in a smaller procession back to the church, unaccompanied by the priest. The musicians ate next; then everyone who wished should have been fed, but the food ran out and not everyone was accommodated.

The Apostles were left sitting in the church all afternoon except during one procession to the *calvario*, or hermitage, with the image of Christ. The image was accompanied by a centurion on horseback and a group of soldiers, resplendent in new costumes with bright tin helmets brought for them from Oaxaca by Doña Paulina. These had been prepared as a surprise and the house had been topsy-turvy getting the costumes finished in time while the Colonel gloomily reminded his wife he had told her not to interfere with customs. His forebodings were belied by the rush of volunteers to act as soldiers, once the costumes were seen. On the return, the Christ image was placed in a niche near the door of the church behind a screen of branches, where it was guarded all night by the soldiers. Alms were placed in a dish before the image by worshipers.

In the evening the *tinieblas* was performed again. After the services the *topilillos* of the church "caught" women to cook atole as they left church; for preference, young unmarried women, at least in theory. They are said sometimes to be chased and brought to the market by force, but this year most of the women were older and came by prearrangement. I actually saw only one effort made to press a woman into service, and she worked up a fine anger and stalked off through the *topillilos* without a hand being laid upon her. In the morning after matins the atole was given to everyone who came.[9]

The church altar was curtained off during the day on Thursday and Friday but not during the night. Friday there was a mass in the morning. About noon the encounter of the Virgin of Dolores and Christ was portrayed. Two processions formed, that of Christ going right from the church, that of the Virgin, left, following two different routes to the *calvario*, each with music, the band dividing up. A pulpit had been improvised in front of the shrine, and there the priest preached about twenty minutes, telling very simply the story of the original occasion. It was made quite a festive event, the Colonel's wife serving a little sweet drink to the schoolteachers and me on the veranda of a neighboring house while we waited for her father, the priest. The two processions, now merged, returned to the church (pl. 10, *a*).

---

[9] Natalio told of his youth when he used to sleep in the market or by the hermitage awaiting the first atole before he went home. He also liked being an Apostle for the food, but afterward he ran away and hid because he didn't like being shut up in the church.

About five in the afternoon there was a Rosary and Father Hernández preached briefly, touching on the creation of the world and man and the redeeming sacrifice of Christ in terms simple enough to be comprehended by a small child. During mass the altar and cross were curtained and the centurion and his soldiers stood before the curtain facing the altar. When the priest left, the curtain was parted and the image of Christ was lowered from the cross by *Los Santos Varones*, the saintly men, dressed in white with white cloths over their heads. The cross was set before the altar against a wooden frame covered with shrubbery of the yiyíai (Sp. *ure*) plant. After removal, the figure was placed in a carved wooden coffin. The shrubbery was then torn from the frame and thrown out to the audience. It was a gay scene as the crowd, mostly men, scrambled and snatched good-humoredly for the branches, which protect against lightning and also have curative values.

After the branches were divided, two processions started. The soldiers and centurion accompanied these, the latter on a horse decked with paper streamers. First went the Santo Entierro (image of the dead Christ), preceded by the cross from which the image had been lowered and followed by most of the crowd. A little distance behind came the Virgin of Soledad, the Virgin of Dolores, and San Juanito accompanied by a smaller group (pl. 14, *a*). At the *calvario* the Santo Entierro was left for the night guarded by soldiers and the centurion, now not in costume.

The following morning, Saturday, mass began at seven. The altar was curtained. About half-past eight the curtain was drawn and the Gloria chanted. Apart from the fireworks outside, this seemed a very conventional ceremony. The altar was ablaze with candles and most of the worshipers had candles. During the singing of the Gloria the big *mayordomía* candles were lit and handed to a row of worshipers in the front of the church, to whom communion was also given. The church was crowded, but there was no excitement or emotional expression visible.

The church was specially decorated for the day. Hanging from the roof were three bunches of green bananas and two bunches of *cocolillos*. This is a traditional decoration. The altar was handsome in gold and white, covered with flowers and medallions or rosettes made of large intertwined leaves. During the long services, it was so cold that the breath steamed and fog swirled through the open doors and unglazed windows until at times the altar was dim from the rear of the church. Outside, by nine, the fog was so thick that objects twenty feet away were invisible.

The Santo Entierro still remained at the *calvario*. In the afternoon, after the Rosary, a procession around the church with one of the virgins was made in the light rain. Then the centurion and his soldiers went in costume to be on guard while the Santo Entierro was removed from the *calvario* back to the church.

That night the town council made atole in the hermitage. Early in the morning there was a procession to the hermitage, considered now as the tomb, and another "encounter" between the Virgin and Christ was enacted. Confetti was thrown over the images as they left the church. After the procession, atole was served in the hermitage until about eleven o'clock.

Variations of interest occur in other towns. At Juquila there are some seventy *mayordomos*, an incredible number, but it is claimed there is a *mayordomo* for every saint in the church. Since the church is crowded with saints, the number may not be far wrong. The *mayordomos* are named anew by the mayor each year. They make a *gasto*, that is, give a feast, at their house before the saint's day for two days during which the candles are made. Aguardiente, tamales, cigarettes, and coffee are served. The band does not attend except to accompany the candles to the church. After the candles are made, there are prayers at the house of the *mayordomo*. The following day the candles are taken to the church and left there for the fiesta. They are burned for matins and vespers. There is no *gasto* in the house on the saint's day, and the saint is not taken to the house. The *entrega* or change of *mayordomos* follows the fiesta. The candles are weighed in the *mayordomo's* house. There is no *gasto* for this but the new *mayordomo* is supposed to burn candles in the church every afternoon. For a big fiesta such as that of San Juan, the *mayordomo* spends three to four hundred pesos of his own money alone. The *castillo*, or firework sets, are apart and are paid for by the town. Only a rich man can be *mayordomo* of San Juan. One wealthy man told me he had been *mayordomo* of San Juan and that it had cost him five hundred pesos.

On the first Friday of Lent, the members of the town council give a small fiesta. Each official brings a present for the priest—eggs, chickens, tamales, maize, beans, or other food. These offerings are hung on a pole which is carried to the *curato* with the Negritos dancing on each side.

Every Friday of Lent a procession makes the rounds of the stations of the cross about the commons behind the church in an anticlockwise direction. The prayers at each station lengthen this procession to three or three and a half hours.

The fiesta of the first Friday of Lent at Cacalotepec was largely a drunken debauch combined with a market (pl. 12, *b*). The first night there was supposed to be a *castillo*, but the fireworks maker did not arrive to make it although he had accepted ten pesos sent him as an advance. Mass was held by the priest from Juquila for the vespers, for the morning and evening of Friday, and for the following morning. A steady stream of people went in and out of the church all day long. Friday afternoon the dancers performed. In the evening, there were vivas for local personages and others, including one for the King of Spain, another for the Pope, but none for the President of Mexico.

There were a great many fights, largely uninterrupted. Even though a man of Atitlan beat his wife badly and tried to drag her off, he was let alone. However, he became involved in a brawl with others and eventually rolled some forty feet down the hillside when he fell off the edge of the plaza, which seemed to calm him considerably. The major fiesta at Cacalotepec is Asunción.

Yacoche has only one *mayordomo*, who is appointed in December. Before the fiesta on February 19 he goes to the summit of Zampoaltepec, where he sacrifices a male puppy. The following day he gives a feast in his home. In February the *fiscales* give the town a feast at which the chaplain is the guest of honor.

Metaltepec has two *mayordomos* who change annually. The main fiesta is June 24 (San Juan). There is a captain who feeds the band at the fiesta.

Atitlan has six *mayordomos* who serve one year. Formerly (up to 1931) a man was said to be tied to the cross to represent Christ in Holy Week. This was done secretly.

At Tepuxtepec, Santo Domingo, on August 4 is the important fiesta. Musicians play but there are no dancers. Two *mayordomos* are named for this fiesta but there is no captain. A turkey is sacrificed before the fiesta at a shrine a few hundred yards from the church. The *mayordomo* serves one year and pays all the expenses except for the *castillo*, for which the town pays. A *calenda*, without lanterns, is held on the same night the *castillo* is burned. The same *mayordomo* also has to give the fiesta of San Francisco September 17. The new *mayordomo* makes a *gasto* (feast) on the occasion of the *entrega*. Musicians play at the house, and tepache is served.

The fiesta foods at Tamazulapan (according to the schoolteacher) are broth of turkey, tamales, tepache, and a little mescal (none for some fiestas). For large fiestas the *topiles* take wood to the house of the *mayordomos*, mayor, judge, and councilmen, and are given tepache at each house and fed, if it is mealtime.

Tamazulapan has only two *mayordomos*, who change each year, being named by the mayor. A fiesta is given for each saint in the church. One must be *mayordomo* twice before one may be mayor.

At Tontontepec there are eleven *mayordomos* (but the same informant said there were two for each saint). They are named by the town council and must serve for one year. They give food to all comers in their house. The fireworks *castillo* is paid for by the town. Formerly, a man had to give two *mayordomías* to be eligible for the office of *mayor*. When the *mayordomo* brings in supplies for the *mayordomía* about a week before, *cohetes* are fired and the drum and flute are played at his home.

A feature of many of the Catholic festivals is the appearance of dancers such as the Negritos of Ayutla. Although the dancers do not perform in the church, they often dance beside or before it. Their appearance only at church festivals makes them clearly part of the Catholic aspect of ceremonialism.

Considerable variation exists in the dances performed at different fiestas. My data are incomplete. At Ayutla the Negritos dance for the fiesta of San Pablo. The dance itself is a straight European country dance with very elaborate steps in a rigid pattern and figures, designed for eight performers (pl. 13, *b*). At one point two dance, the others standing in a circle. This is obviously the fandango common in Oaxaca, although done more vigorously even than the energetic fandango of Ayutla. The music throughout is fandango music. There are many heel-and-toe steps, and hops and skipping steps. The figures are based on combinations of two and four and are constantly re-formed, that is, there is a constant change of partners for temporary

Fig. 1. Rattle used by Negrito dancers at Ayutla. Handle of wood with spoon-shaped hollow opposite the wooden clapper. The clapper is hinged with stiff leather.

periods. The basic formation is in two files, varied by the center four dancing together and by forming two groups of four. Only once is there anything very reminiscent of the widespread Mexican Conquista dance. This is when the pairs strike together twice a light stick about eighteen inches in length. Each dancer carries one of these sticks. There is a change in tempo in the middle of the dance for which the Negritos signal by a prolonged sounding of their rattles.

The performers wear tight knee breeches and jackets of black velvet embroidered with pearl buttons, old but clean and well cared for. When the dancers sit, they always spread a handkerchief to protect their costumes. A half-dozen varicolored bright silk ribbons hang from a band across the shoulders down to the center of the thighs behind. A hat is worn, suggestive of Napoleonic military caps, a sort of zouave cap with much gold fringing and a short vizor, with an oblong cloth down the back of the neck. Hat and cloth are of black velvet. A hornlike object with gold fringe projects up and back from the top. A ribbon tied under the chin holds the hat in place. Stockings and sandals complete the clothing. The dancers carry a castanet rattle (fig. 1) and kerchief of silk in the hands, and sometimes a short baton in either hand. Most striking is a mask worn while dancing. This is very dark brown in color with very natural features, neither Indian nor negroid. A pointed black moustache is painted on. The nose and lips are thin, but the whites of the eyes are slightly exaggerated. There is a slit for vision in place of eyebrows.

The dancers are accompanied by a *viejo* who wears ordinary dress, with a small poncho, straw hat, a bag of maguey fiber, and a long cane of thick reed. The *viejo* mask is of wood, slightly large and slightly grotesque, without negroid features (pl. 11). The nose is bulbous, the eyes open holes, and there is a very realistic beard of gray streaked with brown and black. The mask is of medium brown color with a band across the forehead of brown, red, and a lighter brown. The *viejo*, acting like a feeble old man, imitates the Negrito dance. He dances around the performers in a clockwise circuit, pushes back spectators and jests with them, particularly with old Tata Le, whose beard is strikingly like that of the *viejo*. There is much use of a chicken leg and claw, the leg wrapped in paper, with which he scratches at bystanders. Later he did the same with the *tiznado*. He sang impromptu songs and laughed in a high shrill voice. There were a few obscene gestures with the *tiznado* or others, mostly making grabbing motions at the sexual organs. Later a man dressed as a woman joined the group. The *viejo* pretended she was his wife, but there was no vulgarity (other than verbal) beyond putting his arms about "her" shoulders. The second day at Ayutla there were more *viejos* with larger wooden masks. One was black, the other only black across the lower part. There was little vulgarity in their actions, beyond poking with a stick. All three later ran down the jolly old drunk, Tata Le, and took away his mescal bottle.

Cacalotepec has a Conquista dance without a dialogue. The performers wear an upright feather headdress (pl. 13, *a*). The frame of the headdress is similar to that of the matachin crown of the Yaqui (fig. 2). The feathers are sewn on a cloth which slips over upright sticks attached to the frame. The dancers wear a long white wig, shirt, and short red pants with a little white apron or a cloth, folded triangularly, in front. They carry a small gourd rattle perforated with numerous small holes The rattle is shaken from side to side. In the other hand they carry a collapsible fan. The music is furnished by violins and a guitar. In 1933 there were four *viejos*, with wooden masks, large and slightly grotesque. Two masks were black and two white. Those with white masks wore a large white sheepskin "wig."

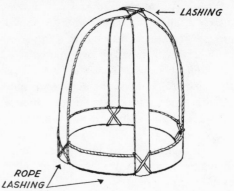

Fig. 2. Base of feather crown worn at Cacalotepec. The feathers are attached upright to the ring. The material of the base is cane. All pieces are flat strips.

How the Conquista is performed here I cannot say, since unfortunately the entire group became too drunk to dance before they finally were all assembled. It would seem to have some relation to a maypole dance, for an elaborate maypole with ribbons was set up for them. A slight attempt to dance showed some of the steps which contained a suggestion of the matachin steps of northern Mexico and more than a suggestion of the matachin music, at least of the Yaqui-Mayo. The steps of both this and the Negrito dance were definitely flat-footed.

Cacalotepec also has a Negrito dance similar to that of Ayutla. The masks are smaller, not even covering all the face and with a pronounced snout and upcurving tusks, obviously piglike, white moustache, and eyebrows. The dress is similar to that of Ayutla dancers but of several colors, not all black. The dancers carry a heavier stick and a larger rattle with two clappers. The dance is less suggestive of the fandango. There is some pantomime, such as thrusting out the snout as dancers pass their partners. The music is almost the same as that of Ayutla.

After the dance a group of "soldiers," a file of about thirty men, mostly young bucks and boys, paraded about town with a weird assortment of guns, under the direction of an individual wearing a cape and with a rubberized cover on his hat. They carried everything from modern repeating rifles to bolt-action Springfields, Mausers, shotguns, and flintlocks, none with any ammunition.

Later this group danced, forming a file on one side of the dance place with all but two of the "Indians" of the Conquista on the other side. Two Indians danced opposite two soldiers, the "white" *viejos* opposite the "black," without form or pattern. They all struck machetes on the ground, first on one side and then the other, while gyrating wildly about, bumping into one another, occasionally advancing or retreating, and sometimes passing or circling one another and clashing machetes. The remainder of the soldiers were in a crouching position, making threatening motions with their guns and, at command of a leader, jumping forward a pace, then back. At each interval, after a short period of dancing, the soldiers moved to another side of the clear space and repeated the performance, changing in anticlockwise direction. After occupying all four sides of the clear space and returning to their original position, the soldiers rushed out and captured the Indians, including those not dancing. Then everyone had a drink and they did it all over again. As a variation, one of the Indians fled and was chased all over the hillside. There was a procession in the intervals in which two small girls marched with the Indians, everyone marching about in a circle. Then they gave vivas to everyone they could think of, including the King of Spain and the Pope—but none for the President of Mexico.

Later, to stringed instruments, there was indiscriminate dancing of the fandango by soldiers and Indians. One dancer at this time was dressed as a woman with a mask, but little was made of it. At the end, the dancers thanked the musicians.

At Juquila there are two dance groups, Negritos and Conquista, the latter with dialogue. According to the schoolteacher, the Conquista is performed more or less as in the valley of Oaxaca.

Tamazulapan has three dances, Negritos, Caballo de Santiago, and a feather dance. The Caballo de Santiago is danced to the sound of drum and flute. One man carries the figure of a horse made of cane. For the feather dance they wear ornaments of feathers, a rosary, and kerchiefs. The music is violins and trumpets. The dance of the feathers is said not to be like that of the Valley in any respect. The feathers are worn like a crown. Masks are worn only by the Negritos. The dances are all for the fiesta of the town in June. There are no *viejos* as at Ayutla. The dancers go to the houses of the captains to dance.

Other towns have dances as follows:

Tlahuitoltepec: Negrito, the same dress is worn as at Ayutla but the music and steps are slightly different. There is a captain for the dancers and the band.

Mixistlan: Negros, Malinche, and Tehuana dances, perhaps another; fiesta is February 22.

Totontepec: Negrito dancers as in Ayutla.

Metaltepec: Negrito and Tehuana dances. For both, wooden masks are worn. The Tehuanas dress like the Negritos but in different colors. They use the same rattle but carry no stick. Neither wears feathers. The Tehuana steps and music are different from those for the Negritos. There are *viejos* for both dances.

Yacoche: a dance by eight performers without masks to music of the violin. It is said to be different from the dances in other towns.

I could discover no organization for the dancers. The method of recruiting is vague and there appears to be no formal leader of the group. Dancers queried said they participated "just for fun." There seems to be no set term of service; men join and drop out as they please.

Together with the functions of the town government, the various Catholic rites and festivals provide the major concrete expression of community solidarity. The annual town meeting and the two or three major fiestas are the only times when most of the population gathers together. The *mayordomías*, with their changing personnel, the involvement of friends and relatives, and the sense of community service also aid in a minor way to solidify the town spirit. As a physical structure the church also is an ever-present recourse in time of trouble, a place to burn candles and pray. The church is an integrating force also since the use and care of the building evoke communal sentiments. In other towns the church and church rituals are more important in themselves, though in Ayutla the weekly market serves to reinforce the importance of the church by bringing more people to the Sunday services.

The day the state government begins to appoint outside town officials and the church rituals are suppressed, the destruction of the scanty communal spirit of the Mixe will begin. The only conceivable substitute for these agencies is the school; but that, in 1933, had made little or no headway, nor is it likely that it will soon wholly take the place of indigenous institutions. Administrators are apt to forget that the essentially mystical sense of group participation must grow from within and cannot be imposed from without.

CHAPTER VII

THE MOUNTAIN SPIRITS

IN THE PREVIOUS CHAPTER I pointed out that the rites and festivals connected with the Catholic church, together with the activities of the secular government, afford the major concrete expression of community cohesiveness. In such a town as Ayutla they are also the principal outlet for the religious impulses of much of the population. Nevertheless, even in so progressive a town as Ayutla there is a certain residue of non-Catholic beliefs and practices. For many persons, it is true, this collection of beliefs has little more value than fairytales among ourselves. Few people have much knowledge of the beliefs and no more than a very slight consciousness of the degree to which they influence the outer conservative fringe of the population.

What forms the outer fringe of Ayutla becomes the dominant element in towns as near as Tamazulapan. There, non-Christian rituals and beliefs are numerous and are universally practiced, sometimes with a degree of secrecy which approaches the reticence of the Pueblo Indians of the Southwest. Such towns have no resident priests. The rites and festivals of the Catholic church are celebrated with little admixture of paganism, but in the consciousness of the inhabitants they have at most an equality with the non-Christian rites. In Ayutla and the progressive towns the community spirit is expressed only in Christian rituals. In Tamazulapan and other conservative towns non-Christian rituals retain a societal function and value which elsewhere is lacking. Furthermore, the rites of a pagan kind have a far more intimate character and partake of the nature of a direct communion with the supernatural, a feature lacking in the functions of the Catholic church. They are most commonly performed alone or in small groups in isolated and lonely places. They have a connection with the most intimate details of daily life in a way which the Catholic rituals do not.

Undoubtedly, the non-Catholic rites of the Mixe at one time had a vital significance far greater than at present. Today, even for the Mixe who practice them most, the pagan rites are almost on the level of magical practices rather than direct supplications to supernatural beings. The performance of a certain act in a certain way with the repetition of the proper formula is believed to bring about a desired result or avoid a threatened evil. There are vague suggestions of supernatural beings involved, but the most concrete statement in connection with the rituals is that they are "offered to the mountain."

That this may anciently have been true also is possible but unlikely. In the neighborhood of Villa Alta, the Serrano Zapotec, who are quite close to the northwestern Mixe and who practice very similar rites, evidently conceive of supernaturals in a concrete fashion. The sacrifices are made to a mountain spirit, Véni yeyú, spoken of in Spanish discourse as *El Rey de las Montañas*, the King of the Mountains. Lightning, rain, and the water serpent are also conceived of as much more definite supernatural entities by this tribe than by the Mixe. Most probably, the Mixe also formerly possessed similar, although perhaps always less definite, conceptions. What evidence exists indicates that the entire vaguely conceived group of supernaturals is connected with the mountains; and consequently, it seems permissible to class them as mountain spirits.

The word "spirits" rather than "gods" is employed advisedly. The use of the word "gods" in Mexican ethnology as well as in the Southwest has been very loose and quite misleading. The term "spirit" or "supernatural" is usually far more accurate, in part from the very fact that it is more general and less specific in its meaning than is the word "gods." Furthermore, the use of the term "gods" has often concealed the fundamental character of the spirits involved and obscured their basic similarities to many more widespread and basic North American Indian concepts.

The pagan rituals center about a number of sacred shrines, and my first knowledge of the rites came through discovery of these shrines. Although I had found one near Ayutla, the people of that town are so secretive that I almost gave up hope of discovering anything about the rituals. Consequently, a love of mountain climbing rather than any particular credence in the vague rumors of turkey sacrifices performed on the summit of Zempoaltepec caused me to ascend the mountain with Francisco Reyes and a youth from Tlahuitoltepec.

The main trail from Tlahuitoltepec to Zacatepec passes within a few hundred yards of the summit. Near its highest point I came upon the first evidence that the stories of sacrifices were true. Near the main trail is a stagnant pool of noxious-looking water in a depression below an overhanging rock. In this many bundles of pine needles were deposited. The needles were all of the long-needled ocote pine, which I did not observe anywhere on the upper part of Zempoaltepec.

Since neither of my two companions could or would vouchsafe any information about the purposes of these offerings and since a heavy fog was rising perceptibly, we hurried to the first minor peak of the summit ridge, stumbling upward among the pines. From some hidden point below us came an occasional shout. "Men from Tamazulapan," said my companions, "shouting to see if there is anyone about before coming to make sacrifices." I was still skeptical until we reached the summit of the first minor peak.

Here all doubts were resolved. A tiny shrine of slabs of rock, one upright on each side, a third for the back, and a fourth covering the back part of the shrine enclosed a space which had obviously been used for offerings. Turkey feathers were scattered within the shrine and for some distance about. Horsehair, bits of wool, and the wrappings of many tamales lay within the shrine, while a log, much marked with blows from a machete, reposed in front. It and much of the contents of the shrine were stained dark with blood. Before and a little to one side was a tiny enclosure of small stones. Within, the ground was covered with small pine cones. Behind this "corral," leaning against a convenient rock, was a queer figure of palm-leaf strips tied to a small stick.

My companion disclaimed all knowledge of the purpose of the shrine, although from Zapotec practice it was obvious that it was connected with petitions of some sort for animals.[1] After photographing the shrine I picked up the figure of palm leaf lying behind the "corral." When my companions still denied knowledge of its purpose, I began to put it in my blanket roll. Instantly both men protested vigorously. "It represented an ox with a yoke which has been left to ask for oxen. You should not take it. Otherwise how will the petition of the poor unfortunate who left it be answered? The stone enclosure represents a corral full of animals and the entire

---

[1] Parsons, p. 233.

shrine is used to ask for animals." "Of whom or what do they ask?" But to that I could get no answer. Perhaps God. Perhaps the mountain. To the perceptible relief of my companions I left the little "ox."

We came upon the main summit suddenly to encounter two men from Tamazula-pan eating lunch about the embers of a little fire. Francisco ran ahead quickly to keep them from running away. A newly beheaded turkey lay on a large rock near by, and one of the men quietly crammed the carcass into a carrying basket and covered it as we came up. They regarded us uneasily for a few minutes while we warmed our tortillas and broiled jerky over the remnants of their fire. But one was an acquaint-ance of Francisco's, and when we had finished our meal, they filled a gourd bowl with tepache from a gourd bottle at their feet and insisted on our drinking. Their eagerness to have us partake of the brew did not end until the bottle was empty. Later, I learned that the completion of the tepache was obligatory.

Their tongues loosened, they gave us some information concerning the sacrificial places. This shrine upon the highest point resembled the one already described. Offerings and sacrifices were made at this place for money, in preparation for jour-neys, and to secure good crops, particularly of maize. Within the shrine were frag-ments of two partly burned candles, clay incense burners, maize leaves, tamales, a small jar of tepache, feathers, cigarettes, and in one spot several coffee beans. Maize meal was also offered, according to our two acquaintances, but there was no sign of it. Feathers, fragments of broken pottery, and maize leaves surrounded the shrine (pl. 16, *b*).

Our two friends also told us the location of other shrines. Two we had passed by without noticing. The first resembles a sweathouse, or temescal, and is used by barren women to petition for children. A large rock with a natural cavity in it closely resembles the flat-roofed sweathouses of the Mixe. This impression has been height-ened by a piling up of rocks to make a copy of the fire chamber (pl. 17, *a*). Fires had been built in this miniature chamber, and at the time, it was full of wood carefully broken to the right size. Feathers and maize leaves were visible inside the main chamber. Branches of shrubbery had been laid on top, the yiyíai plant, much used in Holy Week, and another shrub resembling in its leaves the California holly, or toyon. Close by was a log where turkeys had been beheaded.

The other shrine resembled in its construction the first two described, although placed on a raised base. It was used by hunters who wish to petition for deer. Only one draggled white chicken feather, upright within the shrine, showed that it had been used. Undoubtedly of great antiquity, its lack of use is a testimony to changing living habits.

The final shrine revealed by our Tamazulapan friends lay below the flat summit rock of the mountain, concealed by shrubbery. It showed signs of much use and there were thousands of pottery sherds about it. This shrine was used by potters from Tamazulapan and Mixistlan, the only two pottery-making villages.

Like my own two guides, the men from Tamazulapan resorted to generalities when I sought more specific information. The sacrifices were to "ask" for things or to "pray" for them (Sp., *pedir*). They "asked of the mountain." Thus far and no farther would they go. So it was to be each time I came in contact with these pagan rituals. It was relatively easy to learn of the manner and occasion of the rituals: of their purpose, of the supernatural beings involved, I rarely obtained any information. Our two friends pleaded their long journey homeward and departed into the fog now swirling about the mountaintop. Shortly after, we descended in the opposite direction to lie stormbound and frozen in the miserable village of Yacoche.

Although this was the first time I obtained any definite information on the pagan mountain-spirit cults of the Mixe, it was not my first hint. The young secretary of Ayutla had already said "he had heard" that turkeys were sacrificed at a cave above the town although he did not know what the beliefs were. Later, after I had visited the cave alone, perhaps twoscore people asked me privately and with insistence who had shown me the way to the cave and manifestly refused to believe my story that I had found it unaided.

The Colonel really put me in the way of visiting the cave by extolling the view to be had from the cross at the summit of the cliff in which the cave lies. It was he who pointed out the most practicable trail, and early one morning I started up the hill alone to the cross. For all it looked easy the ascent is a good two-hour climb. The cross is practically a duplicate of the one before the church, set up on rocks, the trees and brush carefully cleared away around it. One or two iris and a number of yellow-flowered succulents growing near by had recently been laid at the foot of the cross. There were a couple of broken pots with water in them and some flowers. A few sherds were scattered about, while in a hole about eighteen inches deep in the rocks before the cross there was an eggshell, opened by breaking off one end.

From the cross a steep trail, the brush recently cut back, led down two or three hundred feet to turn quite unexpectedly into the cave. The cave is only a shallow depression thirty to forty feet deep like a giant clamshell, the rear sloping downward. There were hundreds of potsherds around the mouth and many old carrying baskets. In a natural deep hollow in the side of a boulder on the lip of the cave were numerous crosses of straight twigs, bound with palm fiber. On a little flat spot slightly in front of this were the fresh remains of a good-sized fire. At the back left of the cave is a small pool of stagnant water. Two odd-looking stalagmite formations stood before it. Twigs which stood up before them were now dead and lifeless. Broken potsherds deeply covered the ground near by and part of the bottom of the pool. A little in front of the water stood an obese-looking roughly pyramidal rock about one meter high (pl. 18, *a*). On top were wilted iris and about eight of the cheapest variety of cigarettes. Another cigarette was stuck in a crevice a few inches below the top. The front of the rock was white from maize meal thrown against it, and every crevice was filled with turkey feathers stuck in quill foremost. Once a few iris were laid across the feathers. At the base was a noisome mess of shelled maize of mixed colors, sprinkled with fresh blood, as well as numerous maize husks, and a great many iris. Two maize ears lay flat, apparently without method, one close to the base of the rock and partly concealed by some maize husks, the other on the edge of the mess. One was mostly white with some pink and red grains, the other mostly red with some white. There were an eggshell broken at one end, three or four pieces of broken sherds containing maize meal in a line near and parallel to the base of the rock, and one small jar of tepache. Several short pieces of the broad leaves of an agavelike plant growing near by, with carefully squared ends, lay on the edges of the offerings, together with iris and feathers, some stuck upright. A bundle of maize leaves was tied about a little maize meal soaked in tepache. In front lay a block of wood about a foot long and two inches square with knife marks on it where turkeys had been beheaded. The blood apparently had been caught in the leaves of the agavelike plant, for several showed blood stains and one was still sticky. A little to the left of this was a pile of maize husks and iris leaves carefully covered with three sections of the agavelike leaves. Large flies buzzed lazily about the two messes and a pair of ravens croaked protestingly above the cave.

As yet unaware of how my intrusion would be taken, I found the cave an eerie place. Thick tropical cloud-forest vegetation entirely surrounded it. Agavelike plants grew in the undergrowth and sprang from the rough walls of the cave mouth. The walls were covered with fantastic sheets of limestone, and weird stalactites hung from the sides and roof.

The shrines described so far are to some extent the type of all the shrines to be encountered in the Mixe country. They are situtated either in caves or upon mountaintops. Often they have been completely abandoned, like the shrines I saw on the Cerro Pelado northwest of Zempoaltepec (there are three "Cerro Palados" within twenty miles, so this is hardly a revealing designation) or one on top of the Lightning Peak above Totontepec. A few, however, have additional features, particularly those now in use, and may be profitably described in some detail before discussion of the religious concepts involved.

The Cave of the Spring is near the border of Tamazulapan, not far from Ayutla. A sizable stream comes out from beneath the fallen rocks in front of the entrance. Evidently it formerly had a higher outlet through the cave. At the inner end of a narrow ledge, on the left side as one enters, is the place where turkeys are killed. Evidently tamales and maize ears are left, since many maize husks are strewn about, but none were in evidence at the time I visited the cave. Placed about the cave were old stalks of the wild agave and withered flowers, a number of small jars, and several broken potsherds with pinole, as at the cave above Ayutla. Candles had also been burned and on a tiny ledge above the offerings were three cigarettes and the dried remains of a few iris and geraniums. Turkey feathers were stuck in every crevice of the wall. At the left of the altar, nearer the entrance but behind a thin projecting sheet of rock, hundreds of old potsherds were carefully stacked. To the right of the altar was a rather largish downward opening, about eight feet deep and extending perhaps ten feet farther into the mountain. A numerous collection of maize husks, feathers, and trash apparently had been thrown down the steeply sloping edge of this hole. The bottom was once evidently in the water. In the rainy season it may still be. It was covered with waterworn potsherds, most of them partly buried in the sand and gravel, suggesting that they had been thrown in at a time when water ran here. Small galleries opening off this, too small to enter, also had partly buried sherds in the sand at the bottom. At the extreme rear, about shoulder high, was an opening about two feet in diameter which led to other recesses, but the water fills the floor back of this opening, evidently part of a basin into which the stream dropped from some invisible higher level. There was no sign of sherds in this basin. In the part of the cave some six feet above the altar were remnants of a water-formed ledge or old floor on which rested two or three maize cobs. The pottery all resembled modern Tamazulapan pottery, some of it smoke-blackened. There was no sign of the unique Mixe foot jar. Small caves seen in the neighborhood all had some evidence of casual if not regular offerings, a few sherds or a whole pot. Nowhere did I see miniatures except at Mixistlan, although I did not visit several mountain shrines of Tamazulapan.

Another important shrine is the cave of Yen-ja (this name sounds Zapotec), located just below the road about two and a half hours' walk from Ayutla. A narrow steep opening leads into a large cave with several descending benches and passages extending farther than I cared to explore without ropes or companions and with a failing electric torch. Beginning at the mouth and extending well beyond the range of any light from the door were thousands of potsherds, a few whole ollas covered with bowls, a few maize cobs, and many, many pine needles, remnants of fires, and ocote branches. There was no evidence of sacrifices in this cave although I believe I explored beyond the range of the offerings in each of the galleries.

At Mixistlan there are many ancient house terraces on the summit of the mountain. Much pottery is strewn about, often deeply buried where modern trails have been cut. There are three main shrines, one on each of the three main peaks and one on the slightly raised point between them. There are also numerous smaller places in crevices among the rocks where potsherds and cooked maize have been dropped down. The east shrine appears to be where blood sacrifices are made. A depression in the summit of the rock forms the shrine. The west shrine has two insignificant pits where things have been left. The center shrine was perhaps the most interesting, although there was no evidence of blood sacrifices (pl. 17, *b*). It was topped by a cross (as were the other peaks, although the crosses were almost disintegrated) and was surrounded by thousands of pieces of partly intact pottery and sherds of varying size. Most of the large pieces of pottery had a hole made in one side, but some were crude miniatures. No miniature boot or moccasin jars occur, but I saw several large ones. At the foot of the cross were many bundles of ocote needles carefully twined together near the base with maguey-fiber thread. To some was attached a small bundle wrapped in banana leaf. Other bundles of the same shape were independent of the pine needles. Inside the bundles were several blades of long grass doubled and tied, with a small feather or piece of down inside. This was sprinkled with pinole and first wrapped in clusters of broad leaves from a wild shrub resembling the avocado which grew near by, and then in a piece of banana leaf.

Near Totontepec is a small cave under an overhanging rock on the trail into the town from Yacoche, Villa Alta, and Yalalag. Maize cobs and flowers have been left inside. There is evidence of a long-disused shrine on top of the Lightning Peak above the town.

Near Cacalotepec, almost at the top of the climb on the trail from Alotepec and Atitlan, is a pile of loose rocks which is called the temescal (sweat lodge). Travelers pick a branch of a bush growing below in the river canyon and carry it to the top. When they reach the pile of stones, they throw water on them and then switch their legs with the brush saying, "nuwúpkits, nuwúpkits," "Give it to me." " 'Make my legs warm,' is what they mean," said my informant. Then they leave the branch on top of the pile of stones. A few feet farther on is a small cross with flowers at the foot and several flat stones on which to sit and rest.

I visited many other shrines, but these represent a typical selection. I was told of shrines beside springs, but I did not visit any.

The central event in the rituals at the shrines is usually the sacrificing of a turkey. In a conservative town like Tamazulapan the occasions for sacrificing a turkey are almost innumerable: birth, marriage, death, sickness, completion of a new house, planting, the appearance of the first "flower" on the maize, the appearance of the first ear, the gathering of the first green ears, the harvest, before a journey, the assumption of a public office, and finally just whenever one happens to want something, like money or livestock, sufficiently to feel that a sacrifice would be of assistance. The details of sacrifices in connection with public office have been described (p. 26).

In general, good days are Tuesday, Thursday, or Saturday. On such days sacrifices are made. The following day a little feast, or fiesta, is given in the house. Mondays, Wednesdays, and Fridays are bad days to plant, to marry, to begin a journey, or to initiate any undertaking. Persons born on these days will have bad luck.

No star lore was found and few groups of stars are named. The following are the only names I collected:

Guarache, or sandal, kuk: five or six stars, about one hour before meridian, February 18, 1933.
Arado, or plow, tiktúp. Comes out with the sandal.
Mukmazáp: two large stars rising at about nine o'clock (February).
Kaskú: morning star.
Cruz maza: a group resembling a cross which appears low on the southern horizon. Professor Samuel Herrick, Jr., of the Astronomy Department of the University of California, Los Angeles, suggests that in view of the date this is the false cross rather than the Southern Cross, although both would be visible at the latitude of Ayutla.

The various towns exhibit such differences in their pagan rituals that it will be necessary now to deal with each village separately. Some special topics are treated independently.

Ayutla.—According to Tata Le, the people formerly went to the cave above Ayutla and sacrificed a turkey on any unusual occasion either connected with the crops or personal life, or to request good crops, money, or cattle. They also made use of the Cave of the Spring toward Tamazulapan, as well as other caves and springs.

One important use of sacrifice was in the prevention of sickness. I suspect the former initiatory rites of the new officials (see p. 26), still practiced at Tamazulapan, are to secure the health of the pueblo. Certainly there is considerable belief that the present recurrent epidemics of typhus, such as that in 1933, are caused by the failure of the people to make turkey sacrifices.

Those who do not know the proper way to make sacrifices may hire someone to perform the rites. These persons are called *abogados* ("advocates," "lawyers"). I could learn of no native word for them. They seem to be apart from the curing doctors, although they may be called in to diagnose a sickness. They only cure when the diagnosis indicates that a sacrifice is the proper method. Possibly similar agents exist in other towns, but I did not learn of them.

The cave of Ayutla is particularly the home of the lightning and the wind, although these supernaturals also live in the sky and in various other caves. They also are definitely associated with the summit of Ayutla's Cerro Pelado across the canyon. On the summit of this peak are several shrines, one of which has been in recent use and contains an idol, tsámshut. The year before, one of the schoolteachers had found it and removed it to town. It later disappeared and I found it back in place. I could find no one, however, who would confess to knowing its purposes. Since I was told definitely that this shrine was used to ask the lightning and wind to send rain, presumably the amorphous idol (pl. 4) had some connection with these spirits.

Old Tata Le said only male turkeys and chickens are killed for sacrifices. When a new house is finished, or a child is desired, or there is sickness or some other important event, a turkey or chicken is killed at the cave. Sophisticated Agapito maintained that one who wants money takes flowers to the church, burns candles there, and prays. Afterward the petitioner kills a turkey or chicken in the cave, and later serves tepache in his house. Agapito said, "They ask for things in caves, or at rocks where there is a cross, or of the earth." Tata Le added that offerings of flowers, burning candles, and pinole are made (and evidently tepache; mescal is never offered). Pinole is put in water, if there is any, as at the cave of Ayutla. For animals, the tails of similar cattle and straw images are offered. Pottery vessels left at Ayutla were said never to be of the moccasin shape.

At Ayutla I encountered some belief in dwarfs, *duendes*, mischievous wood spirits, who go about doing harm, tangling horses' tails and manes and tormenting infants. These appear to be Spanish in origin.

Tamazulapan.—Many of the sacrificial occasions in this town have been outlined in the section on shrines. It was said that corn meal is offered in connection with sacrifices here. This was true of the shrines used in the Cave of the Spring and in the cave above Ayutla, but I saw no sign of it on Zempoaltepec.

Tamazulapan has a stone, "perhaps the lightning," which is under the charge of an elderly woman, a different one each year. It is *cosa muy delicado* (a very delicate thing); not everyone may look at it. Ceremonies are performed with it every year on December 31, including a Rosary in the church and "other things." Sentinels are posted so that no one from another village may enter the town.

Yacoche.—There is a niche in the bank below the church bells, where tamales are left. Above town are twin rocks where tepache and balls of corn dough are offered. When there is much sickness or hunger, pinole and turkey stew are taken there, but not cigarettes. Ketsp is the name of the rocks. Sacrifices, ipshúk, are also made at Zempoaltepec.

Mixistlan.—Sacrifices and offerings are made before and beside the church as well as on the peaks above town. Very likely they are also made inside the church. Practically everyone from here goes to Zempoaltepec during May. On their return, which necessarily is through Yacoche, they offer tepache to anyone encountered. If a woman is met, they do not hand her the cup, but place it on the ground for her. (Information from schoolmasters at Yacoche and Mixistlan.)

Metaltepec.—On the day before New Year, the *topiles* used to visit every house with a drum to chase out the devils. Then they stood guard all night beating the drum at the two roads entering the village and killed a chicken in the middle of the road so the devils wouldn't return. Formerly the *topiles* also killed chickens and turkeys in the church and at the foot of the cross in front, burying feathers and tamales.

People at Metaltepec kill a turkey for a death, sprinkling the blood, but do not kill turkeys for birth, marriage, a new house, or sickness. There is no use of pinole or feathers, nor are shrines visited on mountains, in caves, or at springs.

Cacalotepec.—A few still kill turkeys here, but residents never have gone to Zempoaltepec. I suspect the Sierra de Alotepec is more significant for them.

Tepuxtepec.—A small knoll above and west of town is where turkeys are sacrificed. A turkey is killed in the fields for planting. The blood is buried with pinole in the middle of the field. Nothing is done with the feathers. Men are invited to help sow and are taken afterward to the house for dinner, at which time the turkey is eaten.

For the first flower no sacrifice is made. Some kill a turkey in the fields when they harvest; others do not. They do not smoke when turkeys are killed. No use is made of the feathers, and pinole is not thrown in the directions. They do not sleep with their wives for nine days before killing the turkey, but they may have intercourse immediately afterward. Only married men may sacrifice at Tepuxtepec.

There is some assimilation of Catholic and pagan rites, although, as I have indicated, they remain very much apart. In pagan offerings, candles have been taken from Catholicism, and the church uses copal incense. In sickness resort may be had either to Christian or to pagan rites. More striking is the use of the church for pagan rites as at Mixistlan. At Tepuxtepec the *mayordomo* of the fiesta of the patron saint kills a turkey at a shrine uphill from the church before beginning the fiesta. For the fiesta of the patron saint of Yacoche the *mayordomo* kills a young male puppy on Zempoaltepec. On his return he gives a small fiesta at his house.

AGRICULTURAL RITUALS AND BELIEFS

As might be expected from a dominantly agricultural people, there are many rituals and beliefs connected with the crops. These center almost entirely about maize, which is the principal crop. Most of them are distinctly non-Christian in character but there are a few observances connected with the church.

In a progressive town like Ayutla the majority of the people observe only the church rituals. When the seed is prepared, the people bring a little of each kind of seed they are sowing and leave it in tiny piles before each of the saints, with prayers for success of the planting. Flowers are generally left at the same time. Many people do not even do this. Similar practices are observed at Totontepec and Metaltepec. Tamazulapan, conservative, denies the practice.

Conservatives at Ayutla still make offerings to the lightning and wind to secure rain and good crops. These practices are not greatly different from accounts of old observances given by Tata Le. A turkey is killed in the middle of the field just before sowing. A round hole some ten inches across is dug and in it are placed tortillas and tamales. Over these the turkey's blood is sprinkled, and the hole is covered up.

As they cut off the head of the turkey they asked of Tata Dios and the earth as follows:

Metsún duk maiyáten/chaméni chamengók/metsísh móip mokenshúkits.
Now that we are sowing/do me the favor/of giving us maize.

No feathers or pinole are used. Formerly, if a dog was found digging up the tamales, it was put in jail.

At Juquila, seed is not taken to the church. People take a turkey to the field, behead it there, and let it flop about until dead. This is in "respect of the earth so that the land will bear or give."

At Metaltepec, after seed maize was taken to the church, a turkey was formerly killed in the field. The ground was sprinkled with the blood. The neighbors were invited to the house to eat the turkey. At Totontepec a rooster is killed in the house before sowing.

At Yacoche a man sleeps apart from women three nights. Then he goes to the church and prays. Thirteen perfect ears from the previous harvest and all the double-pointed ears are taken to the field. They are undecorated. In the middle of the field at midday a turkey is killed and the ears are sprinkled with blood and pinole. Pinole and blood are buried in the field. The head of the turkey is passed above the seed in an anticlockwise circuit. The ears are kept until the first flower or tassel appears.

Mixistlan has a very interesting ceremony which may be a planting ceremony, although it was described as being for a good harvest. The person giving the ceremony buries young dogs, eggs, the blood of chickens, lime, and ashes before and behind the church and also at the pinnacles above the town. Within the church "similar" ceremonies are performed, and then some of the guests dance. Some are dressed as city dwellers, that is, as Spaniards, some as women. Two or three violins play and they dance *jarabes*. They all drink tepache and mescal. When this ceremony is over they all go to the house of the person giving the ceremony and eat a stew of turkey meat.

At Ayutla, turkey sacrifices and offerings are made in the cave above the town when the tassel appears, when the first ears are formed, and if an animal is injuring the fields. At Metaltepec, the first ears are taken to the church, but there are other ceremonies. At Yacoche, when the first flower appears, the thirteen perfect ears and the double-pointed ears which were sprinkled with blood at the time of planting are ground into dough and made into tortillas and tamales. Blood is sprinkled over green maize leaves, which are then deposited at the summit of Zempoaltepec. There is a "little feast" in the house. This is said to be on July 25.

At Ayutla interesting observances are still fairly general for the eating of the first green maize and the harvest. The same ceremonies are universal in Tamazulapan. When the first ears of green maize are gathered, everyone who helped in the planting is invited. The ears are cooked in an olla in water except for three or four which are roasted in the ashes. When the ears are cooked, the woman of the household takes those roasted in the ashes and hits each guest three times on the small of the back with the ears, saying, "Nuksh niyúk!" ("Go away, hunger!"). Each guest is then given a plate of the boiled ears and a bowl of tepache. The first of the tepache is spilled on the ground with a prayer. When they have finished eating, each guest says doskoyépne, the usual word of thanks at the end of a meal. At the harvest the same ceremony was observed.[2]

The perfect ears at Ayutla are those sacrificed in the cave, according to Tata Le, but those I saw there were far from perfect. Double-pointed ears, then, are put on top of the pile of harvested maize and called *los pastores*, the shepherds. They are not sacrificed and, according to Tata Le, were kept permanently.

At Yacoche a turkey is killed ceremonially in the house when the first green corn is ready to eat in September. Green ears are taken to the church and left there. In the house, tamales are made of the green maize and the neighbors are invited. The guests are not struck with the ear of maize as at Ayutla, but they say, "Hunger is a little man." Part of a tamale and a green ear are burned in the fire before anyone eats. Neither here nor elsewhere did I learn of any custom of building new fire or providing new pots or fire stones at this time.

The people of Mixistlan all go to a place called Tres Ríos, Three Rivers, on August 4 to make sacrifices. This is so that badgers and raccoons will not eat the corn.

Tepuxtepec has an interesting ceremony at the time of the first ears of corn. Early in the morning the owner of the field takes green corn, *quelites* (greens taken from the tender shoots of the bean vines), squash, and tamales, "all the things they sow," and puts them at one side of a spring in which a water serpent is supposed to dwell. He also places there all the double-pointed ears saved from the previous harvest. A turkey is killed, and the blood is sprinkled over the things left there. A prayer is said. Tamales are made at the house and the neighbors are invited. The guests are struck

---

[2] This is similar to Mitla practice. Parsons, p. 279.

on the back of the shoulder with an ear of roasted green corn by the woman of the house, who says, "Go away, hunger!" exactly as at Ayutla.

This belief in a serpent dwelling in a spring brings up the various serpent beliefs which are, as everywhere in Mexico, connected with water and floods and also with crops in indirect fashion. Probably the drought ceremonies are all, at least partly, directed toward the water serpent.

WATER-SERPENT BELIEFS

Ayutla.—A snake, tokchá, with a red and green back resembling a mat, and with horns on the side of the head, lives in a spring (*pozo de agua*). It does not bite, but should a person by misfortune come upon one, it twines itself about him and drags him down. Ordinarily, it does not come out of the water. River floods are caused by this snake. When there is a cloudburst, the snake comes out of the clouds. This happened last year (1932); it rained so hard it was dark, and the snake came out of the clouds. At such times, salt and copal are put in the fire. (Heavy rains are always accompanied by thunder and lightning.)

Formerly there was a lake at the place some miles west of Ayutla still known as La Laguna. A black snake, thick as a tree, once lived there. At night it went "dr-r-r-r-ahg." My informant had often heard it. People used to visit caves near by. About fifteen years ago, the lake dried up. Now there is water when there are heavy rains, but it goes away and the snake has left too.

Yacoche.—Any serpent belief in connection with floods and springs appeared unfamiliar.

Tepuxtepec.—There are serpents which live in springs where streams start. They resemble mats (in the markings on their backs) and have horns like a deer, with seven prongs on each side (fourteen altogether). People don't go there to leave offerings; they are afraid, according to one informant (but see above).

Metaltepec.—There are said to be no snakes in local springs. My informant knew of a spring near Alotepec (Estancia) where there is a water snake.

DROUGHT CEREMONIES

At Ayutla, the progressive town, when there is a serious drought, San Pablo is taken from the church and alms are solicited. These are sent to Oaxaca to pay for a mass by the bishop. The priest goes later with the image to the cross on the mountain above Ayutla and is paid to pray there. The people of the town go along and spend the whole day there drinking a great deal of tepache. This cross is also visited on May 3, the *Día de la Cruz*.

Unquestionably, the conservatives of Ayutla also visit the cave above town or the cave of the spring and sacrifice turkeys in time of drought. This was formerly done quite generally, according to Tata Le, and the people of Tamazulapan still do it.

Agapito says that, when it doesn't rain, people go to some big cave like that above the town. When the schoolteacher stole the idol of Cerro Pelado, people said it did not rain so much.

The people of Yacoche go to the summit of Zempoaltepec to sacrifice turkeys in time of drought.

The turkey sacrifices for drought are individual affairs. There is no form of communal sacrifice, nor any individuals who sacrifice for the benefit of the community.

Progressive Juquila has no observances for drought. But Juquila is a town of traders and is apparently the only Mixe town which normally raises insufficient grain for its own needs. It also has quite a bit of irrigated land and, if there is drought, special attention is paid to putting all the irrigated land in cultivation and getting a good crop. But there are no ceremonies, not even the saints being taken out.

Tepuxtepec has processions of saints for drought or for a waterspout (*aguacero*) for nine days led by the chaplain and the band.

Mixistlan people bathe at a cataract on the border with Chichicastepec when there is drought. They leave tepache, cigarettes, and small balls of maize dough: they behead cockerels and sprinkle blood there.

DISEASE, CURING, WITCHCRAFT, AND DIVINATION

Sickness is considered by the Mixe to come both from natural causes and through witchcraft and supernatural causes. As might be expected, the progressive towns have only a few believers in supernatural causes of sickness, while the conservative towns incline very strongly toward this causation.

To some extent, contagious diseases are known in the progressive towns. With the exception of typhus, they are rare except in epidemics. Nasal infections result from the climate very often but are little regarded. Pneumonia is rarer than one would expect. Stomach disorders are the most common complaint. All these things are normally regarded as "natural" diseases and are generally treated by herbal remedies. In some towns there are men or women known for their ability to use herbs, but their knowledge is slight and very experimental. There are relatively few recognized treatments, and Doña Sotera, my cook in Ayutla, although widely known as a curer, indicated that her method was to seek some herb to cure each individual sickness. "Sometimes I find the remedy, sometimes not." There are a few well-recognized herbs, evidently, but I could find nothing to indicate that herbal curers of the type of Doña Sotera possessed any extensive knowledge.

Most of the recognized herbs seem to be for the treatment of fevers and colds. *Ojos de grilla*, tsápsiai, leaves are placed on the head, chest, knees, and feet, together with a little lard. *Madroña*, kamók, leaves are used in the same way for the same illnesses. They make the patient sweat. *Pasote* and *amole* (these seem to be Spanish names) are taken uncooked in water after rattlesnake bite. There seems to be no ritual.[3] Yiyíai (Sp., *ure*) which is divided in church on Good Friday is much prized as a protection against lightning and as a remedy for "pains," or *dolores*.

Sweating is the sovereign remedy for everything. It is resorted to in practically all illnesses, even slight indispositions. If a man feels a little dull, he will take a sweatbath. Its use in connection with childbirth has been mentioned. According to the sickness, a person goes one or more times into the sweatbath, inhaling the steam.

Catholic processions of saints are resorted to in Ayutla in times of epidemic. On April 2, during the height of the Sunday market, the patron saint, San Pablo, was carried slowly through the market. Gervasio chanted prayers, and his father, old Tata Le, called to the people to give alms to pay for a mass by the bishop in Oaxaca. This was to stop the current epidemic of typhus. The following Sunday the same thing was done.

These treatments are all for more or less clearly defined diseases which are con-

---

[3] Clothes are not thrown away, and bad luck is not thought to follow rattlesnake bite.

sidered due to natural causes. There are others which are of a distinctly different order. My data are somewhat defective in this respect, because in the progressive section of Ayutla there is a considerable skepticism, to say nothing of ignorance, about such practices and beliefs, while the more conservative fringe has adopted a secretive attitude about them. Sacrifices are common in most towns for individual sicknesses or for epidemics.

In general, it would appear that the Spanish folk beliefs concerning bewitchment and disease are little known to the Mixe. Bewitchment with a doll or image in which pins or thorns are stuck, an almost universal practice in the rest of Mexico, was not known to my informants. The evil eye is believed in by a few but there is no general fear of it. *Aires*, winds, are referred to by some but this also is not a very general belief. Whether this is of Spanish or Indian origin is uncertain, although the evidence seems to suggest that it is not an European importation, but rather a latter-day conceptualization of some earlier widespread belief.

Witches or wizards are murdered. Concerning this there can be little doubt, for informants volunteered this information in the conservative villages. When people are sick from witchcraft, there is no way of ascertaining the witch, and most people profess to know nothing about the way in which witchcraft is performed. In reply to questions about the technique of witchcraft, it was usually said that only the witches knew. If people discovered a person was a witch, they killed him. Evidently this murdering of witches is a species of private justice; at best it is performed by a small group, and the civil authorities merely blink at it. But such murders are rare. I could get no admissions about the time or place of assassinations for this cause.

The only information about the way in which witchcraft is performed was a somewhat unsatisfactory admission from Mixistlan. According to an informant there, the practice coincides closely with the patterns of the non-Christian rituals. The person performing the bewitchment beheads roosters and sprinkles the blood at the four corners of the house area or the outside corners of the house of the victim. Offerings of cigarettes, tamales, and tepache are then left at the hilltop shrines near the town. Undoubtedly, there is some formula to be repeated, but I did not get it. Mixistlan apparently has some sort of diviners of whom one inquires the best day on which to perform such a ceremony. These may be like the Ayutla *abogados*, or advocates.

The same ceremony may be performed in order to benefit a person instead of to injure him. The only difference is that the blood is sprinkled at the four inside corners of the house, and presumably the formula repeated is different.

At Tepuxtepec people do not know who the witches are nor how they bewitch. But one knows when one is bewitched because one is "seized suddenly and wishes to die at once. One feels it in the heart. It comes like the air, like a strong wind." This is very suggestive of *los aires* of other parts of Mexico, but the concept and word were unknown to my informants here.

In all the towns from which I obtained any information there is some form of diagnosis of illness. Ayutla has a special type of diagnostician, the *abogado*, apparently without a native name, who has already been mentioned. The *abogado* is called in to diagnose the case, by methods which I could not discover. He decides what is the cause of the sickness and what must be done for a cure. He may specify burning candles in the church, making offerings to the church, or sacrificing turkeys.

In all towns there are *curanderos*, tsö'yup (also herbalists), or curers who first diagnose by feeling the wrists, elbows, and forehead. They at once know the cause of the illness. There is no breathing on the parts or spraying or bathing with mescal. These curers usually cure by sucking out stones, earth, and other things from the patient's body.[4] There is no diagnosis by passing an egg over the body or by breaking eggs in water. There is, however, a class of curers who cure by taking eggs, chickens, and "other things" into secret places in the woods.

Where there are epidemics, sacrifices are made in the shrines. The recent epidemics of typhus are attributed by some at Ayutla to the fact that fewer turkey sacrifices are made in the hills, specifically, that sacrifices are omitted by the municipal authorities of Ayutla at the time of taking office. It will be recalled that these sacrifices are made so that people will not die. In other towns, notably Tepuxtepec and Yacoche, in epidemics, the authorities make a special trip to certain hilltop shrines and sacrifice turkeys (Yacoche) or make pinole and leave it with chicken eggs (Tepuxtepec). At Jareta a rooster is sacrificed.

There is evidently some belief in the possibility of preventing sickness. Doña Paulina boasts that she has never been sick, even in the epidemics. Although she professes not to believe in the affair, she tells in this connection a story of an occurrence at Juquila, where she passed her girlhood. A local family invited her in to eat. After she had finished a meal with a stew of meat for the main dish, she was told that the meat she had eaten was puma meat. After this, she was told, she would never be sick.

At Ayutla the *abogados* sometimes identify the *tono* or personal animal familiar of the patient and attribute the sickness to the sickness of the *tono*. This belief in a *tono* is widespread in Mexico and is allied to general guardian-spirit beliefs in North America. It is believed that each person when born acquires some animal which stands in this peculiar relation to the person. When the animal is sick, so is the person; when the animal dies, then the person dies also. Tonos may be of many sorts—pumas, jaguars, or less formidable animals. My notes lack a Mixe term for *tono*, which is probably of Nahua origin.

One of the schoolteachers at Ayutla was told that one of the boys suffered from a peculiar skin eruption (*granos*) because "his *tono* is the lion [puma]."

Dreams probably also play a part in disease, particularly dreams of the dead. At Ayutla, if a person dreams of the dead, he prays in church and then burns candles in the graveyard. Afterward he serves tepache in his house. The dream indicates that some dead person is suffering greatly or, if one is of the ultraconservative group, it possibly indicates witchcraft. People go to church and pray "because they are frightened." It is also believed that a witch may actually take the form of a dead person in order to frighten the living so that they will die. If this happens, a turkey should be killed in the cave above Ayutla. Those who do not know the proper formula hire an *abogado* to do it for them. There are said to be very few of these dream beliefs now, as compared with those of former times.

A class of divining not associated with illness is performed by people who are neither curers nor *abogados*. These persons, both men and women, divine by casting grains of maize on a mat to foretell the future. I was unable actually to see the

---

[4] At Yacoche it is said sucking doctors are no longer known. Divining by corn-casting is still practiced.

method of doing this, but it would appear to differ from the Zapotec method. Some throw eighteen grains of corn whereas others throw twenty (compared with as high as eighty at Mitla). I could learn of no prayers being said.

SUPERNATURALS

The supernaturals or spirits figuring in these practices are far from clear, as has been suggested. It is fairly certain that some mountain spirit must be involved. It is also probable that there was some sort of earth spirit in view of the fact (see "Agricultural Rites") that some of the sacrifices at planting are to "honor the earth." In this ceremony the blood and corn meal is actually buried in the field. Lightning, wind, and rain are also mentioned as supernaturals and there is evidence that sometimes the sacrificial rites are more or less directly addressed to them.

At Alotepec a visitor told me that during an unusually severe thunderstorm the mayor called the police chief and ordered him to "put this enemy who wants to destroy our church in jail." The police chief unlocked the jail door and, calling the policemen, they struggled with an imaginary being trying to put him in jail.[5]

Another bit of evidence for an earth deity is found in old drinking customs, Formerly, men poured a little liquor on the ground before drinking, saying "pun yetnašrín matunsún bektsh" ("Let God give us this Holy Trinity"). Today, drinking by old men is always ceremonial. The hat is often lifted, occasionally the sign of the cross is made over the bowl, and usually a phrase of thanks is murmured.

Most interesting is the association of several of the supernaturals with the mountain (or cave) spirits and the dead. My evidence is somewhat slender, but there is every reason to believe that the pine-needle offerings noted in connection with the dead as well as the presence of pine-needle bundles in cemeteries are actually offerings to the deceased. The statement that they are "the home of the dead" becomes more significant in connection with their being left in pools and caves and on mountaintops. Furthermore, the wind and lightning are specifically stated to live in caves. Their association with water and rain is obvious, and the association of pools and springs with many of the sacrificial places is suggestive. There is also the fact that the dead can in dreams cause illness and that such illness may be cured by sacrifices at the same shrines at which one appeals for water or rain, good crops, and other benefits. Almost certainly, then, a linkage with interesting implications may be made between the various supernaturals and the spirits of the dead. There is no evidence that the spirits of the dead are actually regarded as rainmakers or bringers of rain. But the highly developed cult of the dead of the ancient Zapotec must almost certainly have had some connection between the dead and rainmakers in its backgrounds,[6] and one can scarcely refrain from speculations regarding the Aztec Tlalocs and the better-known Pueblo kachinas, both of which are basically ancestral spirits who are the bringers of the life-giving and essential rain.

That this connection between the spirits and rain makers is not more strongly defined is almost inevitable from the Mixe environment. The Zapotecs and the Aztecs live in what are comparatively dry climates or climates which have long dry seasons. The Mixe live in a climate in which there is almost no dry season. Two months at most are to be considered a dry season, and even in this period light rains fall

---

[5] Starr (1900), p. 59, has a similar story from Bishop Gillow. Julio de la Fuente's forthcoming book on the Cajones Zapotecs has much useful data on rain and lightning spirits.

[6] Parsons, p. 214.

in most years. Consequently, only in this period is there any possible necessity for an appeal to supernatural forces for the production of moisture. The existence of any ceremonies to produce rain is a significant indication that Mixe culture is non-indigenous, but that it is derived from surrounding cultures which, with their long dry seasons, have a real reason and need for such practices. Mixe rain ceremonies are thus virtually nonfunctional and their presence is of considerable historical significance. The fact that the rain ceremonies are generalized rather than specialized is only to be expected, and there is no real difference in kind between a Mixe rain ceremony and the ceremonies which may be performed for any other important occasion in Mixe life. Rain ceremonies, for example, are definitely subordinated in importance to the ceremonies related to maize. The maize ceremonies do not center about the elsewhere all-important problem of rain production, but rather about crucial periods in the development of the crop, such as the planting, the flowering, the formation of ears, the gathering of green ears, and the harvest. Even the ceremonies for the civil officials outrank the rain ceremonies in importance.

On the other hand, the reported lightning-stone ceremonies of Tamazulapan suggest a definite rain-making function. Alternatively, however, the fact that these ceremonies take place at the same time as the induction of the new officers as well as at the New Year might be argued as indicating the presence of a renovating function. If this argument is offered, the fact that the New Year observances occur on the Christian New Year is not particularly significant. Such shifts have often occurred. Until someone fills in the regrettable gaps in my data for such towns as Tamazulapan and Mixistlan, much of this must remain pure speculation.

Until comparatively recent times, cannibalism may have been practiced in some towns—probably ceremonially. Father Hernández believes it was practiced in Cacalotepec up to at least 1900, an opinion he gave Starr also. Mixistlan also has a wide reputation for cannibalism, which may once have been justified. The young secretary, who in general gave me the impression of trying to conceal knowledge, twice changed the subject to remark that his grandfather had eaten human flesh as a young man. It is possible that he was trying to live up to Mixistlan's reputation, but a more characteristic Mixe reaction would be to deny the practice and certainly not to bring up the subject voluntarily.

The schoolteacher, who has lived eight years at Mixistlan, stated that it was common opinion held in the town that cannibalism was once practiced. He added that it was said they once ate their first-born, believing they thus ensured further issue. War prisoners traditionally were eaten at dances.

CHAPTER VIII

THE FOOD QUEST

THE BACKGROUND of Mixe life is dominated by maize. Maize is the object of most of Mixe labor. It is the principal food, to which all other foods are in the relation of condiments or occasional luxuries. Days and weeks may pass without other nutriment than that derived from maize. If the maize crop succeeds, there is plenty; if it fails utterly, there is famine, perhaps death.

The zenith of the Mixe economic cycle in one sense and its nadir in another fall about the New Year. In December the harvest ends. Short of complete failure of the crop, food is plentiful. Filled stomachs and the cheerful activity of harvesting maize, husking the ears, and filling the storehouses and bins create contentment.

At the same time nature is at its lowest ebb. Although few plants lose their leaves entirely, yet growth comes nearly to a full stop, imparting a drab grayness to the landscape. Leaves and foliage are tattered and worn. The once-green fields of maize are brown and the dilapidated and dried leaves hang dejectedly from shattered stalks.

By the end of January the new economic cycle has begun here and there. The irregular rectangles of fields, here isolated amid forests of pine or the more lush growth of the cloud forest, there covering solidly whole mountain flanks, show signs of plowing, beginning first at the higher altitudes (pl. 12, b). The felling of trees and brush to make new fields or reclaim old ones is under way. By early February the wave of activity has crept down the mountains to the level of Ayutla. Everywhere people are plowing or clearing brush, and many of the fields are neat and trim. Not all, however, for no field is cultivated two years in succession and last year's maize stalks still stand in more and more ruinous state.

The lands to be plowed are roughly cleared of maize stalks and weeds, which are piled and burned. After the plowing, clumps of maize roots, broken stalks, and weeds remaining from the first imperfect clearing are piled in long windrows to await a favorable time for complete burning. About this time the first wildflowers appear in the surrounding woods and along the trails.

By mid-February, planting is under way on the highest and most humid lands where maize takes longest to mature. Smoke from burning brush rises from every peak after two or three days of dry weather. In a month similar activity is under way about the town. People are sorting seed or shelling it at nearly every house. Laggards are hurriedly plowing their last fields, others are putting in the furrows for planting. The first gay neighborhood assemblages close to the village are helping the more forehanded to plant.

Mid-April sees all this activity passed on down the mountain slopes. In another month it will reach the drier lower levels where, by June, if the rains be on time, the last crop will be in. The brief semidry season is normally over and in the higher altitudes the fate of the year's crop is already determined. There remains only to watch and to wait, husbanding the shrinking stocks of maize, sometimes already with the foreknowledge that the year's close will bring not plenty but want and starvation.

The farm lands of the Mixe are held under systems of tenure which vary from town to town. In Ayutla, Tepuxtepec, and Totontepec, and undoubtedly in some other towns, all lands are held under individual title. A man must either own by inheritance or purchase, or else rent lands. If he be a landless man who cannot rent, he is in a difficult situation. He must wander from ranch to ranch, seeking a chance to do a little work for which he will be paid in maize. Or he may be forced to go to other towns or even out of Mixe territory in order to find means to exist. In times of crop failure, even landowners may leave.

The other system of land tenure is one of use. All the land is considered to belong to the community and a man may utilize any piece of unoccupied land, which will be regarded as his for so long as he may use it. But if he moves to another location, anyone may claim and use the land. Metaltepec, Yacoche, and Tamazulapan follow this system.[1]

Juquila follows an intermediate system. Every house and piece of property in the town proper, as well as desirable land close to town, is privately owned and a tax must be paid on the property. But the lands outside the town are communally owned and may be occupied by any of the residents under the use-ownership system. This system is rather anomalous in such a progressive town as Juquila, but it is partly explained by the fact that Juquila is perhaps the only Mixe town which is not an agricultural village. It is definitely a trading and cattle-raising community and consequently has artisans and specialists not to be found in any other Mixe town. No other town, for example, has a resident baker. Juquila has seven or eight. Many people in Juquila do no farming at all.

The agricultural possibilities and secondary products vary enormously from town to town as well as within the range of territory possessed by each town. Ayutla grows first of all maize. In the cold and temperate zones yellow, white, and black maize are sown; in the hot zones on a few outlying Ayutla lands, red maize is grown. In the cold zone of the mountain above Ayutla, planting is done in February, beginning immediately after the fiesta of the patron saint, January 25. This early date is necessitated by the long, cool growing season. About the town the planting is in March and April. In the warm zones planting is in May and June. Here the winter rains are less and moisture conditions forbid earlier planting.

In the temperate zones beans (Sp., *frijol del monte*) of a climbing variety and squash, kapché (Sp., *chilecayote*), are sown along with the maize. In the warm zones another squash, monjé (Sp., *calabasa de biche*), and a bush bean (Sp., *frijol del campo*) only are grown. The latter is sowed separately from the maize. Tepuxtepec has a rather different group of maize varieties, a yellow maize sown in cold country, another yellow type sown in the hot country, and a white variety which will grow in either zone. Only the bean known as tsapshü'k is sown at Tepuxtepec. Yacoche

---

[1] The following additional details are of interest. Ayutla has few communal lands. Each person has title to or rents land. This includes unused forest lands upon which even the right to cut wood is restricted. Small plots belong to the town: the plaza, the site of the brickyard, and a steep hillslope across the canyon upon which any one of the townsfolk may cut wood.

At Yacoche all lands are communally owned. Rights of usage are recognized but revert to the community if lands are not cultivated. Anyone may then appropriate them.

At Totontepec individuals own all good lands except two small plots close to town which are planted to gain funds for the church or are rented, the revenues going for the same purpose. Lands of little agricultural value are communal and are open to appropriation.

Metaltepec lands are communally owned. Special tracts are cultivated communally for municipal expenses.

Schmieder (p. 69) says that lands are held by use rights in *all* villages but that plow lands may be bought and sold. This statement is contradictory as well as incorrect.

has yellow, white, and black maize as at Ayutla in the temperate zone, red in the warm regions. All Mixe maize varieties have large ears in comparison with Zapotec maize at Mitla.

Mixe fields in general look better cared for and better cultivated than valley Zapotec fields. This is, in part, because of the greater height of the maize stalks. An exception is, of course, the temporarily cultivated fields which are used for two or three seasons and then abandoned. For these the brush is cleared and piled and the trees felled with a crude axe made with a blade passing through a wooden handle. The machete is also much used (fig. 3). The whole is then burned, but the large trunks are left in a crisscross network over the land and the maize is planted between

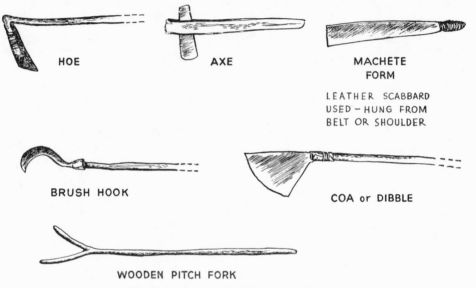

HOE   AXE   MACHETE FORM

LEATHER SCABBARD USED – HUNG FROM BELT OR SHOULDER

BRUSH HOOK   COA or DIBBLE

WOODEN PITCH FORK

Fig. 3. Implements for Mixe horticulture.

them in the ashes. These fields are not neat in any respect, although if they are used again within a few years, the repeated burnings reduce them to some kind of order. Since practically all lands must be rested from one to three years between plantings, there are also large fallow areas which look somewhat dilapidated.

The maize stalks, weeds, and brush on the fields are cut with a hooked machete of peculiar shape (see fig. 3) and then piled in rows with a forked stick (fig. 3). They are allowed to dry and then burned. Fields which are not too steep are then plowed, often twice. Plow fields are called in Spanish *labranzas*, in Mixe, yúup or mogyúup. There are a good many clusters of roots and maize stalks which must be gathered up and burned after the plowing. When the land is to be planted, the plow is again run through the soil a day or two before the planting to make furrows about two feet apart.

The plow is of the most primitive Spanish type, a piece of wood to which is attached a long tongue and an upright handle (pl. 10, *b*). The top part of the point is shod with a piece of iron about eighteen inches in length. The front end of the tongue is perforated to allow passage of an upright wooden pin which hooks over the yoke worn by the oxen. Only oxen are used in plowing. The tongue is bound to the yoke with a strip of rawhide about one and a quarter inches in width. A similar strap binds the yoke to the horns of the oxen. The yoke is a modification of the Zapotec yoke with its queer collar.[2] The Mixe collar is much abbreviated and would appear to have no function whatever, whereas the Zapotec collar is wide enough to rest on the back of the ox's neck.

There is only one steel plow, so far as I know, in all the Mixe territory. Even the progressive Colonel has not bought steel plows. The hilly nature of the country offers little land upon which it would be practical to use an ordinary steel plow, and neither double plows nor side-hill plows are known in Oaxaca—an opportunity for an enterprising implement salesman, if only the people had money to buy the tools.

In making the planting furrows the object is to expose the damp earth underneath the surface. In the actual planting a digging stick about seven feet in length is used. This is usually cut from a young pine sapling. The lower and heavier end is beveled to give a chisellike edge. The planter uses this to scoop away the loose dry dirt until moisture is reached. The stick is then plunged into the moist earth as far as possible and the seed dropped in. Four to six grains of maize are dropped in each hole and an occasional squash or bean seed. A small quantity of squash and bean seeds has previously been mixed with the maize seed. After the seed has been dropped in, it is covered with one or two inches of loose soil by jabbing the digging stick into the uphill side of the furrow.

Some lands called pekmíoch (no Spanish term) are too steep or too encumbered with logs or rocks to permit plowing. Here planting is a little more difficult. The digging stick is again used and the technique is similar except that it is more work to dig down to the moist soil below.

After planting, very little is done to the crop. Sometimes worms attack the seed and the fields must be replanted. More rarely, a plague of crows or ravens, hóii (Sp., *cacalote*), will attack the field and scratch up the seed. Again it must be replanted. If the field escapes these visitations, when the maize is about three feet high the plow is run through between the rows to throw the earth toward the plants. The oxen are made to wear muzzles of leather while cultivating is done. In mountain fields the dirt is sometimes thrown toward the plants with a *coa* (a crescentic blade about four inches long set in the plane of a long wooden handle). More rarely, a crude hoe with metal blade is used (fig. 3). Ordinarily, nothing is done to the mountain fields after planting except to cut away the worst of the weeds, but even this rather careless clearing is not always done. More effort might increase the yield but there is no tradition for intensive cultivation and little necessity. Land is fairly abundant in most of the Mixe towns and it is simpler to plant a little more land than to take the effort required to secure a higher yield.

Despite the fair returns, the thin mountain soil is quickly exhausted. No field is ever planted to maize two successive years. Ordinary plow lands are planted every two or three years, depending on their quality. Mountain fields which are too steep to plow are allowed to lie fallow three or more years before being replanted.

A good deal of care is expended in the selection of seed. At the time of the harvest many pick out the best ears and hang them in bunches from the rafters. This is particularly true of the warmer sections, where there is a considerable interval between the harvest and the next planting time. In cooler climates, as at Ayutla,

---

[2] Parsons, p. 51, pl. 17.

where planting follows on the heels of the harvest, the maize is all stored together. Good ears are sometimes placed apart at once, but many people sort over their maize shortly before replanting time, putting aside the good ears. Since in this region it is necessary to sun maize in good weather every now and then to prevent mold or decay from attacking it, there are various convenient opportunities for sorting. Seed on the good ears is generally selected again, the middle section being taken. The small grains near the tip are never used and frequently a narrow band about the butt of the ear is discarded as well. These are shelled off by hand first, then the remainder is carefully dried and placed in nets on mats spread on the ground or floor. The kernels are then beaten off with a short heavy club. The grain is then gathered up and carefully picked over to remove imperfect grains and pieces of the cob. Grains which show a black spot at the germ end are believed not to sprout and careful people remove them. Very progressive farmers such as the Colonel and his immediate followers also disinfect the seed with commercial disinfectants to protect it from worms.

While the seed selection is being made, plowing is going on and brush being burned on mountain fields. If a man has no oxen for his plow lands, he rents them or is helped by relatives. If men help him plow, he must pay for their services, unless it be a family affair. Not so the actual planting. For this there must be tepache and a feast. No one will plant for money, but there is usually no difficulty in getting plenty of assistance. If a man asks neighbors to help him, however, he must respond to similar invitations from them.

The case of the Colonel is extreme, for he is the biggest planter in Ayutla, but it illustrates the general system excellently. More than a week ahead of the date set for planting, Doña Paulina was busy brewing tepache and assembling food for the feast. Several women upon whom she had claims because of past assistance were given maize to grind. Festoons of dried meat hung in her storehouses or, by day, from wires about the patio. The Colonel's men were busy putting furrows in the plow lands and burning the brush on the steeper slopes to get all in readiness. The day before, they had cut great bundles of planting sticks, hardening the chisel edges a little in the fire. The seed was measured, and careful proportions of squash and bean seed mixed with the maize. There was great making of tortillas in preparation for the following day.

The appointed morning dawned fair and bright. The word had spread widely, for by nine o'clock seventy-five people were hard at work, strung in long lines along the hillslope of the Colonel's most distant field. Each carried a cloth over one shoulder, tied to make a pouch for seed. The Colonel's servants carried large sacks of seed from group to group to replenish the pouches. Old men and women, children, nursing mothers, these last with their infants slung on their backs, worked step by step with the rest. Three generations of one family were pointed out to me. Though it was a merry throng with much laughing and talking, it was distinctly industrious. Everyone worked as if racing with his neighbor and, when the first field was finished, everyone was obviously proud of the speed he had shown.

Two of the largest fields were finished by about one-thirty in the afternoon. The schoolmasters and I had been invited to lunch, and school opened late that afternoon, with but little damage, however, since the majority of the schoolchildren had "played hooky" to join in the planting, or said they had. When the planters streamed in, hot and dusty, they were seated on timbers laid about the patio of the Colonel's house. First a drink of mescal was served, then each received a big gourd bowl of tepache mixed with crushed hominy, called here *posole*. Then the bowls were refilled with straight tepache, the mildest of the several jars prepared, for Doña Paulina had no mind anyone should get drunk before the planting was finished. Food consisted of big bowls of dried beef stewed with cabbage, herbs, and chile, beans, great stacks of tortillas, and bowls of coffee. There were second helpings of everything. While the helpers ate in the patio, the schoolteachers and I ate with the Colonel and Doña Paulina in the house: posole, tepache, chocolate, bread, rice, beef stew, beans, tortillas, and coffee.

After a short rest, the planters returned to finish their work. Only the plow lands close by remained and by five the first of the group began to straggle back. The mescal bottle circulated more freely now and Doña Paulina produced her strong tepache. By dusk everyone had arrived and stew, beans, tortillas, and coffee were served the crowd by the light of a gasoline lantern hung from the center of the patio.

When all had eaten to repletion, there was a lull while the mescal bottles circulated and three or four helpers rushed back and forth from the storehouse bearing bowl after bowl of tepache. At last the orchestra struck up, mandolins and guitars playing gay *jarabes*, and the dancing began.

The fog had crept over the mountain during the afternoon and a fine rain began to fall. The now gay crowd, exhaustion forgotten, paid no attention, although a few moved back under the shelter of the portico. About nine the Colonel himself joined the orchestra with his mandolin, and enthusiasm doubled. This evidence of participation by the ordinarily somewhat aloof Colonel always seemed to please people. By ten the crowd began to thin out. Two of the young men quarreled and, followed by their friends, went into the plaza to fight it out, but the incident was soon over. Ordinarily they would not have left the patio, but they did not feel they should fight in the Colonel's house. By eleven-thirty the rain began to fall heavily and put an end to Ayutla's greatest planting festival.

Such, on a smaller scale, was the round of activity at every household in Ayutla through the planting season. It is a time of abundant food, cheerful companionship, and communal effort. The weather is nearly at its best and at no other time is there as much gaiety and good feeling.

All subsequent work in the fields, a man must either pay for or do himself. Poor people, when their crops are planted, seek work cultivating the fields of the more wealthy. Even the harvest sees no such period of mutual assistance. Close neighbors do not help unless paid to do so. But one who follows the old customs will, when the first green corn is eaten, invite those who helped at the planting to join in a feast. This ceremony and the ritual observances connected with it have already been described (p. 93).

Communal planting customs at the other villages seem the same as those of Ayutla. Only Metaltepec denied the practice.

There are a few other agricultural products besides maize, beans, and squash, but they are of distinctly minor importance. Peas are planted to some extent. They are a recently introduced crop grown more at Tlahuitoltepec than in any other town.[3] Ayutla also plants some. They are either sown among the maize in October, the

---

[3] But Starr (1900), p. 54, mentions them as an important crop at Ayutla.

maize stalks being subsequently cut down, or they are planted on fallow land after plowing. If the latter, they are frequently harvested as early as February in time to be followed by a planting of maize. Peas are always dried, never eaten fresh.

The other important crop is coffee. This is grown in the warmer country below about eighteen hundred meters elevation. Ayutla produces practically none. The cultivation is haphazard. Usually the trees are planted and nothing further is done except to keep them partly free of brush. Some years, if prices are low or the owner is unambitious, the berries may not be harvested. Plantations are frequently abandoned. A plantation with a thousand trees is extremely rare. Most growers have from a few dozen to a few hundred trees, often set out about the house.

Although the Mixe are great coffee drinkers, they consume only a small part of the crop. Coffee forms practically the only export of the Mixe area. It is the one crop which is costly enough and small enough in bulk to be transported, and it is coffee which brings practically all the money which enters Mixe territory. An *arroba*, about twenty-five pounds of shelled coffee, brought from thirteen to fourteen pesos in Ayutla in 1933. In the prosperity years, it brought as high as thirty-five and forty pesos. A good deal of this coffee is carried by the Mixe on their backs to Ayutla or out to Mitla or Yalalag. A considerable amount is gathered also by Mitla and Yalalag traders, who carry it out on burros. The traders of Mixistlan and Tamazulapan, who range far and wide selling their pottery, usually return home with a load of coffee. This they rarely take out to Mitla or Yalalag, but bring it to Ayutla and sell it to traders from Mitla.

Chile is grown only in one or two of the warmer villages, whence it is traded through the area. Some chile is also imported from mountain Zapotec country. Small patches of sugar cane in the hotter sections produce some brown sugar, locally called *panela*, which is made into little round cakes. It is all consumed within the Mixe area. Potatoes are being introduced by the schoolteachers in some of the colder villages and bid fair to be a successful crop. At present a few potatoes are imported from mountain Zapotec country. Some *habas* (pulse) are grown. The most important and generally grown vegetable is cabbage. There is a good deal of fruit grown in a desultory way. Most of it goes to waste. Bananas are perhaps the most important, but various other tropical fruits are traded around the area, mameys, mangos, zapotes, and oranges. Avocados are grown almost everywhere, practically in a wild state since the variety grown appears to be native to the region. In the higher villages, poor-quality cherries, plums, peaches, and apples are planted. It would be inaccurate to say that they are cultivated. If they bear, some of the crop is utilized; otherwise, it is an act of God and no one worries about it.

The last important products are mescal and pulque, derived from the cultivated agave. Pulque is the fermented juice of the plant. Mescal is made by a crude process of distillation of a mash made from the leaves. It is a poor but potent drink, which is not considered locally to be of good quality unless it approaches at least 90 proof. In the hotter country its place is taken by aguardiente, a drink distilled from the juice of the sugar cane.

Irrigation is practiced in some places and under considerable difficulties. Except for tiny patches along the rivers in hot country there is no land level enough to be irrigated easily. Aside from these limited areas of a few acres, water is sometimes conducted along the hillsides in trenches, usually for the irrigation of gardens.

As a matter of fact irrigation for the major products is quite unnecessary in normal years. Even sugar cane is usually grown without irrigation. Sometimes the maize crop suffers. The early crop in the high altitudes is usually planted before the short dry season commences. A few showers may ordinarily be expected during and after the planting season, sufficient to carry the crop over to the beginning of the rainy season. Even without them the crop ordinarily will not be lost. The principal danger lies in the late arrival of the rainy season. Normally, the first tropical thunderstorms begin early in the brief dry season. In 1933 there were two tropical storms in late March and early April. The precipitation at this time, while it may be heavy, is markedly local in character. In mid-May or early June the true rainy season commences. Should it be delayed until after early June, then the crops may be almost entirely lost. In 1933 the Colonel wrote me that the rains had not begun until July, and had then been followed by torrential rains lasting to the end of September, causing great damage and an almost complete crop failure.

Once the rainy season begins, the crop is safe except for locusts. Every few years a plague of these insects passes over the Mixe country from the east or northeast. Their attacks are sporadic; one field is destroyed, another is untouched. In the early fall, perhaps September, the first green ears are available and the people, many of whom have been on short rations for several months, begin to fatten up. At this time the fields may be attacked by great flocks of parrots, crows, or animals that are fond of maize. By November most of the fields have matured. The ears are broken down on the stalk and allowed to dry as thoroughly as the humid climate permits before harvesting. Harvesting begins in December and may continue until late January. This method means that the stalks are of little use for fodder, but the Mixe keep very few animals. Usually the fodder is not gathered at all but cut and burned when the field is replanted two or three years later.

In a few of the lower towns, particularly Totontepec, Metaltepec, and some others where moisture and temperature conditions permit, there are fields called *coamilli* (Aztec) on which are cultivated a smaller-eared quick-growing maize which matures in three or four months. This is planted in January and harvested in June. When I was in Metaltepec in March, a field below the church was over a foot high. Regular types of maize are sown in this town in May, a yellow-and-white variety.

Maize is usually husked before storing. The ears are then stacked up, usually like cordwood, or else piled carelessly in little storehouses of which nearly every Mixe house has one or more near by. Occasionally, maize is stored within the house in a sort of loft made by laying heavy planks across the tops of the walls, but ordinarily only seed is kept in the house. Sometimes a raised wooden bin is put across one end of the principal room of the house. *Habas*, peas, and beans are threshed out by piling them on a mat and pounding the straw with a club. The chaff is winnowed out and the seeds stored in baskets or large jars. Maize usually is not shelled except as needed. If there is any large quantity to be shelled, as at planting time, it is put in a net lying on a mat and beaten with a club. More commonly the next day's supply is shelled in the evening with no other aid than the fingers. Only one mechanical maize sheller is to be found in western Mixe territory.

There is very little use of wild plants, aside from a few medicinal herbs. Some are employed for flavoring foods or in ceremonial. At Mixistlan a root, taragúndi, growing in muddy spots, was said to be much liked as food.

The flesh food of the Mixe is meager. Mutton and pork are little used; the first is practically unknown. They are true Indians, and rarely fry foods. In most towns it is impossible to find enough fat of any sort to fry an egg. Anyhow, there is usually no egg to fry.

Of larger animals the Mixe raise only beef cattle. The humid climate and the many insect pests apparently make even these impossible except in a few of the western towns, notably Ayutla and Juquila. Ayutla does most of the butchering for the whole Mixe territory. There is some butchering of cattle in other towns, but Ayutla meat is preferred, particularly because a system of municipal inspection is used to prevent diseased and unfit animals from being slaughtered and also because Ayutla butchers are more skillful in cutting, salting, and drying.

Milk products are almost unused. Occasionally one can get milk at Ayutla and Juquila. I had it perhaps a dozen times, even though it was the best milking season. Cheese is made only on a small scale and is little used even by the wealthy.

The other source of meat food is chickens and turkeys. They are little used except on ceremonial occasions. Indeed, for most families even the eating of beef is confined largely to such times and eggs also are little eaten.

Game is rarely hunted now. In the outlying ranches occasionally a deer may be shot, and in some of the wilder and less developed regions the tapir as well. The rifle is used, and ammunition is too expensive to be wasted on small game or on the pheasants and turkeys, which seem fairly abundant in places. At Yacoche I saw a young man from Huitepec who was said to be a professional hunter, but his kind must be rare. The disuse of the hunter's shrine on Zempoaltepec is an indication of the decline of hunting. In most of the regions where game is abundant, the jaguar is likewise to be found and hunters hesitate to go alone. Good hunters do not eat the heads of game; they would lose their luck. In a tale (p. 134) use of a snare for deer occurs, but most Ayutla men have no knowledge of hunting except with guns. At Mixistlan people are fond of wood rats, which they catch in traps.

Preparation of food is entirely a woman's work. The mainstay of the diet is the tortilla, which no man would know how to make. Most Mixe men would probably starve if no woman would cook for them. Three meals seem fairly customary. Breakfast is about eight or nine o'clock; dinner, between two and three; and supper, a very light meal, at seven or eight in the evening. Coffee, tortillas, and chile form the diet of most families except at fiesta times. Then meat and tamales may be added. Most Mixe probably do not taste meat for weeks at a time. This was anciently true also.[4]

---

[4] Burgoa, 2:224, 272.

CHAPTER IX

MATERIAL CULTURE

So FAR this discussion has dealt almost entirely with how the Mixe think and feel and act, how they govern themselves, and how they worship. Except for the chapter concerning food there has been no consideration of those concrete objects which form the material expression and subject matter of their existence. That the material aspect of Mixe life should be relegated to the close of this description is entirely in accord with the place it holds in Mixe life and thought. Not that I intend to imply by this relative weighting that the Mixe are essentially mystics or intellectuals. They most certainly are not. Rather, they possess a pragmatism of that extreme sort which causes materialism to defeat itself and become unimportant. Because the practical viewpoint of the Mixe sees no virtue in elaborations beyond whatever makeshift will serve a given concrete end, Mixe material culture is reduced to the most meager terms.

In an early chapter the Mixe lack of standards and order was discussed. This factor alone introduces any complexity into the description of Mixe material culture. Although certain types of objects exist, they vary not only from town to town but within each village. Consequently, when a house type, for example, is ascribed to a given village, actually it is generally only the dominant type.

Housing.—The western Mixe present a wide variety of house types, although a fundamental principle appears very quickly. All houses are rectangular, roughly twice as long as they are wide. The door is always on the side. Windows are almost unknown except at Totontepec, Ayutla, and Juquila, and in these towns only a minority of the houses have windows. The basic roof type is a high, steeply pitched, hipped-gable, thatched roof, often supported independently of the walls. Sometimes the walls are filled in between the supporting posts for the roof. More frequently, especially in the easternmost towns, they are constructed independently of the roof supports, which stand outside the walls.

The typical house construction begins with the setting up of six or more supporting posts. The normal house has six, but for larger structures the posts may number eight, twelve, or even more. Across the tops of these posts are laid roughly squared beams corresponding to the plates in our own construction. These are occasionally mortised at the junction. Upon these plates rest the butts of the main rafters, either held by a wooden pin passing through the plate or resting in holes cut in the plate. For the normal house there are two sets of four main rafters each, forming two pyramidal structures, the tops of which are connected by a ridgepole. Methods of fastening the main rafters at the top vary. They may merely be tied together with withes or they may be flattened and brought in line, a wooden pin passing through holes near the ends (fig. 4). Withes and strips of bark form the only binding material. Two or three horizontal poles of lighter weight are now tied to the main rafters, completing the frame. Lighter poles in upright position are laid over these from the ridge to the plates. Another frame of light poles at about six-inch intervals covers these horizontally. These complete the frame, and the roof is now ready for thatching.[1]

Thatching materials preferred are either a long local grass known as *zacate*, or pine

---

[1] Chinantec roof construction appears the same. See Bevan, pl. 25 and p. 78.

needles. Occasionally, slabs of thin bark from a cypress growing on the north and east slopes of Zempoaltepec are used in near-by towns. The grass or pine needles are gathered in bunches and tied to the outer covering of light poles with bark strips.

Sometimes the supporting posts are dispensed with and the plates rest directly on walls of adobe or puddled clay, but this is probably a later development. Houses with plates resting directly on the walls are commonest in the more advanced towns like Totontepec and are relatively rare in such towns as Metaltepec or Yacoche.

The puddled-clay wall is found only in Metaltepec, Zacatepec, San Pedrito, Yacoche, and Mixistlan, all backward towns except Zacatepec. Consequently, it may

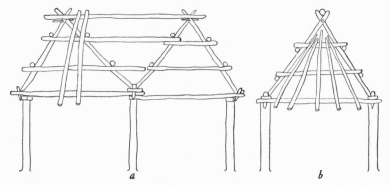

Fig. 4. House construction, showing especially the fitting of the main rafters.
a, side view; *b*, end view.

represent an ancient form and is of particular interest because of its occurrence in northern Mexico and southern Arizona. Forms are constructed within which the wet clay is tamped, the wall being built in sections (pl. 19, *a*). The clay used is highly solidified and must be pulverized before being dampened.

Houses with thatched roofs, even where the plates rest on the walls rather than on an independent support, usually have the front wall some distance back from the edge of the roof to form a veranda or portico. In such houses, regardless of the type of wall construction, the front part of the roof rests on independent supports. The wall is usually carried up only to the height of the eaves, leaving a space open all around, but wider on the side toward the portico. In most of Mixe territory this is a distinct disadvantage, since it allows free circulation of the cold winds and heavy fogs.[2] The space on three sides is frequently stopped up by various makeshifts, pieces of hand-hewn planks, adobes, or branches or bunches of grass and mud. Generally the wider gap toward the portico is left open, although occasionally it is stopped by laying heavy hand-hewn planks across the walls to form a loft.

Within the house, a part is frequently made into a storehouse by laying planks or poles from wall to wall over one end. Occasionally a large house has part partitioned off into a kitchen by uprights interwoven with pliable branches. This partition is rarely plastered with mud. The floor is almost always of earth, although sometimes part or even all may be covered with heavy hewn beams or, very rarely, with cement.

---

[2] Bevan (p. 78) considers the very similar Chinantec house to be very well adapted to the tropical climate in Chinantec territory.

Totontepec is unique in having the kitchen in a small separate room which is entered from the main room. This is roofed in the same manner as the main house, and forms a sort of dormer running into the main roof. Here too (sometimes in other towns, also) part of the main roof is carried down close to the ground outside the walls, forming a storage place for wood or fodder, or, less frequently, a roof for the sweathouse. More commonly, the sweathouse is at one end of the portico or even inside the house itself. Frequently part of the portico is walled off by wattles or upright poles to form the kitchen. In some towns the kitchen is a small separate structure similar to, but less well built than, the main house. The separate kitchen is most common in Juquila.

Ayutla presents the most aberrant house type, a structure very similar to our own log cabin. (See Schmieder, pl. 21.) This is built of logs laid one above another, the corners overlapped by notching the logs. The portico is formed by carrying the top end logs out three to five feet beyond the house wall and laying another projecting log across the house in the middle. The main rafters of the roof rest on the ends of these logs and the roof thus projects beyond the wall on the door side. Sometimes supports are placed under the ends of these logs, but not usually. Near Ayutla the roof is of pine-needle thatch as a general rule, although grass thatch occurs also. These houses, perhaps because of the abundance of pine in this section, are almost always provided with a ceiling of heavy hewn planks.

Whether the log cabin is an introduced feature here or is an indigenous development is hard to say. It is found among the Trique and the more remote mountain Tarascans. Except for the feature of interlocking the corners by notching the logs, the type is not unique in Mexico. Elsewhere in the Mixe region and also in many mountain Zapotec towns one may see house walls made by laying logs up between upright posts, a technique which occurs as far away as Nayarit, where it is very common between Tepic and Santiago Isquintla. It is sometimes seen at Ayutla in place of the notched or mortised corner.

Another general type of house in the region is plainly an introduction within relatively recent times and is probably of Zapotec origin. This is the adobe walled structure with tiled roof. The tile roof is, of course, a Spanish introduction, but the form of the house is evidently a Zapotec stylization. The ground plan is the same as that of the other houses, a rectangular room with one door in the middle of one side. The tiled roof slopes toward the rear. The tiles are generally laid on bricks, making a very heavy roof. The portico is made by another tiled roof, supported in the front by pillars. This roof slopes toward the front. The rafters are inserted in sockets or niches left in the adobe wall for the purpose, the lower end resting on plates running across the pillars in front. The ends of the portico are usually walled. Sometimes part of the front is also walled to make a kitchen. There is also generally a low wall across the entire front of the portico except directly in front of the house door.[3]

Public buildings, schools, churches, and municipal buildings are not typical of

---

[3] The following differences in house types may be observed. These refer only to the dominant types in each village: *Ayutla:* log cabins, thatched roofs, some adobe brick houses with tile roofs in the town proper; *Tamazulapan:* same; *Tlahuitoltepec:* town proper, almost all adobe brick walls with tile roofs, farm houses varied; *Yacoche:* low puddled walls of clay, thatch or cypress-bark roofs; *Mixistlan:* same, walls higher; *Totontepec:* stone in adobe or adobe brick walls, thatched roofs; *Metaltepec:* puddled walls, thatched roofs supported independently of the walls; *Zacatepec:* same, some adobe brick walls; *San Pedrito:* same; *Cacalotepec:* log walls, thatched roofs; *Juquila:* adobe brick walls, thatched roofs.

Mixe construction. Generally they are built by masons brought in from Zapotec territory and are of different styles from the houses. Adobe brick or burned brick is used exclusively in most towns and the roofs are usually of tile or even of corrugated asbestos cement sheets. Many of the churches still have thatched roofs as at Yacoche, Atitlan, and Mixistlan, but in most towns these are now being replaced by brick arches and domes or corrugated asbestos cement sheets.

Temporary field shelters run through a gamut of forms. Lean-to structures of the simplest type are the most common; rafters lean against a ridgepole resting on two forked uprights, the whole thatched with brush. The ends and sometimes part of one side are closed with wattling or cornstalks tied between poles. Occasionally a double lean-to is seen, and on one occasion I saw a conical structure made of bark slabs laid on a tipi-like foundation of poles. All these temporary structures are crudely made of the most convenient materials available. There seems to be no stereotyped form.

No pattern of communal assistance exists in building houses. Usually a man's friends and neighbors help in the construction, but only as the spirit moves them and as it is convenient. In such towns as Ayutla, Totontepec, and the progressive towns in general, assistance is usually paid for. In addition, usually helpers are invited to a feast after the house is finished. Tamales and tepache are served.

In the progressive towns there is no dedication of the house nor any ceremony. In conservative towns, on the other hand, ceremonies are commonly held. A turkey or sometimes a rooster is killed in the house and the blood sprinkled over the floor. Pinole and blood are buried in a hole dug in the center of the house. Those who helped in the construction are then invited to a feast, of which the main constituents are tepache and a stew made of the turkey or chicken which has been sacrificed.

House furnishings are meager. A table, usually serving as house altar, sometimes another table, perhaps two or three chairs, a chest, and a plank bench, often two or three feet wide, and used as much for storage as for sitting, make up the furniture. In some towns low stools, kipkiói, occur. They are about six inches high, made of a section of a log hollowed out on the underside, and with a projection at one end serving as a handle. The handle is sometimes crudely carved to represent an animal head. A considerable number of pottery vessels of assorted sizes, some for storage, others for special uses, rest on the floor or bench. Coils of rope, baskets, bundles, and tools are piled about the walls.

Fairly characteristic of the most orderly Mixe house is that of Don Honrato, the postmaster in Ayutla. It is larger than most houses and is of adobe with a tile roof. It consists of a single room with the door on the middle of the east side. It has the usual veranda, and both room and veranda have an earthen floor. At the south end of the room a corncrib, raised above the floor, occupies the whole wall. Opposite the door is an altar with a canopy of palm leaves. The altar is simply a table, the wall behind it hung with many pictures of saints. Commonly, there are flowers on the table as well as a litter of odds and ends laid down temporarily. The only permanent object on the altar table is the cornet of Don Honrato's nephew, a member of the band. Below the table on a box are the good dishes, used only on special occasions. These consist of a few Oaxaca bowls and some good gourd bowls. Two chests against the wall, one of them the post-office "safe," and a desk with pigeonholes for post-office equipment complete the furnishings, except for benches which fill the remaining wall space. Everything is unusually neat for a Mixe house and there are fewer pots, bundles, bags, clothes, and baskets about. This is partly because there is a special house of the same type of construction used as a kitchen. In most Mixe houses the benches would be completely covered with a disorderly confusion of bundles, baskets, ropes, jars, and so on.

In most of the Mixe towns a varying number of houses have storehouses, tsash (Spanish-Aztec, *tescomate*). Ayutla's are perhaps unique. A mortised rectangular cribwork of logs, resembling a miniature log cabin, is built up to a height of five to seven feet above the ground. It is covered with heavy planks, and on this flooring is built the storehouse proper with low adobe brick walls, thatched gable roof, and at one end a small plank or slab door, which usually is reached by a notched log ladder (pl. 18, *b*).

Juquila's storehouses closely resemble those of Ayutla except that there is no use of adobe in the storehouse proper. This is made in log-cabin style on a plank floor which is raised above the ground by posts rather than by a cribwork. Cacalotepec has storehouses which differ from those of Ayutla in having the base made of thick hewn planks similarly notched and mortised at the corners.

The storehouses at Totontepec are raised only a few inches from the ground by a log foundation upon which rests the usual plank floor. The walls are woven or wattled construction with a full-sized door at one end. The roof, instead of being fully gabled, is hipped at the end opposite the door (pl. 20).

The sweathouse is an important part of many Mixe houses. It is resorted to for all sorts of minor ailments, colds, aching of the body, or any slight indisposition. One of the first things done by the Colonel and his wife on their return from a month's visit to Mexico City was to use the sweathouse. It is used by women when they discover they are pregnant and after childbirth to hasten recovery.

The usual Mixe sweathouse is built in the house or under the portico, but occasionally it is detached. Logs plastered with adobe or adobe bricks are used to build the three-foot-high walls which are topped by a flat pole-and-earth roof. A separate adobe fire chamber is divided from the main chamber by a rock slab upon which water is poured to create steam. The floor is often strewn with fragrant plants, and medicinal herbs are steeped in the water poured on the hot stone. No cold bath follows the vapor treatment, for the Mixe believe the use of cold water when the body is heated is highly injurious.

Dress and ornament.—Dress affords an especially illuminating example of the transmission of culture to the Mixe by the Zapotec. Mixe dress is a combination of pre-Conquest and Spanish elements—the latter, I suspect, being relatively late so far as women's clothing is concerned. The pre-Conquest elements, with one possible exception, are entirely confined to women's dress.

In the backward towns, and to some extent in the progressive towns, women wear an ankle-length skirt which resembles closely the Oceanic sarong. A length of cloth is wound around the body with the corner tucked in. The cloth is white at Tlahuitoltepec, black at Yacoche, blue at Tamazulapan. Over this is worn a peculiar belt consisting of a narrow, figured sash, part of which passes through a tubular length of woven palm strips. The upper part of the body is covered by a huipil, an untailored blouse consisting of a strip of cloth folded on itself and sewed up the sides. A hole is cut out for the head to go through and a slit, made part way down the front, is tied with strings at the top. Short sleeves reaching below the elbow are sewn into the armholes (pls. 5, 6). Since there is no tailoring, the garment when extended is absolutely four-square. At Juquila a low-cut embroidered blouse suggests a Spanish garment influenced by the huipil.

Non-Spanish headdress is seen only at Yacoche and Mixistlan. It consists of a turbanlike arrangement of many strands of loosely twisted yarn worn coronet-fashion around the head. The hair is loose down the back but is tied together at the base of the head with several strands of colored yarn, the ends of which hang down below the hair itself. This tying of the hair with hanging strands is universal in Tamazulapan and is done a great deal in other places, even though the turban is lacking. By color of yarn and manner of tying one may distinguish the women of the various towns. Occasionally, narrow woven bands replace the yarn.

A squarish or oblong piece of cloth is also worn over the shoulders as a sort of shawl. It somewhat resembles the *rebozo* but since it is never worn over the head, even in church, it may be considered strictly a shawl. It also serves as a catch-all for carrying children, supplies, or other articles. For this purpose it is knotted over one shoulder.

That this dress is pre-Conquest and indigenous among the Mixe is far from certain. We have no descriptions of Mixe women's dress from early sources, but the general suggestion is that few clothes were worn. Moreover, every element of the Mixe women's dress is common with that of the Zapotecs. The sash is of special interest. The plaited palm-strip tubes through which the sash passes are not made by the Mixe. Furthermore, the sash itself, which is made only at Tamazulapan in Mixe territory, is the same, even in design characteristics, as sashes still woven in the Valley of Mexico. Consequently, there is a possibility that the whole dress was taken over from the Zapotec under Spanish influence.

This conclusion is inevitable for the modern dress. This is a long ground-sweeping full skirt, pleated about the waist and usually with three or four wide ruffles about it, a blouse with an almost bodicelike effect, usually fitting tightly at the waist with a slight ruffle below (pls. 6; 10, *b;* 12, *a*). This dress is worn only in the progressive pueblos and then not by all the women. We may therefore assume it to be a quite recent introduction. Observe, however, the source of this modernity. This is not a modern Mexican woman's dress; rather it is the distinctive women's dress among Indian groups who were early and successfully missionized. It may be seen among the Mayo and Yaqui of Sonora. It has close relationship, except in the type of material, with the Navaho women's dress, and it is common among many of the Zapotecs. The inference is almost inescapable that the women's dress has been taken over, then, from the Zapotecs and is actually a seventeenth-century Spanish contribution which has only recently reached the Mixe.

Men's dress is a simpler problem. It also is post-Spanish and consists of the usual Mexican cotton "drawers" or "pyjamas" and a shirt (pl. 6). Extremely tight-fitting trouser legs are less common in this region than elsewhere, but the waist is large, so the fly laps far over, and the whole is held up by a white or red sash which wraps around the waist one and a half times or more. The free end is tucked in. The shirts, or more properly blouses, show considerable variation but most of them are embroidered. The general appearance is that of an old-fashioned nightshirt except for the length. The bottom usually does not quite cover the sash and is worn outside the trousers. A U-shaped yoke in front has some embroidery, usually only a few zigzag lines in colored thread about the edge of it. The yoke is sometimes gathered in small pleats. The sleeves are long and are patched with any colored materials which happen to come to hand, so that they become almost quilted with rags of a dozen different colors and patterns. Ayutla men usually own serapes. The red-and-black serape of Tlacolula is the most popular, but many have less expensive commercial cotton blankets.

There is also a tendency to modernity in men's dress. Belts are replacing sashes, regular shirts are replacing the blouse, the shirttail occasionally is placed inside the trousers, and the trousers themselves are becoming convenionally designed.

Footgear has been undergoing some recent changes. The vast majority of men and women wear the simple sandal, a sole of leather with a thong passing between the great toe and its nearest neighbor up over the instep, where it attaches to a loop which fastens again to the sole on each side of the heel. Another loop runs behind the heel, passing over the Achilles tendon (fig. 5). Within the last few years the Yalalag Zapotec sandal, a pointed Moorish-appearing article, has been introduced and is spreading rapidly. The Yalalag sandal is marked by a low heel and a much heavier

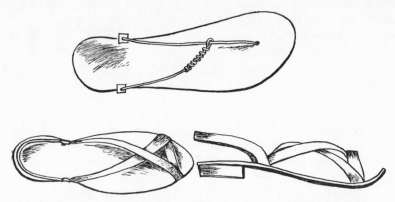

Fig. 5. Mixe sandals. Above, ordinary type; below, Yalalag type.

sole, coming to a sharp point in front and curving slightly upward. It is held on by a broad strap which passes over the toes and fastens to the sole on each side. It is then turned back, the two ends crossing over the instep to fasten again on each side of the heel. Another loop goes behind the heel. A set of buckles provides an adjustment on one side of the instep (fig. 5). The bottom is usually studded with heavy hobnails. In 1926, the year Francisco was secretary, perhaps half-a-dozen people in Ayutla had these sandals. Now nearly everyone has a pair, both men and women, although they are worn principally for "best." Francisco always wears them. In addition, there are about a dozen people who habitually wear shoes, a fashion started, of course, by the Colonel. The Colonel's wife and a Zapotec woman who married into the town are the only women who wear shoes.

All the towns show differences in dress. Those between progressive towns are less obvious. Juquila and Cacalotepec are differentiated from Ayutla only in that the woman's dress comes considerably above the ankle, not below it as at Ayutla. Tamazulapan women wear the conventional conservative woman's garment described, with the saronglike skirt dyed blue, a white huipil, scantily embroidered, a white shawl, and red strings tying the hair. The huipil is tucked in or tied about the waist. The women of Tlahuitoltepec wear the same garment except that the skirt is white and the hair strings black. Yacoche women wear a black skirt and usually a black huipil, although it is sometimes white. The turbanlike yarn headdress has been noted. Mixistlan women dress the same way, except that the huipil is always black. (The black is really a very dark blue.) Yacoche men wear a white sash, those of Ayutla and elsewhere, red. In Ayutla, Totontepec, and Juquila the *rebozo* of black or blue and white has completely replaced the white shawl. When at work, women sometimes wrap it turban-fashion about the head, a Zapotec style. Yacoche and Mixistlan women are also distinguished by enormous collars or necklaces of strings of beads. These often contain forty to sixty strands and weigh many pounds.

Men's faces are cleanshaven, the beard still being plucked. Two coins are customarily used in lieu of tweezers and the "click" of the coins is a regular accompaniment of any conversation.

Minor arts and occupations.—Almost nowhere will one encounter a people so lacking in handicrafts as the Mixe. Those few which they practice are so purely utilitarian, so lacking in decorative elements, that they hardly may be considered arts. They are purely means to an end necessary or considered desirable. This paucity of arts is to some extent due to Spanish influence. Many old techniques have passed away. Thus guns for hunters have done away with netmaking. Nevertheless, Mixe culture must always have been singularly lacking in the multitudinous techniques that usually characterize even the most primitive tribes.

The lack may have been due aboriginally to the constant trade-and-barter system which, with the substitution of money in Spanish times, must go on today much the same as in ancient times. Aboriginally, many of the techniques must have been confined to a few villages. Specialization by villages seems to have been an ancient characteristic through much of the area of high culture in Mexico, and it is particularly observable in Oaxaca in the Mixtec and Zapotec regions, where practically every village has some special technique practiced by most of the population.

Weaving must have been an exception to this principle of specialization. Probably every village did some weaving, although certain villages must anciently have specialized in certain techniques and designs as they do today. A Tlacolula blanket is still to be recognized anywhere. Nevertheless, it is doubtful whether the Mixe did much in the way of weaving aboriginally. Cotton will not grow in most of the Mixe country. They may have used the bast fiber of the leaves of the agave plant, though it is possible that this plant was not cultivated in pre-Spanish times. It does not seem to grow wild anywhere in the region and its fiber is not woven or used in any way at the present time. Even ropes are purchased from the Cajones Zapotec.

Whatever may have been the aboriginal Mixe situation, at the present time weaving is confined to three villages of the western Mixe, the conservative towns of Tamazulapan, Yacoche, and Mixistlan. I was told it was also practiced in some towns of the eastern Mixe, but I do not know whether this is true. The method is pre-Spanish in every respect and the main product is simple cotton cloth, which is used extensively but not universally for clothing in these three towns. It is occasionally traded to other towns for use in women's blouses or huipiles.

The cotton used, as I have said, is traded in to the three villages mentioned. The nearest source is the valley of Oaxaca, but few people from these towns go to Oaxaca. It is more probable that the bulk of the supply comes from the north, from the more distant Chinanteca country which is visited by traders from Tamazulapan and Mixistlan, or from Tehuantepec, which is visited by traders from Tamazulapan. The Chinanteca also supplies cotton to the Zapotec Cajones valley region with its important trading center of Yalalag, also visited by the Mixistlan people. Mitla Zapotec and Yalalag Zapotec traders also visit the Mixe towns, but, so far as I know, they never carry raw cotton. How Yacoche gets its cotton is a bit of a mystery unless it buys from Mixistlan and Tamazulapan. The Yacoche people almost never go out of their own territory even to visit other Mixe towns. Even Tamazulapan and Mixistlan, quite close, are not often visited. Yet Yacoche people use homespun cotton cloth for clothing more than any of the other villages.

Thread is spun on a small wooden spindle about one foot long with a wooden weight near the lower end to act as a flywheel or spindle whorl. The lower end rests in a fragment of broken pottery exactly as may be seen in ancient manuscripts. The spindle is twirled with the right hand, the raw cotton fed out from the left.

Weaving at Tamazulapan is done by only a few persons who live in accessible places and my account is necessarily deficient. The cloth is woven in a strip about two feet wide and about forty feet long. This arrangement must make a very unwieldy set-up when the weaving is first begun. As it progresses, the finished cloth is rolled up on a rod tied to the loom bar at the end toward the operator.

The setting up of the loom must be difficult and complicated, although I did not see it. The preparation of a loom is something which must be seen to be described adequately and I was not fortunate enough to encounter the process. Since it was impossible to live in any of the weaving villages without more extensive resources than were available, to find a loom being set up would have required many days of tramping over steep mountains until one encountered the process by chance. The Mixe, who usually know little of what their immediate neighbors do, are entirely ignorant of the activities of townspeople who may live hours of travel distant. It is also useless to ask to be notified when an event such as the setting up of a loom is to take place. The Mixe are not anxious for an audience. Even seeing weaving done was through chance. On one of my visits to Tamazulapan it was sunny and an old lady was at work. On cold and foggy days, the usual type of weather, she would not have worked.

The method of weaving is the same as that to be seen in many parts of Mexico. There is a simple heddle to reverse the threads of the warp. The weft threads are wound in figure-eight style on a stick forming a shuttle as long as the cloth is wide. Every few inches a slight ridge is made in the fabric by passing the weft thread about the selvage thread at the edge and bringing the weft back through the same shed so that there are two threads together. At longer intervals of eighteen inches or so a red weft is worked in to make a slightly larger ridge. The weaver works in a kneeling position, sitting back on her heels. A strap, much resembling the carrying strap and made of plaited palm-leaf strips, passes behind the back and is attached in front to the loom bar. At each shift of position of the warp threads (i.e., each reversal of the sheds) the weaver loosens the tension a little by leaning slightly forward. The presence of a large native vocabulary for parts of the loom suggests that it is an ancient possession and hence pre-Spanish. Detailed knowledge of the surrounding peoples, however, may show that both vocabulary and loom were borrowed (see fig. 6 for diagrams of the loom and vocabulary).

Some weaving is done at Mixistlan. The schoolmaster stated that herbs used to dye thread or cloth are cultivated. Since all weavers lived in rancherias at a distance, I could obtain no further information in the time available.

In basketry weaving the Mixe again show a paucity of techniques. The only basket made is from cane splints, that is, canes split to make strips a quarter of an inch or so in width. These are woven in the simplest checkerboard type of plaiting in only one form, cylindrical, with a flat circular base. The only variations are in quality of workmanship and size. Baskets are made only at Tepantlali and Zacatapec, which have "hot" lands where cane will grow. The canes are cut green, split,

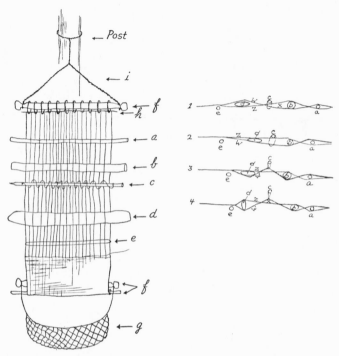

Fig. 6. The Mixe loom. *a, kip,* first shed bar; *b, hagóp,* second shed bar; *c, kavea mats,* string heddle; *d, shamán,* batten; *e, auk,* spreader bar; *f, pitchkíp,* end bar (each end); *h, agwét,* loom string; *i, konjéts,* cord attachment at end; *g, pit chum,* backstrap; *huák méats,* shuttle (not illustrated), a light stick with weft wrapped around it; *pi·t,* thread. On the right are shown successive positions of the sheds and batten in weaving. In position 1, the second loom bar, *b,* is pulled forward close to the heddle and the batten, *d,* is removed from the position shown and inserted at *x.* This gives position 2 with the upper half of the shed, *w,* changing places with the lower half, *z.* After the weft is passed through the shed formed, the second loom bar, *b,* is pushed close to *a* and the heddle is lifted as in position 3. The batten, *d,* is then turned on edge to further separate the two parts of the sheds; it is then withdrawn and inserted and the heddle released, the loom returning to position 1. The warp is about forty feet long when the loom is first set up. As weaving proceeds, the cloth is rolled on the loom bar nearest the weaver. Changing of the sheds is accompanied by loosening of the tension, accomplished by leaning slightly forward. The back strap, *g,* is woven of palm fiber.

and woven before they dry. The baskets are then allowed to dry thoroughly before being used. They are called almost universally by the Aztec name, chicahuite, so much so that, not knowing at the time this was an Aztec term, I assumed it was a Mixe word. There most probably is a Mixe term.

Pottery again is a highly specialized craft. Only Tamazulapan and Mixistlan make pottery. It is difficult to believe this specialization was true formerly, but there is no evidence to the contrary. No other Mixe, even of the most distant eastern group, make any pottery whatever and very little seems to be brought from outside.

Most of the Mixe pottery is carried by the men of these two towns throughout Mixe territory and as far as Tehuantepec to the east, although it is almost never taken to any of the other Zapotec towns. As potters the Zapotecs are vastly superior to the Mixe.

Like all other Mixe operations, pottery is strictly utilitarian. It has no decoration whatever, except for some "design" on Mixistlan pottery which I doubt very much has a decorative intention. It certainly has no decorative effect. This "design" consists of a number of aimless lines of color. When the vessel is first taken from the fire, it is rubbed with the end of a resinous ocote-pine stick, producing lines varying from black to a reddish brown color, depending apparently on the degree of heat (pl. 19, *b*). Since pottery making, particularly at Mixistlan, seems bound up with supernatural sanctions, it is possible that this practice (copal incense is merely the collected resin) has some magical significance.

The actual manufacture of pottery is one of the more complex processes of Mixe art. At Tamazulapan, clay is brought from a special point in the lowest-lying lands of this community. It is allowed to dry, then pulverized by being pounded with a stick until it is a fine powder. This powder is moistened and kept in a large pot. It forms a grayish mass which looks and feels greasy. The temper is added when the clay is to be worked into vessels.

The temper is soft and brittle yellowish rock, apparently micaceous, which is mined at various points about Tamazulapan and Mixistlan. One of the principal sources is quite near the main center of Tamazulapan, where the hill has been quarried out considerably and the vein of rock has been followed back in a wide low tunnel for some twenty feet. This rock is beaten with a club until it looks like a fine powdery sand. When this is mixed with the clay, the potter apparently determines the proportions by feel, testing the clay by rubbing it between thumb and forefinger as she adds the temper.

The base of a Mixe pottery vessel is always small and is pressed out of a flat disk of clay between the fingers. This is placed on a pottery base, a special flat disk of baked clay which is used to turn the vessel so that the working point is always in front of the potter. The sides are built up by the coiling method. A rope of clay about an inch thick is rolled out between the hands until it is from six to eight inches in length. This is then pinched onto the base and thinned out by pressing, first with the fingers, then by being rolled with a piece of corncob on the outside. Resistance to the inward pressure of the corncob is provided by the fingers inside the pot. The rolling on the outer surface makes a marked series of indentations which resemble an elaborate corrugation of the clay; they are later removed by being rubbed down with the same cob. In the rubbing process the cavities in the cob become filled with clay until it presents a smooth surface. Curved cobs are carefully preserved for this rubbing process. Later the outside of the pot is finished off with a wet hand. The rim has particular attention paid to it and is smoothed with a leaf frequently dipped in water.

After shaping, the pottery is thoroughly dried for at least two or three days if the sun is hot, for longer if the weather is cloudy. It is then burned in one of two special places: one below the town near the river, the other near the summit of the mountain above the town. No reason could be obtained for this, although fuel is more abundant at these points than near the village. Nevertheless, it is hard to see how carrying a large quantity of unbaked and hence very fragile pottery several miles is easier than carrying wood. A ritual reason may exist. The burning is always with pine bark.

Most of the shapes of Mixe pottery are not distinctive. In the main they reproduce the forms of the Zapotec pottery, which itself runs through a wide range. Two shapes, however, are unique. One is the shoe, *zapatillo*, which resembles closely the moccasin pot of the Pueblos. This has a real utilitarian value, for, with things which do not require energetic cooking, the moccasin or shoe pot may be shoved under the *comal* or flat dish for baking tortillas, and the contents will simmer nicely or even boil while the handle is clear out of the heat. This shape also has a speculative interest. Though at present it is made only by the Mixe, it is found archaeologically in Monte Alban, generally in miniature. There it has usually the shape of a jaguar's foot, according to Dr. Alfonso Caso. That it was an offering is unquestionable, and the Mixistlan use of miniatures for mountain top offerings by potters, especially learners, is an interesting parallel.[4] The other distinctive shape is less interesting. It is an aryballoid jar with a very small base and mouth and is used most frequently for cooking large quantities of tamales. It also sometimes holds tepache.

Whether pulque is aboriginal or not is an open question. As has been suggested, the agave is probably not native to the area. However, considering the great importance of fermented liquors in ceremonial in all southern Mexico, it is probably a pre-Spanish drink among the Mixe. Again the Mixe show their usual stylelessness. They use improvised materials as they come to hand, and the long, specially shaped gourds and containers so common to most of Mexico for gathering the juice of the maguey plant are almost completely lacking. In fact, I never saw them. Owing to the great raininess of the country the agave is grown only in the drier parts, particularly Tlahuitoltepec, Tamazulapan, and Ayutla. Even here, when the plant begins to bud and the center is hollowed out to collect the sap, a rough shed thatched with pine branches or grass, whatever is close at hand, is erected over the plant to prevent rain from falling on it and diluting the juice. The pulque is mostly consumed locally.

The derivative of pulque, tepache, is certainly a post-Spanish drink, depending as it does on the addition of sugar. The technique was probably learned by the Mixe from the Zapotec.

Tepache is a fairly complicated beverage. Starting as pulque, it is allowed to ferment about three days, more pulque being added each day to keep the fermentation going. Brown sugar is then added, together with more pulque and small pieces of an unidentified root. Sugar is added subsequently, the amount depending on the strength desired. On the eighth day, sugar, melted by the fire, and warm water are added to fill the jars. The following day it is ready to drink. The procedure is indefinite, since it is varied in order to produce different types of tepache. The recipe just given results in a strong, rather bitter tepache. For sweet tepache, the sugar and pulque are not added until one or two days later. Ground cinnamon is added the last day.

In some towns the tepache is strained through a cloth; in others it is not. Yalalag and Tamazulapan do not strain it; Ayutla and Yacoche do.

---

[4] Bevan (p. 44), mentions Tamasuloapam and Mijitlan as Zapotec towns supplying the Chinantec with pottery. I suspect Mixe Tamazulapan and Mixistlan are meant. However, these towns do not make blackware which Bevan reports. Bevan is incorrect in assigning the boot-shaped pot to the Zapotec today. It is now made only by the Mixe.

The other potent derivative of the agave plant, mescal, is also post-Spanish. The methods used are very crude. The leaves are cooked and fermented, the liquid extracted and boiled. There is nothing unique about any of this except that the methods are makeshift. The actual distilling, however, is of some interest. When the liquor is boiled, the steam is caught in a metal boilerlike arrangement. The still itself is of wood and consists merely of a long wooden tube called the *palenque*. From this, one who makes mescal is called a *palenquero* rather than *mescalero* as is usual elsewhere in Mexico. The liquor is rarely distilled more than once, and then only when it is deemed too weak after the first distilling. It is a fiery stuff, which the Mixe drink in great quantities. The local production is inadequate to the demand, and considerable quantities are brought in from the nearby Zapotec country, particularly from Santa María, San Juan del Río, and Yalalag.

In much of the Mixe country aguardiente, a distilled drink from the sugar cane, takes the place of mescal. It is similarly potent but has a sickish sweetish taste which demands a reliable stomach for its consumption. It is distilled like mescal.

Sugar is made by the cane growers in a most simple fashion. The juice is expressed in a primitive wooden hand mill, boiled down, and poured into circular molds. The sugar produced is crude, dark brown in color, often with cane fibers still present. It is sold in little round cakes about one inch thick by two inches wide, tapering slightly toward one side. It is wrapped in banana leaves in long bundles of eight or ten cakes and sold in this fashion without weighing.

Butchering is a rather highly specialized occupation. Certain families make their living almost exclusively in this way, particularly at Ayutla. Here seven or eight beeves are butchered weekly, probably more than in all the rest of Mixe territory. The meat is butchered Wednesday or Thursday in preparation for the Sunday market at Ayutla. Some of it is bought by traders and carried to other towns which derive most of their scanty meat supply from this source. Butchers of other towns— one at Totontepec, another at Juquila, and several at Tamazulapan and Tlahuitoltepec—usually buy their beeves at Ayutla.

The meat is cut up in long strips about fourteen inches long and about one-half inch thick, salted, and hung up to dry. Some bony parts are sold differently, but this is relatively unimportant. At many houses there is tepache on hand on the day butchering takes place and any visitor is served with it. This is undoubtedly a lingering vestige of some ceremonial accompaniment, probably taken over from hunting rites.

Tanning exhausts the list of important techniques of widespread usage. A few others may be mentioned briefly. One is the making of adobes, bricks, and roofing tiles. It is doubtful if even adobes are pre-Spanish in the area. Adobes may be made by anyone, but brick and tile making are community undertakings, usually done under the tekio. One family in Ayutla is making bricks and tiles for sale, but this is a brand-new venture. To get brick or tile from the community efforts, one must often wait a long time and take what is left over from production destined for community purposes, such as the church, municipal buildings, or school. Ayutla has a regular brickyard and a bit of suitable clay land which is retained as communal land. Everything is done by hand and it is a matter of months to get a kiln of bricks. Work went on almost daily in the brickyard under the tekio for nearly three months without a kiln being fired.

Masons almost without exception are imported artisans. One mason at Ayutla is being entrusted with some of the local communal work, but usually outsiders are sent for. Particularly is this true of important repairs and alterations in the church; and with reason, because, though anyone can lay up adobes well enough to build a residence, it takes a certain amount of expertness to lay bricks and stone, and local people get little opportunity to learn or to practice.

To a lesser degree the same thing is true of carpenters. For anything more elaborate than hewing out beams and heavy planks, a carpenter is sent for from outside. There are a few people, particularly at a town like Ayutla where all the land is in private ownership, who make a business of turning out big pine rafters, not, as a rule, because of any special skill, but because they own lands with suitable pine trees. At Totontepec there is even a little export business. The Villa Alta district lacks pine suitable for large rafters and, since a good trail has been built within the last decade, these are dragged by bullocks over the mountain from Totontepec.

Sandals usually are made by the head of the family. However, at Ayutla the pointed Moorish-looking sandal of Yalalag has been introduced in recent years and a Yalalag shoemaker lived in Ayutla until 1933. He not only made these sandals but could, on order, turn out shoes of sorts. Now the only sandalmaker is at Juquila. Some business is, nevertheless, done at Ayutla indirectly. Mitleños send orders by the regular traders to Ayutla, who, at the Sunday market, transmit them to shoe-traders from Yalalag. Apparently no direct trade relations exist between Mitla and and Yalalag.

Most iron and steel tools come from Tlacolula via Mitla or Yalalag and none of the Mixe are blacksmiths. Plow points, machetes, axe blades, *coa* blades, and hoe blades are the principal items bought. Hafting of any tools is always done by the purchaser.

The Mixe are very fond of bread, but nowhere except at Juquila are there any bakers. Bread at Ayutla is brought in once a week from Mitla, a day and a half by burro carrier, and it is poor stuff when it arrives. Totontepec has bread from Yalalag or Villa Alta. Other towns rarely see bread unless they visit the markets at Ayutla or Totontepec or go outside Mixe territory. Exceptions are the occasion of a large fiesta, when there will usually be a fair-sized market in the town, and the arrival of a trader who happens to have bread.

It is of significance that a considerable portion of this catalogue of material culture is not of aboriginal derivation. Particularly is this true of the more complex aspects. With the exceptions of housebuilding, weaving, and pottery-making, none of the more complex techniques are native. Most are Spanish with a few Zapotec additions. That certain Mixe handicrafts like stone working for pointing weapons have vanished through being supplanted by European substitutes is obvious. Yet it is fairly certain that, aboriginally, Mixe material culture must have been even more limited than it is at present.

Trade.—No information on primitive trade and exchange exists. At the present time Ayutla is the most important economic center in the western Mixe area. The focus of this activity is in the regular Sunday market. Mixe come from many of the eastern villages to attend the market. The mechanics of the market are mentioned on page 24. A few more systematic paragraphs are necessary.

The location of the market is in the main plaza. A long, narrow, tile-roofed brick building on the west side of the plaza is the market building, but its use is confined to the sellers of meat and the buyers of coffee. The other traders are located in the plaza. In a rough way the various types of merchandise are segregated (fig. 7). During my stay the mescal sellers were moved from the location shown in the figure because their disorderly patrons disturbed the rest of the market. A few of the vendors erect awnings over their goods, but the majority are in the open. A rainstorm means a hasty end to the marketing.

The most important traders are from Mitla and Yalalag. The two groups are segregated, although they handle about the same types of goods. Mitla traders are all

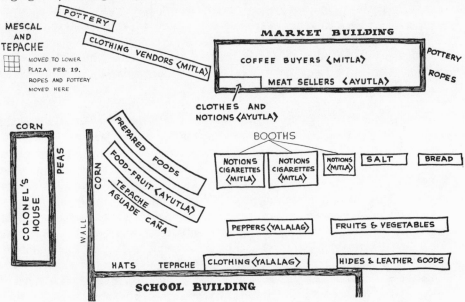

Fig. 7. Plan of the market at Ayutla on Sunday, February 12, 1933, showing segregation of vendors.

men who have brought in fair-sized loads packed on burros and who purchase coffee for the return trip. The Yalalag traders are usually man and wife who have carried in their goods on their backs. They leave Yalalag about four in the afternoon and walk all night, arriving at Ayutla at dawn. They leave in the midafternoon for the return trip, without any sleep. Ayutla traders are ordinarily meat and mescal dealers, but a few sell cloth, and a number of women sell prepared foods, fruits, and tepache. Men from Quetzaltepec, Chimaltepec, and sometimes other towns bring in chili peppers. There are some vendors from the Zapotec towns of Santa María Albarrados, San Miguel del Río, and San Juan del Río. Finally, there may be some vendors from considerable distances who are not regular attendants at the market.

The major goods from Mitla and Yalalag consist of cigarettes, matches, cloth, needles and thread and other notions, salt, candy, bread, and ironwork. The last is from Tlacolula in the valley of Oaxaca. Ropes and twine come from the mountain Zapotec region. Pottery is from Tamazulapan and Mixistlan.

Purchasers at the market areas are as varied as the sellers (pl. 9, b). As a matter of fact, most visitors both buy and sell. In point of attendance, Ayutla, Tamazulapan, Yalalag, and Mitla are represented in diminishing order of importance.

In addition to the Ayutla market there are a good many itinerant traders from Mitla and Yalalag who follow more or less regular routes. In most towns the only markets attended by outsiders are in connection with the fiestas of the patron saints. These are comparable to the regular Ayutla market, but at other times, if there is a market day, it is attended usually by only a handful of local vendors selling fruit, cigarettes, and perhaps a few bolts of cloth. At the large town of Tamazulapan on market day I counted six vendors. There are also some traveling Mixe traders. Tamazulapan and Mixistlan men travel selling pottery and bringing back coffee. Juquila men also travel a good deal. Such traveling traders have a difficult time since they must carry their own food. Mitla traders who have visited the same towns once or twice a year for twenty years or more told me that they could never buy food. Even at Ayutla, where the same men often come every week for years, there is practically no intercourse between the traders and the inhabitants except over business, and the Mitla men have to bring their own food and cook it themselves at the edge of the plaza.

CONCLUSION

No GENERAL SOLUTION of the problems connected with the Mixe can be offered as yet, and any suggestions must be regarded as tentative. The present monograph, an introductory survey of a large but minority group of Mixe, suffers from inadequacies common to most Mexican ethnological work. The time involved was not enough for a thorough study of even a single town, much less of a group as large as the western Mixe. The same statement is, of course, true of virtually all studies of native groups in Mexico which have been made to date. Only the program of the Carnegie Institution of Washington has apparently really envisioned the nature of Mexican and Central American ethnographic problems and made some effort to deal with them adequately. For the remainder of Mexico and Central America there exist only reports which are either accounts of a single subdivision of a tribe or linguistic group, or general introductory surveys such as the present one. In such preliminary investigations the situation is analogous to what would happen if an anthropologist in the United States spent three, six, or even twelve months studying the Siouan-speaking peoples or the Tewa-speaking peoples and if his report was then regarded as having "done" the group.[1] Although it is probable that most groups in Mexico and Central America present a more homogeneous culture than do either of the examples mentioned, the comparison is still a fair one. In instances where a study of a single community has been made, the results are often not unlike the assumption too long made in the United States, that the study of the First Mesa of the Hopi gave us an adequate picture of the entire Hopi group. American anthropologists must disabuse themselves of the idea that when we have one study of each of the major linguistic groups in Mexico there will no longer be anything to do in that field.

In addition to the general and essentially superficial character of the present study of the Mixe, any attempt to place the Mixe with relation to their neighbors is impossible owing to the lack of comparative materials. Excellent as Parsons' study of Mitla is, the Zapotec remain essentially unknown, nor will the situation be greatly altered when Julio de la Fuente's excellent material on the Zapotec of the Villa Alta

---

[1] Parsons' general report on the Tewa of course does not fall in this category, for it represents a number of years of work covering all the Tewa villages.

district is published. Only the most fragmentary materials have yet been published on the Chinanteca, while the Zoque and Mixtec are almost untouched. To make comparisons with Maya-speaking or Nahua-speaking groups when the intervening areas are entirely unknown seems a fruitless procedure.

In general, it is my impression that the Mixe represent a fundamentally archaic group who have perhaps been pushed into an unfavorable environment where they have remained substantially isolated both by the character of the geography and by their own shyness and lack of aggression. As I have already indicated in connection with the discussion of material culture, there seems a strong probability that their original habitat was in a lower and more tropical environment. The recent discovery of a linguistically related group in the lowlands of southern Vera Cruz lends some support to this opinion. On the other hand, Foster's preliminary notes on the Populuca of Vera Cruz show that the culture of the two groups have very little in common except for similarities attributable to Spanish sources or else shared with numerous other groups. Superficial comparison of vocabularies suggests also that contacts between the two groups have not been recent.[2]

The negative character of the archaeology of the Mixe area also suggests that their territory was never occupied by more advanced groups. The only pyramidal structures I saw or heard of in Mixe territory are not more than twelve or fifteen feet high and are not far from the borders of Zapotec territory. The mountain above Tlahuitoltepec is probably elaborately terraced, and I heard rumors of one or two other terraced mountains farther east. Though the chronological position of the terraced hill or mountain in Mexico is not yet well defined, it does not seem likely that, in relation to the pyramid construction, it is a late development. Neither is it likely, on the basis of present evidence, that it is usually associated with very advanced cultures.

A difficulty involved in interpreting Mixe culture as essentially an archaic survival of a tropical lowland is that much of the simplicity of Mixe culture may be a direct outgrowth of the hostile environment. There are also many elements of the culture (such as the modern house type, clothing, and such rituals as the wedding ceremony) which appear to be borrowings from the Zapotec but some of which may belong to the aboriginal culture. Only more detailed study will resolve these questions.

In the field of modern problems likewise, the study does not permit definite conclusions. Any effort to raise the level of Mixe life must cope with the problem of environment and communication. Even should the Pan-American Highway ultimately pass through Mixe territory, it will make little improvement in the accessibility of many of the towns. Moreover, since most of the population will necessarily remain rural, adequate communications and schools can be provided only at so great an expense that I see little probability that the Mixe will be able to maintain them, even though a benevolent central government should provide the initial cost of the facilities. Improvement of the present essentially subsistence economy will be very difficult if not impossible for many of the Mixe because of the nature of available lands and resources. Large-scale transplantation of the population would seem to be the only permanent way of economic improvement. This would be costly and perhaps dangerous, for it would involve transplantation to considerable distances into an entirely different environment and might well have disastrous effects on the

[2] Foster (1940).

health of the population. Extremely difficult psychological problems would also be encountered.

It must be reiterated that the application of outside pressures and influences will require extreme care if unfortunate results are to be avoided. It has been pointed out that the cohesion of Mixe society is extremely tenuous and rests almost wholly on the prestige of the political and ceremonial office holding system and on the ceremonial life itself. Until some substitute can be put into active operation, any tampering with the existing social structure would have most disruptive effects.

Before either the scientific or practical problems connected with the Mixe can be resolved, much remains to be done. Quite apart from the need of study among neighboring groups, the Mixe require additional attention. The central, eastern, and Nexapa Mixe require a general survey. In addition, a number of towns should be studied intensively. Particular attention should be paid to the differences between progressive and conservative towns. Any practical program should first have careful preliminary study to determine not only its probable effects on the social structure, but also the best way of gaining the support of the Mixe for it. Any studies will be difficult because of the isolation, bad climate, difficult travel, and extreme poverty of the region. Studies in the area should not be embarked upon without adequate preparation of personnel and thoroughly adequate resources. Particularly in studies of conservative towns it should be borne in mind that one cannot, as in other parts of Mexico, depend upon the country for food or expect to employ native assistants even as cooks or porters. Neither riding nor pack animals may ordinarily be found. Even where they exist, as at Ayutla, only official pressure would produce them; and in most towns they are nonexistent. Whoever makes the effort, however, should be richly repaid in securing an adequate account of one of the most interesting survivals of aboriginal culture in Mexico.

APPENDIXES

APPENDIX I

THE MIXE COUNTRY

THE ONLY geological and geographical data published about Mixe territory with which I am familiar is that contained in Oscar Schmieder's paper on *The Settlements of the Tzapotec and Mije Indians*. Unfortunately, Schmieder's comments and observations are based on only eight or nine days spent in Mixe territory, and I find myself unable to agree with many of his conclusions. For example, he refers to level summit surfaces which I could not perceive. His illustrations captioned as showing these surfaces seem to be photographs of the broader valleys or terraces existing in the upper parts of some stream drainages. This is true of his illustration in plate 4, *b* (which incidentally is taken from the trail between Tamazulapan and Tlahuitoltepec and not between Ayutla and Tamazulapan as it is captioned). As mentioned in the text of chapter i, the upper parts of some stream valleys are broad and shallow. At other places, these shallow valleys have been cut through the middle by deeply eroded canyons, leaving a bench or terrace of fairly level land on either side of the central gorge. Thus there are many spots at which photographs suggesting level surfaces could be taken if the gorge were kept out of the picture. Several of Schmieder's illustrations are misleading, particularly his plate 5. This photograph is cited to show that the Río de Ayutla (this name is never used locally) has cut back beyond the highest land surface. Although this cutting has taken place in the Cajones Basin, as a whole, with respect to the formation of which Zempoaltepec is a part, it is not true locally of the so-called Río de Ayutla. If Schmieder's photograph in plate 5 had extended farther to the left, it would have shown that the land rises again beyond the head of the river. The general slope of the land toward the south is also much less abrupt than Schmieder indicates. Again his plate 5 is at fault. The southern extension of the Sierra de Ixtlan does not show. It has very much less slope than the foreground ridge, which is all that shows in Schmieder's plate.

Schmieder's cartography is also careless. The contour lines in his map 1 might better have been eliminated as they are so obviously wrong. For example, Ayutla is shown at thirteen hundred meters when it is somewhat over twenty-one hundred meters. Only negligence explains his inclusion of the Zapotec town of Santa María Albarrados in Mixe territory.

The climate within Mixe territory is rather variable, but as a whole it is distinctly different from that of the Zapotec areas. It is generally much more moist and considerably colder even at the same altitudes. Temperature records are completely lacking, but frost is said to be rare except at the higher altitudes. I have seen light frost in late February a few hundred meters above Yacoche (elevation twenty-five hundred meters). I was told of exceptional snowfalls as low as Ayutla. Coffee will not grow above sixteen or seventeen hundred meters and bananas not above nineteen hundred, but this is apparently because of the low annual temperatures rather than actual frost. Maize planted at twenty-three to twenty-four hundred meters is very slow to mature, but apparently it is rarely frosted.

Rainfall is equally variable. Schmieder estimates the lowest rainfall in the western areas as fifteen hundred millimeters, about sixty inches, but my guess is that this is conservative except for some of the pinelands on the extreme western border. The most striking climatic fact is the almost continuous fog which blankets the area, changing frequently into fine drizzles borne on cold penetrating winds. During the latter part of the rainy season in August and sometimes in December there are breaks of a day or two in the weather which provide almost the only times the great mountain views open out to their fullest extent. Only on such occasions may the Pacific be seen from Zempoaltepec.

In most places the vegetation is very luxuriant, and the majority of the forested area is of the tropical rain-forest or cloud-forest type. Nevertheless, there are extensive areas of pine forest, sometimes in pure stands, sometimes mixed with oak. Any interpretation of the occurrence of these types of forest must be entirely tentative, for the situation is evidently very complex. My superficial observations led me to the belief that the present distribution is almost entirely due to differences in soil and moisture conditions. In this I am again at variance with Schmieder, who suggests that the pine forests have been displaced by clearing for agricultural use and that second growths are either dry land-oak associations or the tropical rain forest.

That great changes have been caused by agricultural use of the land is undoubted, but much of this is modern and represents an extension of the permanent and semipermanent field types. There is, however, no conclusive proof that the pines have lost ground in second-growth forests. In the dry lands of the extreme west there are pure oak stands at high altitudes on land which would never have been cultivated, indicating that the absence of pine here is due to ecological factors. In other places I have seen second-growth forests where the oaks apparently have recovered first but are being followed by a healthy pine forest. I also saw areas of first-growth oak forest where young and vigorous pines seemed to be pushing the oak aside. Another point worth mentioning is that the Mixe prefer to clear lands in the rain forest rather than in the pine forest.

A further suggestion by Schmieder that forest fires and the demand for timber have caused reduction of the pine forests is also untenable, in my opinion. Forest fires are extremely rare in the Mixe area, although common in the Zapotec region. I have many times seen the slash and timber of newly cleared fields burned with absolutely no effort to prevent the fire from spreading, and the adjoining forest was too wet to burn. The only reported forest fires have been when the rainy season was delayed until July and a true dry season occurred. Then the rain forest suffered equally with the pine forest. With regard to the effect of lumbering operations I need only say that I have seen the finest of pine logs being burned in field-clearing operations within a quarter of a mile of the plaza at Ayutla. If the demand for pine lumber were in any way acute, these trunks would have been salvaged. Actually, infinitely more timber is destroyed in field-clearing operations than the Mixe have any need for as lumber.

In the region about Zacatepec, San Pedrito, Atitlan, Alotepec, and Cacalotepec (which Schmieder did not see) there are extensive grasslands, owing, apparently, to cultivation. The soil here is sandy in contrast to that of other regions. In this area, the grass makes the land unworkable, with the primitive tools available, in two to three years after being cleared. All these towns are in a serious situation because they have only limited and inferior lands which can still be cleared and cultivated. Wherever the terrain within the grassland area is too rough for even the Mixe to cultivate, the residual pockets of original forest are all of the tropical rain-forest type. The fact that sugar cane can be grown without irrigation in the grassland area indicates that moisture conditions are not responsible for the failure of the rain forest to retake the area. It is very significant for any discussion of the climax vegetation and of the effects of human occupation on the vegetation that the only tree or shrub which is making any headway in reclaiming the savannah areas is the pine. This infiltration may be observed especially clearly at the foot of the trail leading up to Cacalotepec from Atitlan, where, despite frequent burnings of the grass, the pines clearly show a progression into the grasslands. The trunks seem surprisingly fire-resistant, even in small trees, and once needles begin to accumulate beneath the trees, the grass is choked out. Where this process is most advanced and the grass has been almost completely eliminated, a little oak underbrush has appeared, but it seems to have little vigor.

Actually, of course, this discussion in terms of "oak" and "pine" has little meaning. In both dry land and rain-forest associations there are obviously numerous species of oaks involved and there are also at least five species of pine. Most of the pines are of short-needled varieties, the long-needled *Pinus montezumae* so characteristic of much of southern Mexico being of relatively rare occurrence in most of Mixe territory. To be really significant, the changes in vegetation should be discussed in terms of particular species and associations of species.

The following are the towns regarded by the Mixe as being theirs according to a list furnished by the Colonel. The list is divided according to districts as of 1933.

DISTRICT OF VILLA ALTA

Ayutla	Jareta
Tamazulapan	Huitepec
Tepuxtepec	Ocotepec
Tepantlali	Jayacastepec
Tlahuitoltepec	Moctun
Mixistlan	Ametepec
Chichicastepec	Tepitongo
Yacoche	Chinantequilla
Metepec	Totontepec
Tiltepec (not the Zapotec town mentioned by Bevan, p. 8.)	

DISTRICT OF CHQAPAM

Atitlan	Cotzocon
Zacatepec	Chisme
Metaltepec	Puxmetacan
Ayacaxtepec	Ozolotepec
Alotepec	Jaltepec

DISTRICT OF TEHUANTEPEC

Chimaltepec	Mazatlan
Malacatepec	Tutla
Acatlan grande	San José de las Flores

San Juan Guichicovi

DISTRICT OF SAN CARLOS YAUTEPEC

Juquila Mixes	Camotlan
Acatlancito	Huitepec
Cacalotepec	Iscuintepec
Ocotepec	Coatlan
Quetzaltepec	Santa María Nizaviguiti

APPENDIX II

THE COMMUNITY

THE FOLLOWING are the political officials in some other towns (arranged in descending order of rank):

YACOCHE

Alcalde (judge)
Presidente (mayor)
Alternate to the *presidente* or the *suplente*
Fiscales (2)

Mayor (police chief)
Captain of the fiesta (*mayordomo*)
Alternate to the *alcalde*
Topiles (policeman) (2)
Topilillos (church servant) (2)

These are all named at a town meeting. In addition a chaplain (*capillo*) and a secretary are named by the mayor.

TOTONTEPEC

Alcalde
Alternate
Mayor
Fiscales (2)
Regidores (8. The first *regidor* is alternate to the mayor.)
Captain of police (*mayor*)

Lieutenant of police
Topiles (8 groups, each with from 12 to 15 members. Each group has a head who recruits the other members. The groups serve in turn, one week at a time.)
Topilillos (8)
Sextons (2)

METALTEPEC

Alcalde
Alternate
Mayor
Alternate
Regidores (4)

Síndico (boss for communal labor or tekio)
Alternate
Fiscales (2)
Mayores (4)
Police (4)

Topiles (serve as police)

In addition there is a secretary, named by the mayor, and a chaplain, named by the town council.

JUQUILA

Alcalde and mayor (of equal rank)
Alternates (2)
Fiscales (2)

Regidores (7. One is alternate to the mayor)
Mayores (4, serving in pairs alternate weeks)
Topiles (6)

Topilillos (4)

Service as both *alcalde* and mayor is not required. *Alcalde, mayores,* and *topiles* named by town council; *topilillos* by the mayor.

TAMAZULAPAN

Mayor
Alternate
Alcalde
Alternate
Fiscales (2)
Síndico

Alternate
Regidores (4)
Mayores (4)
Lieutenants (?)
Topiles (20)
Topilillos (6)

There are a chaplain, three sextons, and a secretary (regarded as an official but not placed in the hierarchy).

Tepuxtepec

Mayor	Síndico
Alternate	*Mayores* (4)
Alcalde	*Topiles* (4)
Alternate	*Fiscales* (2. Probably rank higher)
Regidores (4)	*Topilillos* (2)

There is also a chaplain appointed by the mayor.

There is little evidence that present political institutions or attitudes are influenced by pre-Hispanic conditions. Whatever the aboriginal political units were, they evidently had some sort of governing chiefs and probably other officials. *Caciques*, or chiefs, are specifically mentioned a few times by Burgoa (for example, 2:273). There are frequent references to chiefs and plebeians in Burgoa, but I find difficulty in considering that a class stratification existed. One could so speak of the majority of the population of a Mixe town as "plebeians" in contrast to the elders or the Colonel, but to do so would certainly stretch the original meaning of the word beyond recognition. There are also legends even today of a king of all the Mixe, Conday. Burgoa also mentions Conday (2:302), but it is impossible to reconstruct any intelligible picture of what is meant.

Actually Conday may have been a leader in much the same sense as the Colonel is today. The Colonel was able to raise a sizable force of men to aid in the suppression of a specific revolt or to organize a large number of pueblos for a specific project such as the building of a road. Ayutla people will say that all the Mixe men are soldiers of the Colonel, but this would be vigorously denied by people in other towns, and the muster rolls kept by the Colonel are far from a register of the adult males of the tribe as a whole.

Actually the road and the truck or *camión* are very much personal enterprises of the Colonel. Some towns which once were in the Regional Council, such as Zapotec Yalalag, dropped out early in the development of the road. In others, I heard much dissatisfaction and disbelief that the road would ever be completed or, if it were, that there would ever be any extension to their own town.

The average Mixe certainly must have some difficulty in seeing the benefits of the road or of the truck. Few of them ever have an opportunity to ride in the truck. Ayutla men must not only work on the road, but carry gasoline on their backs from Mitla to Ayutla; they are not even met at the end of the road and the gasoline carried the rest of the way by truck. The only occasion on which a considerable number of passengers was carried while I was at Ayutla was when the mayors and other officials of the various towns went to Oaxaca to greet the new governor of the state. Then the Colonel was busy all one day taking the officials from Ayutla to the end of the road.

APPENDIX III

TALES

STORIES are very rare among the Mixe. No doubt, intensive work with old people would produce more, but the following are all I encountered.

1. At a spring toward Atitlan, the King of Spain, Montezuma, and Fernando Cortez were born. The place is called Tlascaltepec. They were to have a trial of strength and put up a wager. The next day they fought, but the king said neither had won. (Collected at Cacalotepec. The informant was very drunk and nothing further could be obtained from him.)

2. The crow brought maize to this nation. Who knows where he went to get it? There had not been any maize here. He digs up the maize also from the ground when it is sown and carries away the ear when it is formed. He throws it down or eats it. (Collected in Tepuxtepec.)

3. In Tepantlali they say a man made a lasso for catching deer in the woods. A deer came along chased by a tiger. The deer ran around the noose and the tiger ran into the noose and was caught around the stomach. There were two tigers. They dug up the stick (to which the lasso was tied) and began to run, but the stick caught. How they dug up the earth there! When the people came, they thought it was a deer and followed the track with their dogs. The dogs came to where the other tiger was and at once attacked it. The dog didn't think there was another tiger guarding the one that was caught, and immediately he died. The buzzard came and wanted to eat the tiger. The companion wouldn't let him. When they found the tiger he was sitting upright on his haunches. The rope around his stomach had killed him. (This story was really acted out rather than told and I have interpolated in words some things that were given only in pantomime. Collected in Ayutla.)

4. Our Lord Jesus Christ put a benediction on the earth so there would be maize, but he kept it all in Heaven. A little animal like a bee which comes out in August flew up to Heaven and stole one grain, which it buried. This grain grew and from it came all the maize in the world. (Collected in Ayutla.)

All villages visited denied stories or songs for themselves but generally mentioned that some of the Zapotec villages had short songs and also told stories.

PHONETIC SYSTEM AND VOCABULARY

MIXE WORDS in the text and in the following lists are written in accordance with this system:

a, open, as in Spanish *pan*
e, intermediate as in English "pen"
ĕ, very open
i, closed as in Spanish *cine*
ĭ or ï, closed u
u, open as in German *fuss*
ü, rounded, similar to ü in German *bücher*
ai, as in English "thigh"
g and k, similar to English but with a hard attack and slightly glottalized
p, as in English but with a strong attack
t, interdental or dental
s, similar to English s
ʃ, same but alveolar or post-alveolar with a pronounced hiss
ts, as in English "cats"
sh, as in English "ship"
ch, as in English "church"
x, German ch as in *ich*
w, as in English "wend"
y, as in English "yes"
n and m, as in English but sometimes more nasalized, especially in terminal position.
    Strong nasalization is indicated by the tilde, ñ

Stress is marked, often making unaccented final syllables seem whispered, and I so wrote them at first. There is a good deal of pitch accent, but it does not appear to be functional. The Zapotec say that Mixe can be written in Spanish characters but that their own language cannot. There seemed much individual variation in the pronunciation of sounds in the *s*, *ʃ*, *sh*, *ch* groups; for example *esnái*, *eʃnásh*, *eshnásh*, and *echnách* were all heard clearly at various times. *Tz*, *ts*, *z*, and *s* are also hard to distinguish. However, the phonetics are fundamentally simple. More vowel sounds occur than are written, but I believe they represent merely positional variants, although this needs verification by a competent linguist. Both vowels and consonants are usually long, although again there is some individual variation. Only very marked length is indicated in my notes where it is shown by the raised period, ·. Some glottal stops, ', and breaths,', appear in the notes but they are so rare as to suggest that they are nonfunctional. Other frequent variants seem to be interchanges of *g* and *k* and *ai* and *oi*.

Tamazulapan, Tepantlali, Tepuxtepec, Tlahuitoltepec, and Ayutla are said to speak almost identically except for occasional slight differences in pronunciation. A slightly different dialect is found at Juquila, which is the same as that at Cacalotepec. Ayutla people have difficulty in understanding people from Totontepec because of the use of different words and different pronunciation. My notes suggest yet another dialect for Metaltepec, although this was not mentioned by informants. Isquintepec and Chimaltepec were places mentioned as having a markedly different dialect from Ayutla.

It is an interesting commentary on the ability of some of the Spanish writers that after spending only five minutes studying the phonetic key I was able to read the *Confessonario* of Father Quintana aloud well enough so that Ayutla informants could understand it. Moreover, Ayutla informants identified it immediately and correctly as being written in the Juquila dialect.

VOCABULARY

The following is a partial list of words collected, including names of many of the objects referred to for which native terms were not given in the text. If not otherwise indicated, the words are from Ayutla. If the words are followed by (T) they are from Totontepec, if by (M) from Metaltepec, and if by (J), from Juquila.

NUMERALS

1, *túuk; tuk'* (T); *tug'* (J)
2, *matsk;* also (T) and (J)
3, *tigúg; túuk* (T); *tugü'g* (J)
4, *maktáshk; matáshk* (T) and (J)
5, *magóshk; mugósk* (T); *magúshk* (J)
6, *tudúk; tükúk* (T); *tudúk* (J)
7, *ushtúk; ustuktuk* (T); *ushtúg* (J)
8, *tuktúk; todoktuk* (T); *tuktúg* (J)
9, *tashtúk; tashtuktuk* (T); *tastúg* (J)
10, *mak;* also (T) and (J)
11, *maktúuk*
12, *makmátsk*
13, *maktigúg*
14, *makmátsk*
15, *makmóshk*
16, *maktúk*
17, *makushtúk*
18, *maktuktúk*
19, *maktashtúk*
20, *epsh; ipsh* (T) and (J)
21, *epshtúk*
22, *epshmátsk*
23, *epshtugúg*
24, *epshmatáshk*

25, *epshmagóshk*
26, *epstudúk*
27, *epshushtúk*
28, *epstuktúk*
29, *epstushtúk*
30, *epsmák; ipshmák* (T)
31, *epsmaktúk*
32, *epsmakmásk*
40, *hustíksh; wúshtukupsh* (T)
50, *hustikshmák*
60, *tigúbsh; taugúpsh* (T)
80, *maktápsh; maktupshshúk* (T)
100, *tukmugépsh; mokúpsh* (T)
110, *tukmugépsh hamók*
120, *tukmugépsh kaépsh*
130, *tukmugépsh epshmók*
140, *tukmugépsh haushtíksh*
150, *tukmugépsh haushtíksh mak*
160, *tukmugépsh hĕdugípsh*
180, *tumugépsh hamaktápsh*
200, *matsmugépsh*
300, *tugukmugépsh*
400, *maktashmugépsh*
500, *magoshmugépsh*

GEOGRAPHICAL TERMS AND LOCATIONS

Cerro de Amole, a mountain near Ayutla, *ami ot*

The mountain of Ayutla, *yugótp*

Peak of the mountain of Ayutla, *ko'k kubók*

Cerro Pelado, "Bald Mountain," near Ayutla, *kutagíshp*

Portilla, the pass near the Cerro Pelado, *push sham*

Mata Gallina, a pine flat west of the Portilla, *pektsiyóp*

Lachikukana, a district of Ayutla in *tierra caliente, padsiyóp*

Monte Rosa, a mountain in western Ayutla territory, *kugúch beákpa*

Cerro Grande, a mountain in Ayutla territory, *mukkopgü'shp*

Camino Real, a main trail, *muktúk*

Mountain, *kopk* (J)

Hill, *tun* (J)

Rocky crag, *savil* (J)

Mountainous area, *yuk* (J)

Yacoche, one of the few towns to retain a native name, *yukp*

Arroyo between Tamazulapan and Tlahuitoltepec, *muknú'ch*

ANIMALS

Bird, *hon; hont* (T); *hon* (J)
Eagle, *wets; wiḱtsin* (T); *wits* (J)
Toad, *timyük*
Buzzard, *mitch* (J)
Fish, *aksh;* also (T) and (J)
Flea, *peshk; pishk* (T) and (J)
Louse, *at; üts* (T); *aát* (J)
Bedbug, *nok*
Stinging gnats, *ush*
Flies, *tsatch*
Rabbit, *kói*
Jackrabbit, *tsái*
Rattlesnake, *shagók*
Squirrel, *kui*
Dog, *uk;* also (T) and (J)
Jaguar, *kudshbúk; ka* (M)

Puma, *hamgók; kushupúk* (M)
Deer, *hadjúk*
Peccary, *azengók*
Badger, *tsek*
Fox, *wax·sh*
Costoche, a type of wildcat, *ix·k*
Cuache, a type of wildcat, *pok*
Cattle, *tsap kok*
Pig, *kuch*
Goat, *tsabísh*
Sheep, *tsapásh*
Domestic turkey, *tetútke*
Chicken, *tsaptútke*
Turkey eggs, *titusách*
Chicken eggs, *tutsách*

PLANTS

Maize grain, *téumpta*
Maize plant, *mogyúm*
Maize flower, *kok*
Small green maize ear still with flower, *mokpúch*
Large green ear, *shó'ish*
Dry maize ear, *teuchítzna mok*
Maize leaf, *mogái'*
Yellow maize, *putsmók*
White maize, *po·v*
White maize in hot country, *po·vabishpúts*
Black maize, *kats*
Red maize, *ávishputs*
Chilecayote, a squash, *kotsé; katsí* (J)
Squash, *kapché; tsi* (J)
Sweet potato, *pakmoín; mun* (J)
Chayote, a vegetable, *akshák*
Tomato, *tutkó'n*
Small green tomato, *taspkó'n*
Very small tomato, *tsipkiyó'n*
Maguey, *tsats*
Dry chile, *tutsní*
Chile, *ni*

Green chile, *shushní*
Zapote negro, *tsúik*
Anona, *atk*
Avocado, *kútskpe*
Sugar cane, *washk*
Wheat, *tsapmók*
Potato, *tsapmoín*
Peach, *tsubáksh*
Cherry, *miutpiáksh*
Plum, *túin*
Small banana, *mazuzám*
Large banana (Sp., *platano de castilla*), *watsám*
Tree, *kip; kup* (T); *képi* (M); *kep* (J)
Wood, *pek'yót, kwiyót; yukhót* (T); *yuk* (M); *am* (J)
Fruit, *sá'um; huksh* (T); *utstám* (M)
Flower, *pux; puk* (T); *pux* (M–J)
Pine, *wazín*
Ocote, *tsi·n*
Resin, *ik*
Turpentine, *tsinípk*
Oak, *shok*

NATURAL PHENOMENA

Sun, *shi; shä* (T); *shu* (J); *sheúk* (M)
Moon, *po'; po* (T–M); *po'* (J)
Night, *kots; winíts* (T); *ko·ts* (J)
Daylight, *shu; shu'* (J)
Cloud, *nemók; yo·ts, yak* (J); *hok* (M)
Heavens, *tsap;* also (T), (J), and (M)
Star, *masá;* also (T); *muzá* (J); *mazá* (M)
Fire, *hün,* also *tsaim* or *töip; hü·'t* (T); *hün* (J) and (M)
Ashes, *kuiká* (J)
Smoke, *hünhók* (M)
To burn, *tiói* (T); *tói* (J)
Salt, *kan;* also (T), (J), and (M)
Dry, *tüts; te'úts* (T)
Stone, *tsax; tsa* (T–J); *sa* (M)

Earthquake, *uksh; o'sh* (T); *ush* (J)
Hole, *hut*
Water, *nük; nüg* (T); *nu* (J) and (M)
River, *mükmük; mahanüg* (T); *mwŭnu* (M)
Wet, *shog; shok* (T–J)
Rain, *tuk; tö'* (T); *tu·* (J); *tu* (M)
Wind, *pok; po'* (T); *pok* (J)
Lightning, *azúk; anä'* (J); *manzúk* (M)
Tempest, *aná*
Thunder, *vuzúk* (J); *anáu* (M)
Sand, *tsai, pu'u* (J)
Earth, *gnash* (J)
Morning star, *káshu*
Red, *tsaps;* also (T) and (J)
Green, *sushk; sashk* (T); *sushk* (J)

PARTS OF BODY

Head, *kabók; kabák* (J)
Hair, *wai*
Ears, *tátsk;* also (T–J–M)
Eyes, *wen; wiñt* (T); *wi·n* (J–M)
Nose, *hu·p; hup* (M); *hu'p* (T–J)
Forearm, *ku; kúu* (J); *küü* (T); *kĭk* (M)
Elbow, *kupóksh*
Mouth, *a·; ak* (T); *au* (M); *avák* (J)
Teeth, *túits*

Tongue, *tots; yá·am* (J); *tots* (T–M)
Breasts, *chetsk*
Navel, *putsk*
Thigh, *pái; po'* (T); *púi* (J–M)
Foot, *tek;* also (J)
Hand, *kú'a*
Nails, *shróik; kushrék* (J)
Beard, *awái*

FOODS

Brown sugar (Sp., *panela*), *pak; pá'ak* (J)
Tepache, *paknéx*
Pulque, *kech*
Mescal, *mukních*

Meat, *tsúich*
Bread, *tsapkáik*
Tortilla, *káik*

CLOTHING

Cotton cloth, *wéta*

Serape, *tsabísh*

Reboza, *kasigwóp*

Hat, *kuhúp*

Sash, *tsum*

Shirt, *nishí*

Pants, *eshmúts*

IMPLEMENTS

Coa or cultivating tool, *puráp'*

Plow, *yú'u*

Digging stick, *keksh*

Axe, *potpúpsh*

Machete used in fields, *möts*

Plowshare, *makosóte*

Plates, *tesh*

Olla, *tuts*

AGE TERMS

Infant, *mashúñ*

Boy, *mishuñ; wa·tyúk* (T)

Small girl, *kish, kishchúñ'*

Older girl, *teshchúk*

Adolescent girl, *kishyé'*

Adolescent boy, *yuyákpe*

Man, *yeyúk; yatyík* (T); *yayúk* (J)

Woman, *teshúk; tastík* (T); *toshchúk* (J)

Old man, *ná'u* (T)

Old woman, *amúk* (T)

When woman passes menopause, *tüyeyék pátna*

People, *haíyu* (T); *haíi* (J)

HOUSES AND HOUSE MATERIALS

House, *tük*

Patio, referring here to yard in front of dwelling, not to an interior court, *tahák*

Roof, *pütch*

Adobe, *mú·tch*

Clay, *mönts*

Lime, *ham; ha·m* (J)

Sand, *puk*

Storehouse for grain, *tsash*

MISCELLANEOUS

Yes, *wem* (T); *dun* (J)

No, *ka* (T); *kiáp* (J)

Big, *mük; mu'* (T); *muk* (J)

Little, *mutsk; pik* (T); *mutsk* (J)

Round, *nikyü'k; niyúk* (T)

More, *hawán*

Bridge, *ku·ch*

Soap, *shüts*

Cigarettes, *húik, huk* (T)

Good morning, *mai*

Good afternoon, *ešnásh*

Good night, *gzu·in*

Greeting at a house, *estagai yépsna*

Greeting on the road, *hana beákten* (literally, "Now we see each other")

BIBLIOGRAPHY

BEALS, RALPH L.
1936. Problems in the Study of Mixe Marriage Customs, *in* Essays in Anthropology in Honor of Alfred Louis Kroeber, pp. 7–14. Berkeley.

BEVAN, BERNARD
1938. The Chinantec. Instituto Pan-Americano de Geografía e Historia. Publ. 24. Mexico.

BURGOA, FRANCISCO DE
1670–1674. Palestra Historial ... y Geográfica Descripción ... Mexico.
  (Note: The copy belonging to the Bancroft Library, University of California, Berkeley, was employed, in which the two works are bound as Vols. 1 and 2.)

FOSTER, GEORGE M.
1940. Notes on the Populuca of Vera Cruz. Instituto Pan-Americano de Geografía e Historia. Publ. 51. Mexico.

GILLOW, BISHOP E.
1899. Apuntes Históricos. Mexico.

KROEBER, A. L.
1931. The Seri. Southwest Museum, Papers, 6.

MASON, J. A.
1940. The Native Languages of Middle America, *in* The Mayas and Their Neighbors, pp. 52–87. New York.

PARSONS, E. C.
1936. Mitla, Town of the Souls. Chicago.

QUINTANA, P. FR. AUGUSTIN DE
1733. Confessonario en Lengua Mixe (reprint by the Count de Charencey, n.d.).

REDFIELD, ROBERT
1930. Tepoztlan. Chicago.

ROYS, RALPH
1940. Personal Names of the Maya of Yucatan. Carnegie Institution of Washington, Contributions to American Anthropology and History, Vol. 6, No. 31.

SANTA MARÍA Y CANSECO
——. Relación de Nexapa, *in* Papeles de Nueva España.

SCHMIEDER, OSCAR
1930. The Settlements of the Tzapotec and Mije Indians. University of California Publications in Geography, Vol. 4. Berkeley.

STARR, FREDERICK
1899. Indians of Southern Mexico. Chicago.
1900. Notes upon the Ethnography of Southern Mexico. Davenport, Iowa.
1902. Physical Characters of the Indians of Southern Mexico. Chicago.

PLATES

PLATE 1

a. West from Ayutla. This view to the west from the cross above Ayutla should be compared with Schmieder, plate 5. The slope to the south mentioned by Schmieder is not obvious in my picture, which shows the background more clearly. Ayutla is somewhat to the right and below the foreground of the picture. The drainage is all into the Cajones River except for the section in the upper left of the background, which reaches the Tehuantepec River. The lighter patches are fields.

b. Northeast from near Jayacastepec. The great canyon northeast of Zempoaltepec. Totontepec is on the near slope of the most distant ridge. The trail from Totontepec to Juquila crosses country like this for most of the distance of fifty-eight miles.

a

b

PLATE 2

a. Zempoaltepec from the northeast, viewed from the Lightning Peak above Totontepec. This view is the reverse of that in plate 1, *b.* The cloud formations are typical, showing the banded occurrence of clouds and fog.

b. North from Ayutla. View north from the cross above Ayutla. Field patterns show clearly in the foreground and middle distance. Yalalag lies in a valley behind the third or fourth ridge.

a

b

PLATE 3

a. A view in the cloud forest. Trail between Yacoche and Totontepec. The elevation is above nine thousand feet. Details are
blurred by the almost constant fog.

b. Stone idol from near Ayutla, in shrine on the Cerro Pelado
across the canyon west of Ayutla.

a *b*

PLATE 4

a. Woman from Tamazulapan at the Ayutla market. The skirt is handwoven cotton dyed with indigo. A baby is slung on the back in the white cotton shawl.

b. A Mixe couple. Francisco Reyes of Ayutla and a friend. Francisco was my principal informant. The dress is typical of Ayutla for Sundays and fiestas except that Francisco is not wearing his hat.

a   *b*

a. Ayutla from above, showing scattered nature of the settlement. More than half the houses are included in this view.

b. Part of Jayacastepec viewed from the church. The settlement is along the top of a spur of Zempoaltepec.

a

b

PLATE 6

a. Totontepec from the Lightning Peak. The compact character of the settlement is in marked contrast to Ayutla. At this
distance the settlement cannot be distinguished from mountain
Zapotec towns.

b. Tamazulapan. View from the plaza of the town, showing
scattered location of houses and the combination of adobe brick
walls with thatched roofs.

a

b

PLATE 7

a. Mixistlan. The nuclear settlement at Mixistlan showing summit ridge and one of the peaks. The church, school, and municipal building are slightly left of center. From any side it is at least an hour's climb to the settlement from the main trails.

b. Ayutla plaza on market day. The prepared-food and tepache vendors are in the foreground. Before the second arcade is the patron saint's image being taken on procession to collect funds for a mass by the bishop in Oaxaca against the typhus epidemic.

a

b

PLATE 8

a. Holy Week procession returning to church from the Shrine of the Calvary. The picture is taken from the church tower and shows the market building (lower right), schoolteacher's house (upper right), and the Colonel's house (upper left).

b. Mixe types. The man at the right is one of several exceptionally tall persons in Ayutla. A plow leans against the wall behind the group.

a

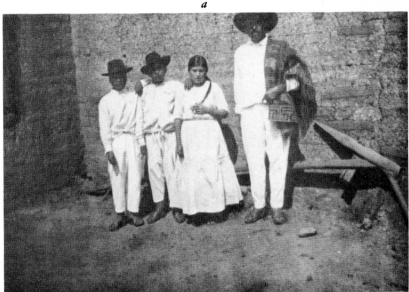

b

PLATE 9

Masked clown (*viejo*) posed to show the mask.

PLATE 10

a. Women relatives of the new *mayordomo* dancing at the change of *mayordomos* for the Santa Cruz.

b. Plaza of Cacolotepec during the fiesta of the first Monday of Lent. The thatch-roofed building in the foreground is the school. With the exception of a small area to the left of the school, this view shows all the level land in Cacalotepec.

a

b

PLATE 11

a. "Indians" of the Conquista dance in Cacalotepec. Notice the wigs of sheepskin. Musicians are in the background and the inevitable bottle is being passed on the left.

b. Negrito dancers performing at the fiesta in Ayutla. A *viejo* is burlesquing the dancers in the right foreground.

a

b

PLATE 12

a. Holy Week procession along a trail from the church to the Shrine of the Calvary at Ayutla.

b. Two *viejos* fighting a "bull," a framework worn by one of the *tiznados*. The house of the Colonel is in the background.

a

b

PLATE 13

a. Church door decorated for the fiesta at Ayutla. Men and boys always lift their hats as they pass before the door.

b. Graveyard at Ayutla, showing the decorated crosses and graves.

a

b

PLATE 14

a. Offerings hidden behind the fence of the graveyard at Ayutla.

b. Major shrine on the summit of Zempoaltepec. Primarily used in connection with maize-growing. Materials at the left are the refuse of previous offerings. An incense burner and a small olla of tepache are visible within the shrine. Taken immediately after the conclusion of a turkey sacrifice.

a

b

PLATE 15

a. Shrine used by barren women on Zempoaltepec. The shrine resembles a temescal or sweathouse. The view shows the "firebox" with wood piled up for burning.

b. Shrine on the peak of Mixistlan. Observe the fallen arm of a cross and the bundles of ocote-pine needles. The latter are the "house of the dead."

c. Shrine in the cave above Ayutla. The white on the rock is corn meal. Iris leaves and turkey feathers are distinguishable, as well as fresh blood on the agave leaves at the left.

a

b

c

PLATE 16

a. Typical Ayutla storehouse. The bottom cribwork of logs is merely a support for the adobe-walled thatch-roofed storehouse. The only entrance is through the square windowlike door, reached by the notched ladder, upon which a blanket is hung. The platform at the left is a frequent feature of houseyards where pottery may be placed out of reach of the dogs.

b. Rammed earth wall of a house at Mixistlan. The cracks show the sectional construction clearly.

a

b

PLATE 17

a. Storehouses at Totontepec, with the church in the background. The floor is of wood slightly raised above the ground and the entrance is through a full-sized door. Fences are rare, but this shows the typical construction.

b. Mixistlan pottery showing the decoration made by drawing lines with a pitch-pine stick (ocote) while the pottery is still hot from the kiln.

a

b